Island
Entrepreneurs

The East-West Center is a public, nonprofit educational institution established in Hawaii in 1960 by the United States Congress. The Center's mandate is "to promote better relations and understanding among the nations of Asia, the Pacific, and the United States through cooperative study, training, and research."

Some 2,000 research fellows, graduate students, and professionals in business and government each year work with the Center's international staff on major Asia-Pacific issues relating to population, resources and development, the environment, culture, and communication. Since 1960, more than 25,000 men and women from the region have participated in the Center's cooperative programs.

Principal funding for the Center comes from the U.S. Congress. Support also comes from more than 20 Asian and Pacific governments, as well as private agencies and corporations. The Center has an international board of governors. President Victor Hao Li came to the Center in 1981 after serving as Shelton Professor of International Legal Studies at Stanford University.

The Pacific Islands Development Program (PIDP) at the East-West Center helps meet the special development needs of the Pacific islands region through cooperative research, education, and training. Its quality in-depth research provides island leaders with information on alternative strategies to reach development goals and meet the needs of the island peoples.

PIDP serves as the secretariat for the Pacific Islands Conference, a heads of government organization, and for the Standing Committee, composed of island leaders. PIDP's projects—requested and reviewed by the Standing Committee—respond to the development themes discussed at the First (1980) and Second (1985) Pacific Islands Conference. This process is unique within the East-West Center and in other research and educational organizations serving the Pacific.

Island Entrepreneurs

Problems and Performances in the Pacific

Edited by Te'o I. J. Fairbairn

ᚥ *An East-West Center Book*
Pacific Islands Development Program
East-West Center

Copyright © 1988 The East-West Center
All rights reserved
Manufactured in the United States of America

Library of Congress Cataloging-in-Publication Data

Island entrepreneurs : problems and performances in the Pacific /
edited by Te'o I. J. Fairbairn.
    p.   cm.
    "March 1988."
    Includes index.
    ISBN 0–86638–107–4
    1. Small business—Oceania—Case studies. 2. Entrepreneurship-
-Oceania—Case studies. 3. Businessmen—Oceania—Case studies.
    I. Fairbairn, Te'o.
HD2346.O3I77 1989   88–16434
338'.04'099—dc19   CIP

Distributed by
University of Hawaii Press
Order Department
2840 Kolowalu Street
Honolulu, Hawaii 96822

To my family—
Hedy, John, Nari, and Karene

Contents

List of Maps

Preface

A BOOK on indigenous entrepreneurship in the South Pacific is timely, given the evidence throughout the region of a heightened interest in the development of entrepreneurship, as well as in the private sector as a whole. Almost all Pacific island governments perceive the need to foster indigenous businesses not only as a crucial component of the private sector—which is increasingly recognized as the only certain source of dynamic economic growth—but also as a means of achieving valued social objectives including a more balanced pattern of development and employment expansion.

This book highlights the major aspects of indigenous entrepreneurship and business development in the South Pacific. It focuses on the motives of indigenous entrepreneurs for going into business, their training and educational backgrounds, their methods of establishing and operating businesses, the reasons attributed to their successes, and the various problems encountered in operating small businesses. The book also discusses policy measures that can foster indigenous entrepreneurship, as well as development issues with special significance for small businesses.

The contributing authors have diverse backgrounds and include college professors, professional researchers, development bankers, and officials of international agencies. Several are Pacific islanders with considerable experience in policy formation relating to small business development.

Many book contributors have authored individual country studies on the Cook Islands, Fiji, Marshall Islands, Tonga, Papua New Guinea, and Western Samoa. These case studies were conducted under the auspices of the Pacific Islands Development Program (PIDP), which has published detailed reports for each country. This book presents the results in chapter form to highlight and disseminate major features of these studies.

Other chapters focus on selected major issues of development that were raised in the case studies. These chapters are devoted to the role of development banks (particularly as a catalyst for business development), the access of small businesses to various sources of credit for development funds, and the ever-increasing participation of women as entrepreneurs.

The information and insights presented in the book can help to provide a more complete understanding of the process of indigenous entrepreneurship in the region. As such, it can serve as a useful basis for government policy formation in the areas of entrepreneurship and the private sector. In addition, the book should be a useful reference for students and professional researchers in the field of small business development in the South Pacific as it relates to economic growth.

Acknowledgments

I would like to thank the individual authors for their respective contributions. I owe a special debt to Barbara Yount, PIDP senior editor, for her editing expertise and for her production coordination work—both of which were vital ingredients to the successful completion of the book. Particular thanks are also due to Forrest Hooper and Titilia Barbour of PIDP for their secretarial support, which was always rendered efficiently and enthusiastically. I also wish to express my appreciation to Mary Yamashiro, who volunteered to proofread the book. The financial assistance from PIDP is gratefully acknowledged.

PART I

Integral Aspects of Entrepreneurship

CHAPTER I

Introduction to Entrepreneurship in the South Pacific

Te'o I. J. Fairbairn

IN THE South Pacific region, indigenous entrepreneurship[1] and its potential for promoting the development of the private sector (and, in turn, the economy as a whole) are at the forefront of current development thinking. The various reasons for the emphasis on indigenous entrepreneurship involve both economic and non-economic influences. A thriving indigenous business sector can significantly generate employment and foster a strong private business sector leading to economic expansion and growth. A strengthening of indigenous entrepreneurship is necessary if the island peoples are to make a substantial contribution to the growth process.

In addition, indigenous entrepreneurship can restore more balanced economic structures, promote greater self-reliance, and strengthen national identity and cohesion. In support of indigenous entrepreneurship, many Pacific island countries have introduced a variety of supporting measures and schemes, including taxation incentives, to translate this potential into practical reality.

The current situation

The concern for indigenous participation in business is understandable in the context of the current state of entrepreneurship and business development in the region. If the participation of indigenous groups is compared with that of non-indigenous groups, a sharp demarcation emerges in the pattern of ownership and control, with non-indigenous groups being overridingly dominant. Characteristically, large multinational corporations are active in many key areas of the economy and are particularly dominant in economic and financial areas such as manufacturing, mining, forestry, and services including insurance, banking, tourism, and trading (Fairbairn and Parry 1986). Smaller foreign-owned operations, many operating as joint ventures with significant local participation, are also active, as are enterprises under the control of local non-indigenous groups including Asian immigrant groups and persons of mixed ancestry. The operations associated with these non-indigenous groups frequently are as large and sophisticated as those under the control of multinationals.

In sharp contrast to non-indigenous business, the indigenous business sector is poorly developed, essentially occupying the periphery of the commercial sector as a whole. Individual business operations tend to be extremely small in size and family based; many involve only one or two operators—typically the owner and one or two members of the immediate family. Operations are often conducted from small temporary makeshift premises and even from the owner's residence. More often than not they serve rural and peri-urban centers, and their activities are concentrated in a few selected areas—usually those requiring only limited managerial and technical skills such as retail trading, taxi and food services, and light carpentry.

The failure rate has apparently been high, reflecting low levels of operating efficiency and an inability to compete with other groups. Because of their small size and restricted mode of operation and organization, many indigenous enterprises fall within the ambit of the so-called informal business sector.

Although generally peripheral, the relative position of indigenous entrepreneurship differs markedly from one country to another. As will be shown in the following chapters, participation by indigenous entrepreneurs in the commercial life of the Cook Islands and Western Samoa, for example, has been fairly extensive and reasonably successful. Achievements in these countries can be contrasted with the situation in Fiji and the French territories of New Caledonia and French Polynesia where indigenous entrepreneurship is at an abysmally low level of development. In Fiji the contrast between the participation of Fiji-Indians and indigenous Fijians in the business life of the country is particularly striking and continues to pose serious problems for policymakers.

Why have the indigenous peoples of the Pacific region fallen so far behind in business? The following chapters will help to provide answers, but some insights can be gleaned from past studies such as those by Belshaw (1964), Finney (1973, 1987), Epstein (1968), Watters (1969), Bollard (1984), and Lamont (1983). These studies suggest that the two leading constraints have been limited experience and know-how, which probably reflect policy deficiencies in the past. Also relevant is weak motivation—a problem related to the continued existence of value systems and preferences that are essentially rooted in the traditional cultures. Lack of mobility also serves to prevent would-be entrepreneurs from expanding their mental horizons and from learning about new business opportunities. In addition, a range of institutional barriers limits access to vital resources (particularly finance and advisory and managerial assistance) that indigenous entrepreneurs need to start and sustain their operations.

Nonetheless, the Pacific islands region has produced many outstanding indigenous entrepreneurs. Finney (Chapter 8) introduces several entrepreneurs from the Highlands of Papua New Guinea who, within a relatively short period of time, have succeeded in building up diversified business empires worth millions of dollars. Individual success stories are also found in other Pacific island countries, some of which are well known throughout the region. Among such leading personalities are Mere Samisoni who operates Hot Bread Kitchen stores in Fiji and in at least two other Pacific countries; Tsutomu Nakao who maintains several businesses including manufacturing and export/import operations in Tonga; Va'ai Kolone who has built up several business interests from an initial start as a cocoa planter in Western Samoa; Papiloa Foliaki who operates buses and a motel in Tonga; and Warren Paia who controls real estate, stationery, and computer businesses in Solomon Islands. These are some of the stars in an otherwise dull firmament who have achieved major breakthroughs and who are serving as role models for others.

Early Pacific entrepreneurs

Indigenous entrepreneurship did not always occupy such a lowly status in the commercial life of the Pacific islands. The economic history of many Pacific island countries shows that entrepreneurial activities were often pursued vigorously during pre-European times and that traditional skills associated with such activities often provided a basis for exploiting the new economic opportunities generated by contact. Many instances can be cited of entrepreneurial activities that thrived under the traditional culture. Thus, in her study of the Gazelle Peninsula of Papua New Guinea, Epstein (1968:29) found evidence of regional markets that thrived during pre-contact times and a form of "primitive capitalism" in operation that was characterized by clear-cut concepts of ownership of resources, employment, profit, and accumulation of wealth. An extensive trading network had been established through which "inland natives produced a surplus of taro and other food crops which they sold to coastal Tolai and in turn bought fish, salt water, wild fowl as well as lime" (Epstein 1968:22).

Similarly, entrepreneurial activity, typically manifested through trade, was pursued throughout many Pacific islands, especially between relatively adjacent geographical groups. In Fiji, for example, coastal peoples traded regularly with neighboring groups, including those on other islands, and with inland inhabitants of the various islands. Moreover, trade contacts had been established with Samoa and Tonga in which fine mats, kava (yaqona) roots, and foodstuffs figured prominently. Women also formed part of the traditional trade flow, especially those women of high rank who were in demand for marriage purposes. According to Samoan legends, even whole islands moved intra-regionally; it is believed that the island of Manono—which lies just off Upolu toward Savai'i—was brought from Fiji by a renowned warrior chief and erstwhile entrepreneur named Lautala!

A notable feature of the economic development of several Pacific island countries was the efflorescence of entrepreneurial activity that occurred during the post-contact period. This is illustrated by the Cook Islands during the 1860s—40 years after initial contact. Here, a highly developed system of entrepreneurship emerged under the leadership of a group of "chiefly entrepreneurs" (Gilson 1980:54). These traditional chiefs had gained control of the export trade (principally with visiting whalers), involving the sale of items such as pigs, poultry, fruit, and vegetables. As heads of their lineages, these entrepreneurs took it upon themselves to organize the production, control, and marketing functions and to operate schooners that traded throughout the Cook Islands group, as well as to Tahiti and even as far south as New Zealand. Unfortunately, this promising beginning came to an abrupt halt with annexation in the early 1900s, when the New Zealand administration stripped the chiefs of virtually all their powers to conduct trading activities.

The rise and fall of chiefly entrepreneurs in early Cook Islands history is closely paralleled by the experience of the neighbor island of Tahiti. According to Finney (1971:18), trade between Tahiti and the outside world during the early 19th century was dominated by a few leading chiefs who applied their chiefly prerogatives to commercial relations with Europeans. These "trader chiefs" became leading figures in the pork trade and in the sale of coconut oil, arrowroot, mother-of-pearl shells, and pearls. However, as with the Cook Islands, this period of entrepreneurial endeavor ended abruptly in the early 1840s due to the French takeover (1842), constraining missionary laws, and depopulation.

More recent examples of vigorous entrepreneurial performance resulting from contact with Europeans and the consequent introduction of the cash economy are provided by certain tribal groups in Papua New Guinea. As chronicled in the well-known works by Epstein (1968), Finney (1973), Salisbury (1970), and Crocombe and Hogbin (1963), indigenous entrepreneurship advanced rapidly as traditional leaders sought to build up prestige and social status through success in business. Apparently, these factors have accelerated the pace of monetization and economic development in post-contact Papua New Guinea.

The importance of indigenous entrepreneurship

Why do Pacific island countries attach so much importance to indigenous entrepreneurship? The two main reasons are (1) to exploit the development potential of indigenous entrepreneurship as a means of promoting private sector growth and (2) to achieve a more balanced pattern of development by narrowing the existing gap between indigenous and non-indigenous entrepreneurship. The first entails economic aspects, the second mainly social and political factors.

Economic enhancement of the private sector

On the economic side, there are many reasons why Pacific island countries have recently been emphasizing private sector development. One reason is a recognition of the dynamic role of the private sector in promoting economic growth. Almost all Pacific island countries are beset with difficult problems during their development, including restricted resource bases, small domestic markets, geographic isolation, paucity of capital and technical skills, and vulnerability to external market forces (Fairbairn 1985:70). These obstacles impose severe limits to achieving national development objectives, including employment expansion and economic diversification. Faced with these realities, Pacific island countries have increasingly turned to the private sector as a key element in promoting economic development. The dynamic skills of entrepreneurs can identify profitable investment opportunities and can marshal the requisite capital and related resources to exploit these opportunities.

Another major economic factor is an increasing awareness of the merits of the private sector in achieving efficiency in resource utilization. The recent history of Pacific island countries invariably shows a heavy dependence on government not only in providing essential infrastructure and regulatory services but also in operating enterprises in manufacturing, services, and other productive sectors. In general, the level of performance in these sectors has not been impressive, with many government enterprises operating at low levels of efficiency and often requiring heavy budgetary subsidization for their survival. With mounting pressure on government finances in recent years, which reflects low levels of economic activity arising largely from unfavorable trade balances, Pacific island governments have been forced to restrict their direct involvement in the economy and to encourage a greater reliance on free market forces to guide resource utilization. A notable part of this process has been the government's withdrawal from certain productive areas and the consequent privatization of public enterprises and other government-owned assets.

The specific contribution that indigenous entrepreneurship can make to the private sector—and hence to the national economy—derives essentially from its integral role in the small-scale business sector. As such, the arguments in favor of small business in general also apply to indigenous entrepreneurship. Small businesses can play a dynamic role in promoting income and employment expansion through their unique capacity to

- Operate on a viable basis with relatively little capital,
- Adopt labor-intensive techniques consistent with resource endowments characterized by surplus labor,
- Sustain activities that are more likely to be dependent on local material resources,
- Display resilience in operations because of family based characteristics,
- Serve as a practical training ground for entrepreneurs.

As a recent publication on entrepreneurship has emphasized, indigenous businesses are able to "operate in communities where large firms could not survive and are well adapted to supplying goods and services appropriate to local needs. . . . [and as a consequence] they not only can widen consumer choice but also in time can reduce the reliance on inappropriate goods and foods imported from overseas" (Hailey 1987:4,8).

From the perspective of economic development, however, the small-scale indigenous business sector can present serious problems for policymakers. Official attempts to foster indigenous business have often proved costly when weighed against the results. One consequence has been a waste of resources. Also small businesses generally lack the capacity to conduct research and development activities that could benefit consumers through lower prices, new products, and related innovations. Moreover, because of their small size, small businesses are not in a position to realize significant economies of scale.

Balanced development

The second major reason for the importance attached to indigenous entrepreneurs is related to the need for more balanced development to narrow the existing gap between indigenous and non-indigenous business. There is a growing dissatisfaction with the status quo, which is overwhelmingly dominated by multinational corporations and other non-indigenous groups in the business life of the region. The leading objectives are to reduce the power (and sometimes the political influence) of the foreign corporations, to reverse any apparent trend toward the erection of neo-colonial economic structures, to expand the opportunities for indigenous peoples to participate actively in the development process, to achieve a more equitable distribution of income, and generally to foster a pattern of development that is conducive to social and political stability and, in consequence, economic maturity. On the last point, Cole notes that, "Economic maturity is reached only when a diversified and multifunctional business network in the hands of native citizens has developed" (Cole 1968:63).

The political perils of an unbalanced business structure in favor of outside groups were recognized by Papua New Guinea soon after independence in the mid-1970s, as Finney points out in Chapter 8. Regarding coffee plantations, the Papua New Guinea government introduced various schemes, including the so-called Plantation Redistribution Scheme, to aid Papua New Guineans to buy out expatriate owners. In addition, the government has identified specific categories of business activities as "reserve areas" for the exclusive participation by Papua New Guineans.

The recent military coups in Fiji were triggered ostensibly by the concern of the military for law and order following the installation of a government dominated by Fiji-Indians. The real causes of military intervention and sociopolitical instability have yet to be identified. However, a major factor probably relates to long-standing grievances on the part of indigenous Fijians over their virtual exclusion from effective participation in the commercial business sector.

Pacific Islands Development Program (PIDP) research project

In attempts to stimulate indigenous entrepreneurship, policymakers in the region have been constrained by lack of basic information. The earlier pioneering studies by social anthropologists such as Finney and Epstein provided many valuable insights into Pacific island entrepreneurship, as did the later studies by economists such as Bollard and Lamont. However, some of these studies, notably those by Finney and Epstein, were essentially anthropological in perspective and somewhat academic in orientation. Moreover, these studies covered only a few countries, and the results have become somewhat dated.

The need for detailed up-to-date information that would be useful for policy formation in this vital area was a principal concern of members of the Pacific Islands Conference Standing Committee at its inaugural meeting in Pago Pago in 1981. The Standing Committee requested that PIDP initiate a major project on indigenous entrepreneurship and business development. In proposing such a project, the Standing Committee recognized the need to conduct an in-depth policy-oriented study that would promote a clearer understanding of indigenous businesses in the region and that would identify possible strategies and policies for accelerating indigenous involvement in the economy. Specifically, the study was designed to identify and analyze the various socioeconomic factors contributing to success or failure of indigenous business ventures. Such a study entailed an examination of (1) the nature of indigenous entrepreneurship, (2) the alternative forms of business organizations and arrangements, (3) the extent of government support programs, and (4) policy proposals to stimulate indigenous entrepreneurship.

The project began in 1984 with field studies in seven selected Pacific island countries to collect primary data. Comprehensive surveys were conducted in each country, entailing intensive interviewing of enterprise owners by PIDP staff members and associates. Based on detailed prepared questionnaires, the surveys were complemented by interviews and discussions with leading government officials in the field and representatives of the private sector and voluntary organizations. The data were then processed and analyzed at the East-West Center. The results of each country study have been published and distributed throughout the region.

The project also sponsored a regional workshop on indigenous business with funding from the Canadian International Development Agency. The participants at the workshop, which was held in Apia in 1986, produced a set of recommendations for strengthening indigenous entrepreneurship in the region. (See Chapter 13 and the Appendix.)

An outline of the present work

This book has been inspired largely by the PIDP project described above. It presents the main findings and conclusions from six case studies: Cook Islands, Fiji, Marshall Islands, Papua New Guinea, Tonga, and Western Samoa, supplemented by chapters on selected aspects of indigenous business development and on the experience of Australia. In a sense, the value of this volume is its synthesis of the results from the separate studies and its guidelines based on the collective experience.

Part 1, which comprises two introductory chapters, sets the stage for the rest of the book. In Chapter 2 this author defines the concept of entrepreneurship and reviews its treatment in the over-all literature. The discussion also shows how economists have dealt with entrepreneurship in formal analysis and analyzes the vital relationship between entrepreneurship and economic growth —a relationship that previously has been only partially explored.

Part 2 comprises Chapters 3–8, which are the book's core section. These chapters present the results of the country studies described above and represent the basic rationale for this volume.

Part 2 begins with the country study on Fiji (Chapter 3), which was prepared by John M. Hailey based on his original country report (Hailey 1985). Problems regarding the definitions of an entrepreneur and of a small business are discussed, as well as those aspects of early colonial policy that have ramifications for the present disadvantaged position of indigenous Fijian entrepreneurs. Given the racial dimension of entrepreneurship in Fiji, the chapter draws attention to the performance of Fiji-Indian businessmen relative to other ethnic groups.

The Cook Islands (Chapter 4), prepared by this author, is based on the original country report written with Janice Pearson (Fairbairn with Pearson 1987). The analysis covers 47 sample indigenous enterprises, which represent a cross section of the country's business sector as a whole; these businesses are located on the main island of Rarotonga and the outer islands of Aitutaki and Atiu. Particular attention is given to the various institutional barriers obstructing indigenous business.

C. Ross Croulet prepared the country study on Western Samoa (Chapter 5) based on the original report he wrote with Laki Sio (Croulet and Sio 1986). A total of 70 enterprises were surveyed, including many commercial farmers and fishermen. The study emphasizes the complex nature of the relationship between traditional status and modern business.

The analysis of the Marshall Islands (Chapter 6) by John J. Carroll is based on a survey of 86 businesses (Carroll 1986). A sizable sample of non-indigenous enterprises is included for comparative purposes, and emphasis is on the impact of government policy on business development and on the overall business structure.

The country study of entrepreneurship in Tonga (Chapter 7) by S. Deacon Ritterbush extends over a broad cross-section of businesses (Ritterbush 1986). The analysis not only encompasses a large sample, totaling 197 entrepreneurs, but also includes a sizable group of commercial farmers and fishermen. Observations on the importance of traditional "ascribed" status in Tonga provide insights on the special nature of Tongan entrepreneurship.

A different approach is used by Ben R. Finney in his study of indigenous entrepreneurship in the Highlands of Papua New Guinea (Chapter 8). Finney adopts an individual case history approach in documenting some of the most successful entrepreneurs in Papua New Guinea operating within a traditional cultural milieu. Finney's chapter, based on a larger report (Finney 1987), is particularly revealing because he relates his observations to the results of his studies in the late 1960s and the early 1970s.

Part 3 comprises chapters dealing with significant issues in small business development. S. Deacon Ritterbush and Janice Pearson (Chapter 9) discuss women in business, in recognition of their increasingly important role in the commercial life of the region and the need to augment their participation. This author (Chapter 10) examines the sources of capital funds and the various factors that have constrained indigenous entrepreneurs' access to these funds. Laisenia Qarase (Chapter 11) discusses the various sources of capital available to indigenous Fijian entrepreneurs, as well as the role of the Fiji Development Bank in promoting indigenous business.

Aspects of small business development in Australia at the federal and state levels are examined by William James Sheehan (Chapter 12). He outlines the various government policies and programs to foster small business growth. The Australian experience illustrates the range of support measures available to promote small business in a large industrialized country.

The book concludes with an assessment of the evidence and findings. General conclusions are drawn about the leading constraints on Pacific entrepreneurship and the factors contributing to success. Recommendations are made on various policy measures to strengthen indigenous entrepreneurship.

NOTE

1. As used here the expression "indigenous entrepreneurship" essentially refers to Pacific islanders who own and operate a business or several businesses, whether large or small, formal or informal. Entrepreneurship in an economic context is discussed formally in the next chapter. In addition, the authors of the country studies have personal definitions of entrepreneurship, which reflect their own perspectives.

REFERENCES

Belshaw, C. D.
　1964　*Under the Ivi Tree—Society and Economic Growth in Rural Fiji,* University of California Press, Los Angeles.

Bollard, A.
　1984　*T-Shirts and Tapa Cloth: A Handbook of Small Rural Business for the Pacific,* South Pacific Commission, Noumea.

Carroll, J.
　1986　*Entrepreneurship and Indigenous Businesses in the Republic of the Marshall Islands,* Pacific Islands Development Program, East-West Center, Honolulu.

Cole, A. H.
　1968　"The Entrepreneur," in Papers and Proceedings of Eightieth Annual Meeting of the American Economic Association, *American Economic Review,* Vol. LVIII, No. 2 (May), Washington.

Crocombe, R. G. and G. R. Hogbin
　1963　*The Erap Mechanical Farming Project,* Bulletin No. 1, New Guinea Research Unit, Canberra.

Croulet, C. R. and L. Sio
　1986　*Indigenous Entrepreneurship in Western Samoa,* Pacific Islands Development Program, East-West Center, Honolulu.

Epstein, T. Scarlett
　1968　*Capitalism, Primitive and Modern—Some Aspects of Tolai Economic Growth,* Michigan State University Press, East Lansing.

Fairbairn, Te'o I. J.
　1985　*Island Economies: Studies from the South Pacific,* University of the South Pacific, Suva.

Fairbairn, Te'o I. J. and T. G. Parry
1986 *Multinational Enterprises in the Developing South Pacific,* Pacific Islands Development Program, East-West Center, Honolulu.

Fairbairn, Te'o I. J. with J. Pearson
1987 *Indigenous Entrepreneurship in the Cook Islands,* Pacific Islands Development Program, East-West Center, Honolulu.

Finney, B. R.
1971 *Big-Men, Half-Men and Trader Chiefs: Entrepreneurial Styles in New Guinea and Polynesia,* Working paper No. 12, Technology and Development Institute, East-West Center, Honolulu.
1973 *Big-Men and Business: Entrepreneurship and Economic Growth in the New Guinea Highlands,* The University of Hawaii Press, Honolulu.
1987 *Business Development in the Highlands of Papua New Guinea,* Research Report Series No. 6, Pacific Islands Development Program, East-West Center, Honolulu.

Gilson, R.
1980 *Cook Islands 1820–1950,* Victoria University Press, Wellington.

Hailey, John M.
1985 *Indigenous Business in Fiji,* Pacific Islands Development Program, East-West Center, Honolulu.
1986 *Indigenous Business Development in the Pacific,* (ed), Final Report of the Regional Workshop, Pacific Islands Development Program, East-West Center, Honolulu.
1987 *Entrepreneurs and Indigenous Business in the Pacific,* Research Report Series No. 9, Pacific Islands Development Program, East-West Center, Honolulu.

Lamont, J.
1983 *A Little Bit of Everything: A Study of Small Entrepreneurs in Vanuatu,* Institute of Rural Development, Nuku'alofa.

Ritterbush, S. Deacon
1986 *Entrepreneurship and Business Venture Development in the Kingdom of Tonga,* Pacific Islands Development Program, East-West Center, Honolulu.

Salisbury, R. F.
1970 *Vunamami: Economic Transformation in a Traditional Society,* University of California Press, Berkeley, Los Angeles.

Watters, R. F.
1969 *Koro: Economic Development and Social Change in Fiji,* Clarendon Press, Oxford.

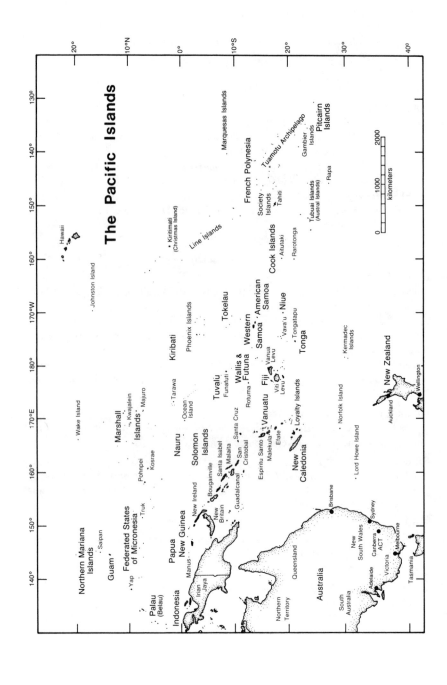

The Pacific Islands

20°N
10°N
0°
10°S
20°
30°
40°

130° 140° 150° 160°W 170°W 180° 170°E 160° 150° 140°

Hawaii

Johnston Island

Kiritimati
(Christmas Island)

Line Islands

Marquesas Islands

French Polynesia

Tuamotu Archipelago

Gambier
Islands

Pitcairn
Islands

Society
Islands
Tahiti

Tubuai Islands
(Austral Islands)

Rapa

Cook Islands

Aitutaki

Rarotonga

Phoenix Islands

Kiribati

Tarawa

Ocean
Island

Tokelau

Western
Samoa

American
Samoa

Niue

Vava'u

Tonga

Tongatapu

Wallis &
Futuna

Wallis

Rotuma

Fiji

Vanua
Levu

Viti
Levu

Tuvalu

Funafuti

Kermadec
Islands

Wake Island

Marshall
Islands

Kwajalein

Majuro

Nauru

Kosrae

Pohnpei

Solomon
Islands

Santa Isabel

Santa Cruz

San
Cristobal

Malaita

Guadalcanal

Bougainville

Vanuatu

Espiritu Santo

Malekula

Efate

Loyalty Islands

New
Caledonia

Norfolk Island

Lord Howe Island

New Zealand

Auckland

Wellington

Northern Mariana
Islands

Saipan

Guam

Federated States
of Micronesia

Yap

Truk

Palau
(Belau)

Papua
New Guinea

New Ireland

New
Britain

Manus

Indonesia

Irian
Jaya

Australia

Northern
Territory

Queensland

South
Australia

New
South Wales

Brisbane

Sydney

Canberra
ACT

Adelaide

Victoria

Melbourne

Tasmania

0   1000   2000
kilometers

CHAPTER 2

Entrepreneurship and Economic Growth

Te'o I. J. Fairbairn

ENTREPRENEURSHIP has long been acknowledged as a dynamic factor in economic growth; yet economists have not found it easy to define its role and to integrate it into formal economic analysis. Problems arise over basic definitions and identification of the functions performed by entrepreneurs, as well as their significance. Lack of agreement on these issues has been largely responsible for the differing perceptions of the role and importance of entrepreneurship and for various theoretical interpretations. Attempts to come to grips with these problems have been compared to the never ending search for the veritable Heffalump—a popular creation in children's literature (Kilby 1971:1). This large and important creature has managed to elude all those who have attempted to capture him although many pursuers claim to have caught sight of him. The search for Heffalump continues. Similarly, economists and other researchers in related disciplines continue the search to grasp the essential nature of entrepreneurship and its role as a dynamic force in economic development.

The role of entrepreneurs: a formal perspective

In economic literature, the entrepreneur has been variously depicted as a risk-bearer, a supplier of capital, an innovator, a manager, a gap-filler, or a combination of these and related functions.

The notion of the entrepreneur as a risk-bearer dates back to the early 18th century but is associated mainly with Knight (1921) who viewed entrepreneurs as a specialized group of people who bear uninsurable risks and deal with uncertainty in the quest for profit. The entrepreneur's role as a supplier of capital was

espoused by Adam Smith (in Harbison 1961:310) who saw him as
a proprietory capitalist—a supplier of capital and, at the same
time, as a manager who intervenes between laborers and consumers. The innovatory role was given primacy by Schumpeter
(1934), who saw the entrepreneur as enabling new combinations
of factors of production and distribution. His role as a manager
was stressed by J. B. Say (cited by Kent 1984:2) who envisaged
the entrepreneur as one who brought together the factors of production (and assumed risk) in such a way that new wealth was
created.

Several contemporary economists have stressed other functions
or particular elements of the above functions. Leibenstein (1968:
73), for example, argues that the entrepreneur is essentially a gap-
filler, especially in coordinating inter-market activities; Kilby
(1971:28) sees him as one who perceives market opportunities and
gains command over scarce resources; and I. M. Kirzner (cited by
Kent 1984:3–4) describes him as one who perceives what others
have not seen and acts upon that perception.

Several economists, including Marshall (1961), take a more
comprehensive view and see the entrepreneur as carrying out a
combination of functions including risk-taking, management and
organization, and innovation.

Schumpeter's representation of the entrepreneur as an innovator who carries out new combinations of resources was a major
breakthrough in the analysis of entrepreneurship. As Kilby
(1971:3) writes of Schumpeter's contribution ". . . his innovation
represents not only the first dynamic concept of the entrepreneurial functions, but he is the first major writer to put the human
agent at the center of the process of economic development."
According to Schumpeter, the innovative entrepreneur was a
heroic figure who was at the heart of the process of economic
development. His role encompassed that of introducing new
goods and methods of production, opening new markets, exploiting new sources of materials, and rearranging markets. These
functions are distinct from purely managerial tasks but are crucial
for ensuring economic growth and the avoidance of the stationary
state. Because the innovation phase of a major initiative may be
short-lived, an individual's status as an entrepreneur will tend to
be ephemeral.

The traditional treatment of entrepreneurship has focused on the entrepreneur as an individual, but several recent attempts have been made to broaden the concept. Harbison (1961:311), for example, argues that with the increased complexity of business firms, the entrepreneurial functions, such as risk-taking and innovation, are no longer performed by a single individual but rather by a hierarchy of individuals. In essence, the entrepreneur is an organization that comprises all people required to carry out entrepreneurial functions. Harbison maintains that such an "entrepreneurial organization" can be treated as a resource like labor or capital and can be measured quantitatively.

Another perspective is the concept of the family as entrepreneur (Nafziger 1984:314). Here, basic decisions affecting the enterprise are made within the family or clusters of families rather than by an individual entrepreneur, although a single member, usually the father or the eldest son, may play a dominant part. This concept of entrepreneurship has particular relevance for business development in the developing countries.

The significance of entrepreneurship

Neither the function nor the significance of entrepreneurs is specifically treated in economic theory dealing with growth, on the one hand, and the behavior of the firm, on the other. In the case of growth theory this neglect is shown in neo-classical models that represent the most sophisticated extension and refinement of classical thinking (see Swan 1956; Solow 1956; Meade 1961). In these models a unique equilibrium growth rate is derived based on the interaction between three basic variables: capital accumulation, population growth, and technical change (representing growth in productivity), allowing for factor substitution. The entrepreneur, who is scarcely mentioned, plays a managerial role, largely behind the scenes; he is responsible for making decisions and adjusting the key variables, including the factor inputs necessary for equilibrium growth. His part in introducing major innovations is not explored.

An underlying assumption of the neo-classical growth models is that at any given time the supply of entrepreneurs, or entrepreneurial services, is highly elastic in response to economic incentives. As these incentives improve as a result, say, of economic development, the supply of entrepreneurial services expands more than proportionately. In the absence of market imperfections, entrepreneurship is ruled out as a constraint to expansion so that the level of entrepreneurial activity at any time is largely influenced by demand factors.

A simple explanation of the growth in entrepreneurial services is given in Figure 2.1. The rate of return on entrepreneurship, R (which may be regarded as an entrepreneur's "wage" measured in some way), is represented by the vertical axis and the supply of entrepreneurial services, S, by the horizontal axis. SS represents a supply curve that is highly sensitive and hence elastic to R as opposed to other predominantly non-economic influences. (The fact that it is not perfectly elastic means that it is influenced to some extent by sociocultural factors.) The demand for entrepreneurial services at varying rates of R is depicted by DD whose position is assumed to be determined by the level of economic activity.

In Figure 2.1, an increase in the supply (or actual availability) of entrepreneurs can be illustrated by assuming that the demand curve shifts from its initial position at DD to D_1D_1 as a result of economic expansion. Given that the SS curve remains unchanged,

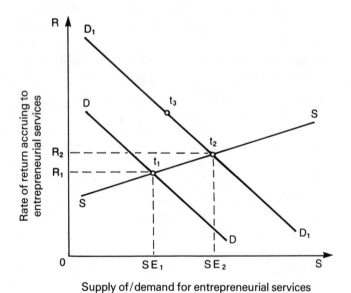

Supply of/demand for entrepreneurial services

Figure 2.1. The growth of entrepreneurial services

the induced shift in demand leads to a new equilibrium at point, t_2, where D_1D_1 intersects with SS. This new equilibrium is associated with SE_2 level of entrepreneurial services and R_2 rate of return as opposed to the initial equilibrium, t_1, associated with SE_1 entrepreneurial services and R_1 rate of return. As a consequence of the shift in demand, the level of entrepreneurial services in use has expanded by SE_2–SE_1, an expansion that is proportionately greater than the change in R, given by R_2–R_1.

The above example shows that a high elasticity of supply imposes less of a constraint on the expansion of entrepreneurial services in use and hence on achievable levels of economic development. Point t_3 in Figure 2.1 represents an alternative equilibrium position that would have resulted had the supply curve been highly inelastic. Such a position represents only a small growth of entrepreneurial services as compared with t_2 but is associated with a rate of return much higher than R_2.

As they stand, the economists' growth models do not promote an understanding of the role of entrepreneurs in the growth process. One reason is due to the assumption underlying supply elasticity, namely, that entrepreneurs are always available and are highly responsive to entrepreneurial rewards. Particularly in the case of developing countries, such an assumption may be untenable, given that the process of building up entrepreneurial skills may still be in the early stages. More generally, and as pointed out by Kilby (1971:26), entrepreneurial responses may be obstructed by various factors such as market imperfections and inefficient government policies that serve to impede factor mobility, ignorance of available opportunities, segmented markets, and pervasive administrative controls. An additional problem arises from a failure to specify entrepreneurship as a separate factor input so that its contribution to economic growth becomes inseparable from other components that are usually lumped together as "technical change."

The entrepreneur does not fare any better under the theory of the firm as a productive unit. In this case, his decision-making powers are largely managerial, directed at maximizing profit through the adjustment of output, the production process, and the like. He becomes a passive agent responding to fortuitous external developments, leaving no room for entrepreneurial initiative. This passive role has been highlighted by Baumol:

> Look for him (i.e., the entrepreneur) in the index of some of the
> most noted of recent writings . . . on activity analysis models of the
> firm. The references are scanty and more often they are totally
> absent. The theoretical firm is entrepreneurless—the Prince of Den-
> mark has been expunged from the discussion of Hamlet (Baumol
> 1968:66).

Nonetheless, in standard microeconomic theory the management factor bears heavily on the assumptions regarding costs. The
intensity with which management is used by a firm over the relevant range of production affects the level of efficiency, which is
reflected in the familiar U-shaped average cost curves, both short
and long term. Regarding major entrepreneurial innovation, current microeconomic theory seems to provide little help in analyzing its impact and consequences. In principle, a major innovation
would create a monopoly situation with the corollary of monopoly profit; but current theory does not provide clear guidelines on
what happens after that (Baumol 1968:68), although the possibility of product and/or process imitation, as envisaged by Schumpeter (1934) as a means of restoring competitive conditions, offers
one possible alternative.

The hiatus in formal economic theory contrasts sharply with
the importance attributed to entrepreneurship in the growth process by many economists. Schumpeter's innovating entrepreneur
and his central role in economic growth have been noted above.
While not necessarily based on Schumpeter, other observers have
acknowledged the critical role of entrepreneurship in the growth
process. N. Kaldor states:

> . . . the innovating entrepreneur . . . is found to have an honorable
> place, or even a key role . . . (in) economic expansion and . . . the
> most plausible answer to the question of why some human societies
> progress so much faster than others is to be sought . . . not so much
> in fortuitous accident . . . or in favorable natural environment
> . . . but in human attitudes to risk-taking and money-making
> (quoted by Denison 1962:163).

Baumol (1968:17) states: "I am convinced that encouragement
of the entrepreneur is the key to the stimulation of growth." Similar views have been expressed by Hirschman (1958), McClelland
and Winter (1970), and other prominent observers.

Although several attempts have measured the sources of economic growth at the empirical level, some lend substance, albeit indirectly, to the above views concerning the importance of entrepreneurship (Solow 1957; Denison 1962).

Using U.S. data on private non-farm GNP from 1909 to 1949, Solow sought to segregate variations in output per head due to technical change from those due to changes in the availability of capital per head. An aggregate production function, together with historical data on output and factor input, was used as a basic analytic framework for deriving and isolating technical change.[1] Technical change, which is assumed to be neutral (in that marginal rates of substitution remain unchanged), is taken to be a shorthand expression for any kind of shift in the production function due to "slowdowns, speedups, improvement in the education of the labor force and all sorts of things . . ." (Solow 1956:312). Solow's main conclusion was that gross output per manhour doubled over the period, with 87.5 percent of the increase attributable to technical change and the remaining 12.5 percent to increased use of capital.

Like Solow, Denison (1962) attempted to measure the sources of economic growth in the United States but used a more disaggregated approach and a longer time period, 1909–57. Dension proceeds by isolating the contributions arising from individual factor inputs (capital, labor, and land) and from increases in output per unit of input or productivity. Again, entrepreneurship is not specifically touched upon, but Denison found that over the period, the growth rate of real national income per person employed was 1.44 percent per year of which capital accounted for 17.3 percent, labor (adjusted for quality changes) 41 percent, land –4.8 percent, and productivity 46.5 percent (Denison 1962:149). These results cannot be compared directly with those of Solow's partly because of differences in the classifications of specific factor inputs, but the results do generally confirm the significance of productivity and technical change in economic growth.

The relevance of Solow's and Denison's findings for this analysis lies in the link between technical change and entrepreneurship. As pointed out by Baumol (1968:66), technical change is associated with innovation, which requires entrepreneurial initiative in its introduction. Thus the entrepreneur cannot be ignored because he is a substantial source of economic growth.

The supply of entrepreneurs

The analyses of the supply of entrepreneurs have been dominated by sociologists, psychologists, and several economists who have relied on essentially non-economic explanations. As pointed out above, a central assumption of mainstream growth theory was that the supply of entrepreneurs was highly elastic and that ". . . failures in entrepreneurship are attributable to maladjustments in the external environment" (Kilby 1971:3). The forces determining the level of entrepreneurial performance at any given time had to be looked for on the demand side.

The dominance of non-economic explanations of the supply of entrepreneurship is given in Kilby (1971:6–26), which shows that of the seven leading theories of entrepreneurial supply, four were psychological theories and three sociological (he later discusses one economic theory). Such theories highlight a variety of non-economic causal factors influencing supply—religious forces, low social status, child-rearing practices, education, the need for personal achievement, and related factors. Among the more notable of these theories are those by Schumpeter (1934), Hagen (1962), and McClelland and Winter (1970).

Schumpeter's entrepreneur, through his innovative activities, was the driving force in economic growth. However, Schumpeter relied on non-economic factors to explain the motives of the entrepreneur—factors that are present in any society, developed or developing. According to Schumpeter, the factor that determines the level of entrepreneurial activity relates to certain psychological influences—the will to found a private kingdom, the will to conquer, and the sheer satisfaction derived from achievement (Schumpeter 1934:93). Except for the first factor, pecuniary rewards are of secondary importance as entrepreneurial motives. And given that new opportunities for innovation are always present, entrepreneurship will depend on how powerfully these motives operate throughout society.

Hagen (1962) stresses the importance of ideological factors in entrepreneurship. He maintains that over time the loss of traditional status and respect has driven certain minority groups to bring up their children in ways that give them a strong urge to regain their former status. Such social—essentially deviant—groups are illustrated by the Jews in Europe, the Chinese in Southeast Asia, and the Ibo in Nigeria. Success in business is seen as one means of compensating for the loss of traditional status.

McClelland, a psychologist, sees entrepreneurship as being promoted by a particular human motive—the need to achieve or *n* Achievement. This concept is associated with a type of personality that places a high value on success, personal initiative, curiosity, and a rational and practical approach to problem solving. Success is measured in attaining excellence for its own sake rather than in accumulating money, position, or power. Childhood experience, coupled with education, religion, and other environmental factors, plays a part in promoting achievement and, in turn, entrepreneurship. Business is viewed as a powerful means by which individuals with high achievement can excel. When this motive is highly developed, it follows that the supply of entrepreneurs will be correspondingly high (McClelland and Winter 1970).

Supply factors in the South Pacific

The conditions governing the supply of entrepreneurs in the South Pacific region are still not fully understood, although the series of country studies of indigenous business conducted by PIDP will help fill the information gap. Some valuable insights also have resulted from studies carried out by anthropologists and sociologists during the 1950s and 1960s. Foremost are studies by Crocombe and Hogbin (1963), Finney (1971, 1973), Epstein (1968, 1970), and Salisbury (1970) in the context of the then territory of New Guinea; Belshaw (1964) and Watters (1969) in Fiji; and Finney (1971) in French Polynesia. These studies generally focus on the experience of particular social or tribal groups within these three countries, but they nonetheless point to several features that may have a wider interest. Several aspects are worth noting.

The first aspect relates to the studies of the Goroka and Tolai peoples by Finney, Epstein, and Salisbury showing that these groups, by virtue of the traditional culture, have a predisposition toward entrepreneurial activity and thus can adapt readily to the business opportunities offered by the modern cash economy. Both the Gorokans and the Tolais are strongly achievement oriented and see business success as a means of attaining upward mobility and hence individual prestige and so-called "big-man" status in the

community. Adaptation was further facilitated by certain characteristics of the traditional subsistence economy, including the use
of shell money to facilitate trade, an emphasis on the accumulation of wealth, and the ability to enlist the support of clansmen
and followers.

Although this entrepreneurial potential can provide a promising
base for modern business development, it does not in itself ensure
success on a sustained basis. Finney (1973:180) points to the need
for complementary resources, particularly land, to provide the
opportunities for entrepreneurial investment and regular contact
with the cash economy. Epstein (1970) and Finney (1971) maintain that once past the initial phase of contact with the outside
economy, further business success can be realized only by upgrading management and technical skills and by expanding the entrepreneur's horizons through exposure to new business possibilities.

A second feature relates to aspects of entrepreneurship in Fiji
stemming from the studies by Belshaw and Watters. These studies
point to the paucity of indigenous entrepreneurs in Fiji that can be
attributed to lack of official encouragement, on one hand, and the
attitudes of a conservative traditional leadership more interested
in politics and administration, on the other. The achievements of
several successful Fijian entrepreneurs were examined, and these
were found to conform to Hagen's notion of social deviants, in
that individuals have turned to economic activity as an outlet for
frustrations over traditional authority and as a means of gaining
power, prestige, and self-expression (Watters 1969:215). Whether
they were social deviants or people with disturbed family backgrounds (Belshaw 1964:154), these entrepreneurs apparently continued to observe, use, and manipulate customary practices and
traditional institutions to achieve their economic goals.

In observing that changes in the vocational preferences of Fijian
leaders are likely to be a slow process, both Belshaw and Watters
saw the value of training and the creation of a favorable policy
environment as being the most effective ways to increase the supply of entrepreneurs.

A third contribution is Finney's (1971) study of Tahitian entrepreneurs that highlights the role played by *demis* or "half-Euro-
pean" persons in the business life of Tahiti, the main island of
French Polynesia. Of French-Tahitian ancestry, the *demis* are the
most Europeanized of the mixed-blood Tahitians and account for

between 10 and 15 percent of the Tahitian population. Occupationally, they have been prominent as businessmen, public servants, and white collar employers, and their success can be attributed to the fact that they have adopted European attitudes, which are reflected in their business operations. Success can also be attributed to the way they conduct business with their Tahitian *(Ma'ohi)* cousins—a relationship that is essentially exploitive (Finney 1971:24).

The *demis* and their business achievements can be analyzed in terms of Hagen's marginal deviant group, but the association between entrepreneurial success and race and the adoption of European values has particular interest for Pacific island countries with mixed ethnic populations.

Two recent contributions

Sociologists, anthropologists, and others in related disciplines will continue to make important contributions to the entrepreneurship debate and thereby help to promote a clearer understanding of the factors that influence the supply of entrepreneurs. Economists, for their part, will need to grapple with these issues and attempt to go beyond approaches based on arbitrary assumptions, which essentially amount to agnosticism. The recent contributions by Kilby and Baumol are signs that economists are responding.

Kilby (1971) provides a useful analysis of the functions or activities of entrepreneurs in contradistinction to entrepreneurial attributes. He lists 13 functions that the entrepreneur himself might have to perform for the successful operation of his enterprise. Two functions—perception of market opportunities (novel or imitative) and command over scarce resources—are accepted as entrepreneurial in terms of the postulates of the economists' models. The remaining functions are largely administrative, managerial, and technological in nature and differ fundamentally from the entrepreneurial functions in that they can be purchased in the market place. These functions are as follows:

> purchasing inputs, marketing of the product and responding to competition, dealing with the public bureaucracy, management of human relations within the firm, manager of customer and supplier

relations, financial management, production management, acquiring and overseeing assembly of the factory, industrial engineering, upgrading process and product quality, and introduction of new production techniques and products (Kilby 1971:27).

Kilby's analysis delineates the multitude of tasks that are normally connected with the operation of an enterprise and provides a yardstick for distinguishing between entrepreneurial and managerial/administrative tasks. It also provides a taxonomy for evaluating entrepreneurial performance and, as such, endows the concept with greater operational application.

Baumol (1968:69) points to the shortcomings in current theory, especially its failure to help understand the determinants of the supply of entrepreneurs. Given that these shortcomings are likely to persist, he argues for a theory that focuses on the rewards for entrepreneurship and their determinants (e.g., policy measures to reduce risk and to make taxation systems more attractive). The emphasis is on what can be done operationally to encourage entrepreneurship through direct policy action rather than relying on a slow evolutionary process of stimulating growth. According to Baumol, the merit of this approach is that

> Without awaiting a change in the entrepreneurial drive exhibited in our society, we can learn how one can stimulate the volume and intensity of entrepreneurial activity, thus making the most of what is permitted by current mores and attitudes (Baumol 1968:71).

Concluding comments

Although the literature on entrepreneurship is extensive, significant differences remain in perceptions of the functions of entrepreneurs and how to deal with them in economic theory. Economists generally agree that entrepreneurship plays a vital, if not a dominant, part in economic growth, but they have not succeeded in measuring its contribution. Economists have generally not dealt with the factors that govern the supply of entrepreneurs, and the available insights stem largely from the works of non-economists.

Formulated essentially within the context of western industrial structures, traditional concepts of entrepreneurship and its role in the economic process need to be modified in any consideration of the problems of the developing countries, including those in the South Pacific. Some elements of established theory are useful, but others are not; much depends on the particular circumstances.

Schumpeter's concept of the innovating entrepreneur, for example, appears to have limited value in understanding entrepreneurship in many developing countries where the entrepreneurial task appears to lie more in applying, modifying, and adapting existing knowledge rather than in implementing ideas based on new discoveries. Furthermore, the fact that large closely integrated families or kinship groups continue to persist in many developing countries means that the focus should be on the family as the entrepreneurial unit rather than on the individual. The evidence derived from micro-level studies by sociologists and anthropologists also points to the need for a careful analysis of the indigenous culture and the social environment to gauge the extent of non-economic constraints and to gain an appreciation of conditioning response factors that might help would-be entrepreneurs adapt successfully to the requirements of modern business.

NOTE

1. The aggregate production function (assuming neutral technical change) takes the form:

$$Q=A(t)f(K,L)$$

with Q representing output; $A(t)$, the multiplicative factor measuring the cumulative effects of shifts over time; and K and L representing, respectively, capital and labor inputs in "physical" units. Solow uses this production function as a basis for isolating the effects of technical change over time, first, by differentiating totally with respect to time and then applying the results (with some rearrangement of terms) to time series of output per man hour, capital per man hour, and the share of capital in total output. (Solow 1957:312–3.)

REFERENCES

Baumol, W. J.
1968 "Entrepreneurship in Economic Theory," *American Economic Review,* Vol. LVIII, No. 2, (May), American Economic Association, Washington, pp. 64–71.

30 *Te'o I. J. Fairbairn*

Belshaw, C. D.
1964 *Under the Ivi Tree—Society and Economic Growth in Rural Fiji,* University of California Press, Los Angeles.

Crocombe, R. G. and G. R. Hogbin
1963 *The Erap Mechanical Farming Project,* Bulletin No. 1, New Guinea Research Unit, Canberra.

Denison, E. F.
1962 *The Sources of Economic Growth in the United States and the Alternatives Before Us,* Supplementary Paper No. 13, Committee for Economic Development, New York.

Epstein, T. Scarlett
1968 *Capitalism, Primitive, and Modern—Some Aspects of Tolai Economic Growth,* Michigan State University Press, East Lansing.
1970 "Indigenous Entrepreneurs and Their Narrow Horizons," in M. W. Ward (ed.), *The Indigenous Role in Business Enterprise—Three Papers from the Waigani Seminar 1969,* pp. 17–26, Bulletin No. 35, New Guinea Research Unit, Canberra.

Finney, B. R.
1971 *Big-Men, Half-Men and Trader Chiefs: Entrepreneurial Styles in New Guinea and Polynesia,* Working Paper No. 12, Technology and Development Institute, East-West Center, Honolulu.
1973 *Big-Men and Business: Entrepreneurship and Economic Growth in the New Guinea Highlands,* The University Press of Hawaii, Honolulu.
1987 *Business Development in the Highlands of Papua New Guinea,* Research Report Series No. 6, Pacific Islands Development Program, East-West Center, Honolulu.

Hagen, E.
1962 *On the Theory of Social Change,* Dorsey Press, Homewood, Illinois.

Harbison, F.
1961 "Entrepreneurial Organization as a Factor in Economic Development," in B. Okun and R. W. Richardson, *Studies in Economic Development,* pp. 311–319, Holt Rinehart and Winston Inc., New York.

Hirschman, A. O.
1958 *The Strategy of Economic Development,* Yale University Press, New Haven.

Kent, C. A.
1984 *The Environment for Entrepreneurship,* D. C. Heath & Co., Lexington.

Kilby, P.
1971 *Entrepreneurship and Economic Development,* The Free Press, New York.

Knight, F. H.
1921 *Risk, Uncertainty, and Profit,* Houghton Mifflin Co., Boston.

Leibenstein, H.
  1968 "Entrepreneurship and Development," *American Economic Review,* Vol. LVIII, No. 2 (May), American Economic Association, Washington, pp. 72–83.

Marshall, A.
  1961 *Principles of Economics* (9th edition), Macmillan, London.

McClelland, D. C. and D. G. Winter
  1970 "Achievement Motive and Entrepreneurship" in G. M. Meier, *Leading Issues in Economic Development* (second edition), pp. 663–673, Oxford University Press Inc. (USA).

Meade, J. E.
  1961 *A Neo-Classical Theory of Economic Growth,* Oxford University Press, New York.

Nafziger, E. W.
  1984 *The Economics of Developing Countries,* Wadsworth Publishing Co., California.

Salisbury, R. F.
  1970 *Vunamami Economic Transformation in a Traditional Society,* University of California Press, Berkeley, Los Angeles.

Schumpeter, J. A.
  1934 *The Theory of Economic Development,* Harvard University Press, Massachusetts.

Solow, R. M.
  1956 "A Contribution to the Theory of Economic Growth," *The Quarterly Journal of Economics,* Vol. LXX (February), pp. 65–94, Harvard University Press, Massachusetts.
  1957 "Technical Change and the Aggregate Production Function," *The Review of Economics and Statistics,* Vol. XXXIX, No. 3 (August), pp. 312–320.

Swan, T. W.
  1956 "Economic Growth and Capital Accumulation," *The Economic Record,* Vol. XXXII, No. 63, pp. 334–361, Melbourne University Press, Melbourne.

Watters, R. F.
  1969 *Koro: Economic Development and Social Change in Fiji,* Clarendon Press, Oxford.

PART 2

Studies of Entrepreneurship by Country

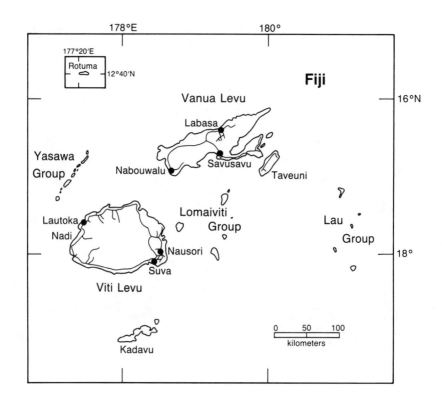

CHAPTER 3

Fijian Entrepreneurs: Indigenous Business in Fiji

John M. Hailey

FIJIAN entrepreneurs have been long overlooked as an integral component of development in Fiji. But in the economic and political climate of post-coup Fiji, the promotion of a viable Fijian business sector is integral to the balanced development of the Fiji economy. This chapter highlights the salient features of Fijian entrepreneurship, examines the role of the indigenous Fijian business community in the Fiji economy, and reviews the performance of Fijian entrepreneurs.

Introduction

Fiji is an independent country comprising more than 300 islands with a total land area of 18,376 sq km scattered over the South Pacific. The two largest islands and centers of economic activity are Viti Levu (10,429 sq km) and Vanua Levu (5,556 sq km). The outer islands are much smaller, and some two-thirds remain uninhabited. The scattered location and isolation of the islands create transportation and communication difficulties; thus economic activity is concentrated in a few centers on Viti Levu and Vanua Levu.

According to Fijian legend, the great Chief Lutunasobasoba led his people across the sea to the new land of Fiji. Most historians agree that in Fiji the Melanesians and the Polynesians mixed to create a highly developed society long before the arrival of the Europeans in the 19th century. In 1874 Fiji was ceded to Britain; to ensure the economic viability of this new colony, plantation agriculture was encouraged as was the development of the cash market economy. Between 1879 and 1916 Indians came as indentured laborers to work in the sugar plantations. After the indentured system was abolished, many remained in Fiji as independent farmers or businessmen; by the end of 1985 the Fiji-Indian community with an estimated population of 349,000 made up 50 percent of the population and as such was the largest single ethnic group in Fiji.

After independence in 1970, Fiji justifiably prided itself on its apparently harmonious multi-racial society, but this harmony was shattered on 14 May 1987 when a military coup overthrew the recently elected government of Dr. Timoci Bavadra. The repercussions of this coup include an escalation of political and social tensions and an exacerbation of existing economic problems. Since independence the Fiji economy not only had failed to diversify but also had experienced per capita growth rates in real terms of only 1 percent per annum. In the 1980s the economy was hard hit by the world recession, high interest rates, and low commodity prices; GDP growth rates were erratic, and the number of people with regular paid employment had decreased. The economy continued to be propped up by the sugar industry, which accounted for 59 percent of export revenue in 1985 while gold accounted for 11 percent, canned fish 6 percent, and coconut oil 4 percent. The manufacturing sector had failed to expand and, since independence, was estimated to consist of only 11 percent of the nation's gross domestic product (GDP).

More optimistically, new investments by overseas corporations in the minerals, timber, and tourism sector promised new economic opportunities, but their viability seems to have been jeopardized in the aftermath of the coup. Other repercussions of the coup include the curtailment of new investment plans, the devaluation of the Fiji dollar, falling foreign reserves, a reduction in export earnings, and a freeze by some aid donors on future aid commitments. But the long-term implications may be most accurately assessed in the context of Fiji's growing population. At present one-half the population is under 21 years of age, and in 1984 it was estimated that some 3,800 new income sources would have to be created each year until the end of the century to meet expected employment demands. This expectation was ambitious then; because of the post-coup economic downturn, it is now unrealistic.

The coup appears to have exacerbated the existing structural problems that had beset the Fiji economy. Thus initiatives to promote Fijians in business should be viewed against this background. The Fijian business, as an interdependent component of the business sector, is integral to the local economy. Given the aspirations of the Fijian people, indigenous entrepreneurs are expected to play an increasing role in the development of Fiji.[1]

Evolvement of Fijian entrepreneurship

Between the time of independence and the author's research in Fiji in 1984, a surprisingly buoyant, thriving, private business sector had developed in Fiji. This period has been one of entrepreneurial experimentation, business innovation, and commercial vision—a time when Fijian involvement and interest in business had flourished. Granted, many of the entrepreneurial experiments undertaken by Fijians had failed, often as a result of poor planning and mismanagement of resources. Yet given the extent of competition, and especially the lack of exposure of most Fijians to business practices, some failures could have been expected, even though the failure rate of Fijian businesses appears to be no worse than that of small businesses in other countries. In general, Fijian interest in entrepreneurship was rekindled in the 1970s, and a foundation of Fijian involvement in the commercial sector was re-established.

Trade and commerce had flourished in the Pacific before the arrival of Europeans. Early European visitors to Fiji recorded that the local economy was well developed and clearly regulated (Wilkes 1845:301). Fijian entrepreneurs had developed international trading contacts with Tonga and Western Samoa, and regular trading links existed within the Fiji group of islands. But the arrival of Europeans in the 19th century and the expansion of the cash market economy introduced European mercantile concepts of business and entrepreneurship that were alien to traditional Fijian enterprise. As a result, two or three generations of Fijians withdrew from active participation in the economy because of increasing competition from non-indigenous business interests. This withdrawal was instigated by social pressures, vested interests, and even restrictive colonial legislation.

European business interests thus dominated the local business

sector. In fact, business practices became so synonymous with
Europeans that to most Pacific islanders, entrepreneurial practices
became institutionalized as belonging to these interlopers (Belshaw 1955:155). Islanders who emulated European commercial
practices were often regarded as social outcasts or even as deviants
(Finney 1972:124). Later the numbers of expatriate businessmen
operating in Fiji were swelled by migrants from India, many of
whom had originally arrived in Fiji at the end of the 19th century
as indentured laborers to work in the sugar plantations; having
rejected repatriation, they remained in Fiji. These new migrants
prospered in several commercial areas including retail, transport,
and sugarcane and are now an integral component of the business
fabric of Fiji.

In modern Fiji the cash market economy is well established, and
the culture has adapted under its influence as entrepreneurs
increasingly exploit market opportunities. But given the limited
Fijian participation in business, commercial practices are still alien
to the way of life of many Fijians. The business ethos associated
with the cash market economy, measurable economic returns,
individual acquisitiveness, and the profit motive are often incompatible with the traditional Fijian communal society. Thus any
attempt to encourage Fijians in business could be seen as a threat
to traditional values and to a way of life.

Economic realities, however, dictate that Fijians should participate increasingly in business. This situation is particularly true in
post-coup Fiji, where the Fijian business community is expected to
reduce the economic gap between Fijians and other races and consequently to ensure that Fijians have some control over their commercial destiny. As a result, a conflict occurs between traditional
values and the necessities of modern business that creates a fundamental dilemma, which influences the thinking of many politi-
cians, planners, and entrepreneurs in Fiji.

This dilemma may explain why, since independence, only limited resources have been allocated to support Fijian entrepreneurs.
Certainly, no short-term panacea is available, and any investment
in the Fijian business sector should be assessed only in the long
term. Any attempt to encourage Fijian entrepreneurs must be sensitive to these issues. As a result, this author's 1985 report on business in Fiji concluded that the government should formulate a
cohesive policy to support indigenous Fijian entrepreneurs; other-

wise, they will have no chance of competing on equal terms with other races. This conclusion is especially true of post-coup Fiji.

Fijian entrepreneurship: a definition

Most definitions of entrepreneurship in the general literature are based on research carried out in the urban industrialized economies of the developed world. These definitions are based on societies with cultural values that have little in common with those of the Pacific islands in that they stress individualism and acquisitiveness, measure success in financial terms, and emphasize the entrepreneur's role as a change agent. These values are alien to Pacific cultures and to the isolated predominantly rural island economies.

Former Minister of Labour, the late Ratu David Toganivalu, suggested that "frugality and acquisitiveness are disciplines that run against the grain of all that is natural in our way of life" (Toganivalu 1979:23). A common aphorism succinctly states that commerce is about selling; Fijian society is all about sharing. Thus the more appropriate definitions of Pacific entrepreneurship emphasize the impact of communalism rather than individuality, reciprocity rather than acquisitiveness, and social gain rather than financial profit. For instance, in traditional Fijian society success and profit were intangibles measured in terms of the status and self-esteem derived from fulfilling inherent social commitments. Material loss was compensated by social gain and enhanced prestige.

Similarly, contemporary Fijian entrepreneurs appear to be motivated as much by personal gain or social recognition as by financial reward. For instance, a majority of urban Fijian entrepreneurs interviewed had entered business as a means of freeing themselves from traditional bonds and thereby asserting their individuality (Hailey 1985:70).

Efforts to define the role of the entrepreneur have been beset by conflicting opinions and theories. Clearly, many definitions are the product not only of ethnocentric bias but also of linguistic constraints. Many Pacific languages do not have the necessary vocabulary to describe Eurocentric perceptions of entrepreneurship. For example, no obvious Fijian words describe the concept of "risk

taker," "innovator," or even "business." If such words do not exist
in the Fijian language, does this mean these concepts do not exist
in traditional Fijian society? Can one therefore surmise that entrepreneurial activity is alien to Fijians? Obviously, such linguistic
and semantic questions need to be re-examined. If the concept of
entrepreneurship is as deceptive and illusory as it appears to be,
then it must be unfathomable to those not inculcated in European
or American nuances and values. This is true when the Fijian
entrepreneur is evaluated in terms that are alien to *vakaviti* (the
Fijian way of life).

Moreover, attempts to analyze Fijian entrepreneurship have
often resulted in contradictory interpretations. For example, Belshaw (1964) and Watters (1969) disagreed as to whether Fijian
entrepreneurs were creative innovators or mere opportunists. Belshaw in his book *Under the Ivi Tree,* which is based on research in
the Sigatoka Valley, argued that entrepreneurship for many Fijians
was a "creative outlet, a release from frustrations," which allowed
the individual to flourish. It was, he suggested, "the non-conform-
ist (in Fijian terms) who is likely to make the greatest effort to
become an entrepreneur" (Belshaw 1964:157).

Watters in a study of the economic development of Koro, an
island in Lomaiviti, argues that the Fijian entrepreneurs were not
so much creative innovators as individuals who merely exploited
existing opportunities. They appeared to exploit possibilities discovered by others but had the drive, skills, and the wherewithal to
do so successfully (Watters 1969:206).

Belshaw also concluded that for reasons related to the entrepreneurs' personality, education, or religion, these individuals became
increasingly detached from local society and so were able to pros-
per. Whereas later research by both Rakoto (1979) and Hailey
(1985) contradicts this perception and instead stresses the strong
links that Fijian entrepreneurs maintain with their village and the
local community in general.

Rakoto, in his study of Fijian sugar farmers in the Sigatoka Valley, identified the most successful commercial farmers as those
who were staunch supporters of traditional ceremonies and community obligations. The least successful farmers were those who
apparently isolated themselves on their own land and became
alienated from their community (Rakoto 1979:180). This research reinforced the perception that Fijian entrepreneurs can be

understood only by analyzing their relationships and aspirations within the context of the local community. The community—as a source of capital, labor, and support—is for most small Fijian businesses often their major market. As such, Fijian entrepreneurs jeopardized their endeavors by isolating themselves from their local community and all its concomitant obligations.

This background highlights a major dilemma facing the Fijian entrepreneurs today. Do they run their businesses as individualistic, risk-taking, profit-maximizing businessmen; or do they accept and work within the local cultural mores and communal obligations? If they reject Fijian values, not only is a viable way of life threatened but also they risk business failure by becoming alienated and ostracized from the local community. In so doing, they may threaten important customer relations, alienate a potential source of labor or capital, and create divisive personal tensions.

In an attempt to understand the Fijian entrepreneur, some of the issues must be resolved in the conflicting definitions of Fijian entrepreneurship. In my original study, the Fijian entrepreneur was defined as "a Fijian *(i taukei)* who shows practical creativity, combining resources and opportunities in new ways to benefit the individual, the family, and the community in general."

Similarly, an appropriate definition is needed for "small business" because the Fijian business sector is dominated by small businesses. Legal definitions of small business differ from country to country, and international criteria are inappropriate in the context of Fiji.

The criteria used in assessing the size of a business can include the number of employees, the annual sales turnover, the level of profit, the size of assets, the decision-making structure, and the degree to which control is separated from ownership. Such criteria are often either too complex or inaccurate for the Pacific. For instance, many small businesses in the Pacific rely on relatives to work on an irregular or part-time basis. Thus an assessment of the size of a company based on the number of regularly paid employees does not accurately reflect its size. It would also be inaccurate to rely on a company's figures for sales turnover, profit on assets, or cash ratios because of incomplete bookkeeping or tax accounting procedures.

In Fiji a small business has not been defined for government policies in support of the small business sector. Fiji's Eighth Development Plan does refer to "small, medium, and cottage industry as an enterprise requiring up to $100,000 in initial total fixed capital" (Government of Fiji 1980, Vol. 1, 9.7.16). But this definition does not reflect the reality of Fijian business, which has virtually no involvement in the industrial sector and in which the estimated mean value of initial total fixed capital invested was a mere $7,978 (Hailey 1985:67). Thus a small Fijian business was defined as "an independently owned and operated business that has a small share of the market and an annual turnover of less than $50,000[2] and that was personally managed by its owner, who relies on five or fewer regularly paid employees" (Hailey 1985:36).

The Fijian entrepreneur

Based on the author's original study, certain characteristics mark entrepreneurial activity in Fiji (Hailey 1985). The Fiji-Indian and part-European communities are concentrated in the urban and peri-urban areas, whereas two-thirds of the Fijians interviewed operated businesses in the rural areas and outer island groups. These data support the Fijians' strong rural ties and accurately reflect the proportion of the Fijian population living in rural areas. At least one-half of the Fijian entrepreneurs interviewed ran small trade stores, while the rest operated transport and service businesses or commercial farming or fisheries ventures. None of those interviewed ran manufacturing industries, a sector dominated by expatriates or Fiji-Indian companies. The numbers of Fijians running small businesses in the service sector suggest that these businesses are relatively easy to start and manage, needing fewer sophisticated business skills and a smaller capital investment. Unfortunately, this situation also means that the retail, transportation, and service sectors are saturated with small businesses competing directly against each other. There even appears to be a strong tendency to imitate existing businesses; this "copy cat" mentality not only creates problems for existing businesses in small markets but also reflects a lack of confidence to innovate or grasp new market opportunities.

The parochial nature of business in Fiji is reflected in the fact that nearly two-thirds of those interviewed served local markets. Their narrow horizons suggest that entrepreneurs are not fully aware of the market opportunities in Fiji. This situation is surprising because 58 percent of the Fijian entrepreneurs interviewed were migrants who ran businesses outside of their original province. Apparently, they were part of the pattern of migration that marks contemporary Fijian life. Increasing numbers of Fijians are moving to urban centers or seeking tourist-related employment in western Viti Levu (Hailey 1985:72). Also the small proportion of entrepreneurs who have any contact with overseas markets reinforces this inward orientation.

The parochiality of the business community in Fiji is determined somewhat by traditional values and cultural mores. Thus business in Fiji is a man's world as befitting the patrilineal nature of Fiji society. This state of affairs is reinforced by the limited training opportunities available for women, the lack of management positions for women, and the suspicions of the traditionally male-dominated business and banking community (Hailey 1985: 86). Despite these constraints, an increasing number of well-educated Fijian women, some 20 percent of the Fijian entrepreneurs interviewed, had opened businesses in urban areas. Such women entrepreneurs have succeeded by tapping specialist market areas, (e.g., Hot Bread Kitchen Shops) or by using the sexual and racial loyalties of their customers, (e.g., hairdressers or seamstresses). Although many businesses were registered in men's names, in fact the wives played an active, if not dominant, role in the business. The husband acted as the "front man," while the wife was the driving force, essentially the manager of the business (Hailey 1985:85).

Most entrepreneurs interviewed were over the age of 40 and were well-established members of their communities with strong family ties and social responsibilities. The relatively high average age of entrepreneurs in Fiji has important implications for the successors of entrepreneurs in times of illness or death and for business training programs for Fijians (Hailey 1985:70).

The Fiji-Indian entrepreneurs appeared to have spent much of their working life in business, while in contrast the older Fijian entrepreneurs generally established their businesses only after a period of other employment. In other words, they started businesses in which they had no previous experience despite their years of previous employment. For example, a taxi driver turns to fishing or an accounting clerk to hairdressing. This pattern reinforces the perception that many Fijians are still "experimenting" with business and are not bound by precedent. Furthermore, many entrepreneurs do not make the most appropriate use of their skills and appear unconcerned about the likelihood of failure (Hailey 1985:75).

It has been suggested that only the better educated entrepreneurs will succeed in business, but there was limited evidence in the 1985 study to support this supposition. A review of the data clearly shows that previous work experience and early exposure to business practices are major predeterminants of business success. This was well exemplified in that two-thirds of the highly successful Fiji-Indian entrepreneurs interviewed had received only a primary education, and that three-fourths had never undertaken any formal vocational training (Hailey 1985:74). In fact, most Fijian entrepreneurs had higher levels of education and had traveled overseas more often than their Fiji-Indian counterparts; yet their business performance did not reflect these supposed advantages. The least educated Fijians were running the smallest, least sophisticated businesses in the retail and transport sector, apparently a reflection of their lack of skills and their limited horizons.

A central concern of the original study was that the Fijian entrepreneurs were disadvantaged by lack of early exposure to business and limited commercial experience. Any child who was brought up in a business environment and who from an early age worked in the business was inculcated in the business ethic. This was commonly the case in the Fiji-Indian retail sector where stores are handed down through the family. The limited number of Fijians who had any family background in business emphasizes the gap that Fijian entrepreneurs still have to bridge if they are to compete on equal terms with other races. To accelerate this process, policies that provide practical experience and that are integrated with vocational training programs should be implemented. Moreover, banks or business advisers should not discriminate against their less educated clients who attempt to raise finance or seek training because their practical experience could well be an asset.

In general, the research showed that the average Fijian entrepreneur was a middle-aged man with extensive family and community commitments who, having finished one career, had gone into business with relatively little commercial or management experience. Despite these drawbacks and the relatively high failure rate, at least three-fourths of the Fijian entrepreneurs interviewed were optimistic about their future business prospects although this optimism could be symptomatic of the "experimental" approach adopted by many Fijian entrepreneurs. Unfortunately, their unrealistic assessment of the potential profitability of their business frequently led to rapid unplanned expansion that collapsed in bankruptcy (Hailey 1985:80).

Fijian businesses

The survey data confirmed that most Fijian businesses had been established by their present owners and that three-fourths had been in existence for less than five years; by comparison three-fourths of the Fiji-Indians interviewed had been in business for at least six years or more. The relatively youthful nature of Fijian business and its relatively short life span further reflect the "experimental" approach adopted by many Fijian entrepreneurs, which was noted above. (One aspect that deserves further research was that Fijian entrepreneurs from the outer islands who had established businesses in Viti Levu were more likely to have survived profitably for more than five years.)

Three-fourths of the businesses in the survey were legally categorized as "sole traders," a business entity that is cheap, easy to form, and in keeping with the relatively unsophisticated nature of most Fijian businesses. Also of interest was the absence of legal partnerships among Fijian businesses. Given the communal nature of Fijian society, such partnerships could fulfill a useful role by allowing, for example, members of a *mataqali* (the traditional lineage group or clan in Fijian society) to work together, pool their talents and savings, use local labor, and develop *mataqali* land. But a review of the interviews with the Fijian entrepreneurs underscores their attitude that partnerships, particularly with other members of a *mataqali,* were riven by jealousies, threatened by the expense of meeting communal obligations, and often suffered from conflicting purposes. Most Fijian entrepreneurs have avoided relying on members of their extended family or *mataqali* as business partners.

Even though Fijians may not be prepared to enter into business partnerships with their family, they are willing to employ their family or relatives as low-cost labor. Sixty percent of the total work force employed by Fijian entrepreneurs was composed of relatives. The use of irregular family labor meant that businesses could operate long hours, keep wage costs low, and avoid the expense and time associated with employee insurance and tax. Family labor was essential if indigenous businesses were to survive profitably. It must also be noted that while two-thirds of Fijian-owned businesses employed fewer than two regularly paid employees, only 20 percent employed more than five employees. These data imply that at least four-fifths of Fijian businesses could be defined as "small business" using the definition described in this study.

Fijian businessmen invested a surprisingly large proportion of their time in their business activities, on average over 67 hours per week. This belies the picture of the lazy, worthless Fijian but does suggest that inexperienced Fijian entrepreneurs are probably not making productive use of their time because the profits generated from hours worked were relatively small. Whether this rate of return was sufficient to justify the hard work and long hours entailed in running a business in Fiji is questionable. Moreover, only one-half of the Fijians interviewed reinvested their profits. These entrepreneurs often failed to distinguish between personal expenses and business needs. These factors became intertwined, and business reserves were often used as personal savings.

The overall rates of return on original investment were generally low, ranging from 0.1 percent for agricultural ventures to 2.5 percent for retail businesses (Hailey 1985:68). These figures suggest that relatively unsophisticated retail businesses can be started with surprisingly little capital and can still generate some return on investment. This reinforces the view of many Fijians that running a retail store is a source of "easy money." However, these figures generally reflect a mediocre rate of return on capital, not to mention time and energy. A better rate of return could be achieved in a savings account.

An additional concern was that Fijian businesses had limited markets and were beset accordingly with cash flow problems. The sales revenue of an average Fijian business was estimated to be $466 per week, whereas Fiji-Indian businesses generated $1,355 per week, and part-European or Chinese businesses generated up to $8,000 per week (Hailey 1985:79). The low sales turnover common to many Fijian businesses meant that the business could not enjoy the benefits of economy of scale, that bulk purchasing was impossible, and that the business therefore carried a limited range of often overpriced goods. For example, the average price charged in Fijian-owned retail stores was 20 percent higher than that in Fiji-Indian-owned stores. With higher prices and a smaller selection, customers shopped elsewhere, and banks were unwilling to lend money on the basis of such poor sales projections. This vicious circle is the death knell of many Fijian businesses and encapsulates many problems faced by Fijian entrepreneurs.

Fijian business: success and failure

After an initial period of entrepreneurial experimentation, the skills of indigenous entrepreneurs in Fiji need to be consolidated. The expanding local market needs to be tapped by successful Fijian entrepreneurs based on the increasing spending power and changing aspirations of the Fijian people. Obviously, any assessment of the performance and personality of a successful entrepreneur is subjective and value laden. But the evidence suggests that successful Fijian entrepreneurs share several characteristics; above all, they are personally ambitious within the framework of their own business goals. In interviews, they emphasized their integrity *(na tamata dina)* and reliability *(na tamata nuitaki)*, as well as their personal charisma in fostering business contacts, maintaining customer relations, and exploiting local resources. Many also admitted to relying heavily on the support of their spouse or family in their business success.

In addition, the survival and profitability of most Fijian-owned businesses seem to depend on the entrepreneur's management expertise, marketing ability, and entrepreneurial personality. The necessary management expertise includes personal maturity and responsibility, which are reflected in a reputation for reliability or professionalism; clear personal goals and concise business objectives; a well-developed business plan; effective coordination and control of all business resources; and a working knowledge of the techniques to effectively use these resources. Successful entrepreneurs were also able to maintain their market share and customer loyalty by offering high quality goods or services at competitive prices.

The Fijian entrepreneur still faces the very real threat of business failure, so much so that there is a pervasive assumption that businesses owned and operated by Fijians will fail and collapse in bankruptcy. This assumption, which is not supported by the bankruptcy data in Fiji, has bedeviled efforts to encourage indigenous business (Chandra and Hailey 1984:3). The implicit expectation of business failure has become so ingrained in island thinking as to become a self-fulfilling prophesy; consequently, many businesses are started with the owners harboring the latent expectation of failure (Hailey 1985:21). The reasons for business failure appear to be similar to those faced by small indigenous businesses in other developing Pacific islands (Hailey 1987:98). These problems include a lack of management experience and business skills, undercapitalization resulting from a failure to raise sufficient funds, uncoordinated government policies, inadequate infrastructure, the lack of appropriate training and advice, a paucity of information on markets, the unavailability of incentives or subsidies, and the expense of meeting the obligations and commitments inherent in Pacific island societies.

The following two problems illustrate the extent of this challenge for Fijian entrepreneurs.

Lack of capital

The lack of capital is a main cause of business failure in Fiji. Undercapitalization results from the failure of entrepreneurs to raise sufficient start-up funds or operating capital to ensure long-term survival. The impact of undercapitalization is reflected in recurrent liquidity problems, a limited range of stock and equipment, substandard business premises, poor location, little effective promotion or advertising, inability to finance expansion plans, and especially recurrent instability. Undercapitalization appears to be a recipe for business failure.

In general, banks in Fiji appear to have adequate financial reserves, and it would have been inaccurate to suggest that there was a shortage of business capital in the country. Instead, the problem appears to be one of how Fijian entrepreneurs can gain access to these funds. Bankers claim they are willing to lend to any viable commercial proposition, but potential Fijian clients frequently failed to prepare a viable loan proposal. In addition, they appeared ignorant of basic bank practices and loan procedures (Hailey 1985:101).

The entrepreneurs were generally critical of the unsupportive attitude of banks in Fiji. In general, Fijian entrepreneurs relied on informal sources of capital; two-thirds of those interviewed had used their own capital or the savings of their family and friends or had borrowed money from money lenders to finance their business activities (Hailey 1985:68). Most entrepreneurs interviewed assumed that banks favored large borrowers and purposely made loan procedures difficult for small indigenous businessmen. This perception was supported by the contention that banks demanded loan guarantees and collateral that local entrepreneurs could rarely afford. Furthermore, most entrepreneurs complained about the high rate of interest charged and the short payback period.

Respondents also noted that the Fiji Development Bank's Industrial and Commercial Loans to Fijians Scheme (see Chapter 11) received a diminishing proportion of the total investment funds available. This resulted in increasing competition among Fijian entrepreneurs for these limited funds and raised the question of the Fiji Development Bank's role as a lending institution with a particular mandate to promote Fijian enterprise. Most entrepreneurs felt that the banks discriminated against them, but they reserved their strongest criticism for the commercial banks that, apart from lending expensive short-term working capital, appeared to avoid any lending to indigenous business. The general lack of capital was structurally inherent in the Fijian business environment, and the unsympathetic attitude of local banks merely exacerbated this state of affairs.

Lack of government guidelines

Fijian entrepreneurs have been hampered because government has never established clear policy guidelines to either define or prioritize the role of indigenous Fijian business in the local economy. Furthermore, no attempt has been made to coordinate the efforts of government agencies and Enterprise Support Organizations, which were established specifically to promote Fijian business.

These include the Industrial and Commercial Loans to Fijians Scheme of the Fiji Development Bank, which was established in 1975; the Business Opportunity and Management Advisory Service (BOMAS), which was established in 1975 to provide training and advice exclusively to Fijian entrepreneurs; and the Economic Development Board (now renamed the Fiji Trade and Investment Board), which was established in 1980 to encourage new investment in Fiji.

The relationship between BOMAS and the Fiji Development Bank exemplifies the problems and the related frustrations that result from the lack of coordination between these agencies. Since its inception BOMAS has prepared feasibility studies of potential Fijian business to assess whether the business proposal is realistic and viable. On the basis of these studies, it makes a recommendation for financial support from the development bank. But over 40 percent of the recommendations have been rejected by the bank. The conflict between these agencies purporting to help Fijian business not only delays the client's business plans but also generates unnecessary confusion and frustration. Another example of this lack of coordination is the bank's recently established Management Advisory Unit designed to provide training and advice to the bank's Fijian clients, which duplicates the role of BOMAS and creates further confusion among their respective Fijian clients.

The service provided by BOMAS is meager because the government has failed to invest sufficient funds or recruit suitably experienced staff. BOMAS can be further criticized in that the great majority of its staff is based in Suva, and thus few Fijian entrepreneurs in the rural areas had heard of BOMAS. Moreover, this organization was established with the expressed purpose of training Fijian entrepreneurs, but only about 10 percent of the BOMAS budget was actually spent on training.

In conclusion, the Enterprise Support Organizations established to promote Fijians in business have not fulfilled their roles and have even created additional problems for Fijian entrepreneurs. BOMAS is constrained by limited funding and insufficient staff. The Fiji Development Bank's Industrial and Commercial Loans to Fijians Scheme offers a declining proportion of the bank's total assets (despite a healthy operating surplus) and little lending flexibility to small Fijian clients. The Economic Development Board's Annual Report for 1983 showed that only one privately owned

Fijian-controlled business had received assistance from the board (Hailey 1985:58). There appears to be little cost-effective coordination of advisory or training programs offered for Fijians. The confusing array of extension programs is marked by conflicting advice and inappropriate materials as well as by an obvious duplication of resources. Given this background, the major recommendation in the author's original study was that the government of Fiji should develop a cohesive integrated policy to coordinate all aspects of support for small enterprises. Only then, it was argued, would many of the structural problems of indigenous Fijian entrepreneurs be overcome.

Conclusion

Pressure to encourage Fijian participation in business is increasing. As pointed out in the original study, "A successful Fijian business community can reduce the economic gap that has developed between Fijians and the other races. Non-Fijian entrepreneurs have consolidated their market position and now dominate business opportunities. If this pattern continues and the economic gap between the races widens, political and social stability in Fiji will be threatened" (Hailey 1985:105).

With the benefit of hindsight, these words ring ominously true in an analysis of the varied political and economic factors that led to the military coup and that have threatened Fiji's stability. In the past, even the limited commitment in support of indigenous entrepreneurs has proven counterproductive. In the context of post-coup Fiji, it is imperative that Fijian entrepreneurs be encouraged by policies that will stimulate, support, and sustain their efforts if they are to thrive and succeed in business.

But this potential can be achieved only if Fijians are willing to integrate their personal values with the rigors of business practice and available business resources. The future of Fijian business depends on whether the individual entrepreneurs can resolve the inherent contradictions between contemporary business practices and the communal commitments that are integral to the Fijian way of life.

NOTES

1. This chapter is based on the author's report entitled "Indigenous Business in Fiji," which was submitted to the government of Fiji in 1985. This report was based on extensive research in Fiji including interviews with over 80 local entrepreneurs, numerous government officials, business advisers, and bankers as well as archival research. The interviews with the entrepreneurs were based on a standard questionnaire designed to obtain information on the entrepreneurs themselves, their business problems, success factors, their attitudes toward government initiatives, and their views on current policies. The majority of those interviewed were Fijian entrepreneurs; smaller numbers of other ethnic groups were also interviewed for purposes of comparison. Those entrepreneurs interviewed operated various types of businesses of varying sizes in different parts of Fiji, including the outer islands. This diverse sample was assumed to represent a cross-section of non-subsistence commercial ventures in contemporary Fiji. The majority of those interviewed worked in the retail and service sectors of the economy.

2. F$1.00=US$0.88 in 1984.

REFERENCES

Belshaw, C. S.
   1955 "The Cultural Milieu of the Entrepreneur, A Critical Essay," *Exploration in Entrepreneurial History,* Vol. 7, No. 3, pp. 146–163.
   1964 *Under the Ivi Tree: Society and Economic Growth in Rural Fiji,* Routledge and Kegan Paul, London.

Chandra, S., and John M. Hailey
   1984 "Business and Bankruptcy in Fiji," *Fiji Accountant,* Fiji Institute of Accountants, Suva.

Finney, B. R.
   1972 "Big-Men, Half-Men and Trader Chiefs," in T. S. Epstein and D. Penney, eds, *Opportunity and Response,* C. Hurst, London.

Government of Fiji
   1980 *Eighth Development Plan, 1981–85,* Central Planning Office, Suva.

Hailey, J. M.
   1985 *Indigenous Business in Fiji,* Pacific Islands Development Program, East-West Center, Honolulu.
   1987 *Entrepreneurs and Indigenous Business in the Pacific,* Research Report Series No. 9, Pacific Islands Development Program, East-West Center, Honolulu.

Rakoto, A.
   1979 "Motivation Research in Rural Development," in A. Mamak and G. McCall, eds, *Paradise Postponed,* Pergamon, Sydney.

Toganivalu, D.
  1979 Interview, *South Pacific Islands Business News,* Suva.

Watters, R. F.
  1969 *Koro: Economic Development and Social Change in Fiji,* Oxford University Press, Melbourne.

Wilkes, C.
  1845 *Narrative of the United States Exploring Expedition,* Gregg Press, Philadelphia.

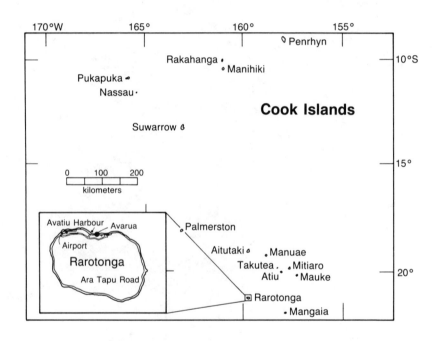

170°W   165°   160°   155°

Penrhyn

Rakahanga
Manihiki   10°S

Pukapuka
Nassau

Cook Islands

Suwarrow

15°

0   100   200
kilometers

Avatiu Harbour   Avarua   Palmerston

Airport   Aitutaki   Manuae

Rarotonga   Takutea   Mitiaro
           Atiu   Mauke   20°
Ara Tapu Road

                 Rarotonga

                   Mangaia

CHAPTER 4

Indigenous Entrepreneurship and Business Development in the Cook Islands

Te'o I. J. Fairbairn

CURRENT development approaches in the Cook Islands rely heavily on the performance of entrepreneurs as the driving force behind the private sector. In this capacity entrepreneurs are expected to play a key role in strategies to fulfill national development objectives such as raising living standards and promoting greater economic independence. According to the Cook Islands First Development Plan 1982–1985 (Government of the Cook Islands 1984: 16), all private sector groups in a position to contribute actively to development will be encouraged to do so—planters, growers associations, processing units, manufacturers, tourism groups, trading organizations, and voluntary associations.

The emphasis on entrepreneurship and private sector development is understandable, given the need to restore and enhance the productive capacity of the economy, which originated from the desire for greater national self-reliance. The emphasis is also due to social factors—a wish both to stem emigration and, in the case of indigenous entrepreneurs, to foster greater local participation in the growth process.

This chapter analyzes various aspects of the major entrepreneurial group in the country—indigenous entrepreneurs. The analysis focuses on the experience of entrepreneurs on the main island of Rarotonga: major characteristics, reasons for going into business, operational problems and constraints, success factors, and government support measures capable of overcoming existing problems. The exercise is based on a larger study of entrepreneurship in the Cook Islands (Fairbairn with Pearson 1987) carried out under the auspices of the Pacific Islands Development Program (PIDP) as part of a region-wide survey of indigenous business

development. A major aim of the initial country study was to gain
a better understanding of indigenous entrepreneurship in the Cook
Islands, which could assist in the design of soundly based development policies in this area.

The background

The Cook Islands is located between 156° and 167° west longi-
tude and between 8° and 23° south latitude, some 3,000 km
northeast of New Zealand. It comprises 15 inhabited islands with
a total area of only 237 sq km dispersed over an area of almost 2
million sq km of ocean. The eight islands comprising the Southern
Group (see Table 4.1) are mainly volcanic in origin while the seven
islands of the Northern Group are all atolls. Rarotonga, the largest island, is the country's commercial and administrative center
and also hosts an international airport. Population is currently an
estimated 17,500 of which just over 9,000 live in Rarotonga.

The Cook islands achieved self-governing status in 1965 "in
association" with New Zealand after being under New Zealand
administration since 1901. Under this arrangement, New Zealand
undertook to assist the Cook Islands government in external
affairs and defense if requested, while allowing Cook Islanders, as
New Zealand citizens, to move freely in and out of New Zealand.
The new political status formalized other arrangements favorable
to the Cook Islands—free and unrestricted access for Cook
Islands' products to the New Zealand market and regular assistance in the form of budgetary support.

The economy is dominated by the service sector although
involvement in subsistence activities remains extensive. Major
service elements are public administration, wholesale and retail
trade, tourism and related activities, communications and transportation, and finance. In 1983 the gross domestic product (GDP)
generated within the service sector totaled $10.7 million out of a
total GDP of $13.5 million or 79 percent (Government of the Cook
Islands 1985: Table 1.3).[1]

This left only a modest share of GDP (21 percent) from the "productive" sectors comprising agriculture, manufacturing, and construction. (These proportions do not take into account subsistence
activities, which remain unrecorded.)

The present economic pattern is the result of significant struc-

Table 4.1. Cook Islands: some physical and demographic characteristics

Island	Distance from Rarotonga (km)	Land area (sq km)	Population 1971	Population 1981	% Change	Density (1981) persons sq km
Rarotonga	–	67.1	11,478	9,530	-17	142
Aitutaki	259	18.3	2,855	2,335	-18	127
Atiu	215	26.9	1,455	1,225	-16	45
Mangaia	204	51.8	2,081	1,364	-34	26
Manuae	230	6.2	2	12	–	2
Mauke	278	18.4	763	681	-11	37
Mitiaro	263	22.3	331	256	-23	11
Takutea	219	1.3	–	–		
Total Southern Group	238[a]	212.3	18,965	15,403	-19	73
Manihiki	1,204	5.4	452	405	-10	75
Nassau	1,246	1.2	160	134	-16	112
Palmerston	500	2.1	62	51	-18	24
Pukapuka	1,324	1.4	732	796	+9	569
Rakahanga	1,248	4.1	339	272	-21	66
Suwarrow	950	0.5	–	–	–	–
Penrhyn	1,365	9.8	612	608	-1	62
Total Northern Group	1,120[a]	24.5	2,357	2,266	-4	93
Total Cook Islands	679[a]	237.0[b]	21,322	17,754[c]	-17	75

Source: ESCAP/SPC 1983:2 and 26; Government of the Cook Islands 1984:9.
[a]Mean distance.
[b]Does not sum because of rounding.
[c]Includes 85 persons at sea.

tural changes that have taken place over the past two decades. Such changes include a sharp decline in agriculture (due mainly to sustained emigration and the apparently disproportionate effect it had on production) and a burgeoning government bureaucracy sustained largely by foreign aid from New Zealand. Another major factor was the successful development of service industries, particularly tourism and related activities and philatelic sales. ("Rent" incomes from the licensing of fishing rights and earnings from tax havens and offshore banking facilities are two recent additions.)[2] However, the relative position of the productive sector has probably improved over the last few years as a result of a considerable slowdown in emigration and some government success in reducing the size of the public sector.

Export earnings totaled $6.5 million in 1984 and are characterized by a fair degree of diversity. Leading export items include clothing (manufactured from imported cloth), copra, pawpaw, pearl shells, bananas, and fresh vegetables. Export earnings are small in comparison with payments for imports, which totaled $36.2 million in 1984. Such disparity between the value of exports and imports is characteristic of the trade situation and highlights the importance of invisible earnings and related transfers, particularly foreign aid and tourism receipts, as balancing items in the balance of payments.

Current government planning efforts highlight the need for raising the prosperity of the people of the Cook Islands and for attaining a larger measure of economic independence. These and related aims are reflected in a range of development strategies and policies to strengthen efforts in the infrastructural, transportation, telecommunications, training, development finance, and agricultural areas. As noted earlier, the private sector played a leading role in the development of opportunities in the main growth sectors such as agriculture, tourism, fisheries, and agroprocessing. A range of measures have been introduced to facilitate and encourage this process including financial concessions, subsidization in selected areas, and concessionary finance through the Cook Islands Development Bank (CIDB).

The survey

Basic data for the study were collected by two principal investigators (John Tau and George Michael, PIDP associate fellow and intern, respectively) during field visits over the period May–July 1985. The author also participated in the surveys in June 1985. Most of the team's time was spent in Rarotonga, where the surveys involved not only the collection of basic information from a sample group of entrepreneurs but also the interviewing of nonindigenous business people, including those associated with multinationals, government officials, and representatives of non-government organizations. Short visits were made to the two outer islands of Aitutaki and Atiu mainly to collect basic information on the indigenous business situation.

The survey team was able to cover 28 sample enterprises during the time allocated for the survey on Rarotonga. Care was taken to establish a representative sample group of businesses, especially in

Table 4.2. Rarotonga survey sample by industry

Type of industry	Number in sample	%
Motel/hotel (accommodation)	2	7
Manufacturing	2	7
Crafts and clothing	3	11
Restaurant/bar	2	7
Transportation	4	14
Technical and other professional services	5	18
Construction	2	7
Retail shops	5	18
Agriculture	3	11
Total	28	100

NOTE: Manufacturing comprises soft drinks and clothing; transportation is mainly taxi service and tour companies; technical and other professional services include activities such as secretarial services, panel beaters, welding/steelwork, and motor repair; agriculture refers mainly to commercial farming for export.

relation to business type and size of operations. Table 4.2 shows the survey sample classified by broad industry group.

Each entrepreneur was interviewed fairly intensively, usually on the business premises. These sessions lasted approximately two hours and covered aspects such as general background information, nature of entrepreneurship, business structure and performance, operational problems, and factors generating success. For this purpose, a comprehensive questionnaire was used, and usually after each interview the survey team made an independent preliminary assessment of the results, particularly current problems and success factors.

With a few exceptions, all the sample businesses were essentially family operations in which ownership was vested with the entrepreneurs and their families and, in some cases, close relatives. Formally, the sample group was organized into 18 companies limited by shares, mainly proprietary limited companies, eight partnerships (mainly husband and wife), and a few sole traders. (This pattern emerged after several adjustments were made to the original list of enterprises.) Ethnically, the sample entrepreneurs comprised 8 Maoris, 17 mixed Maori-Europeans, a Fijian, a New Zealand-Maori, and a European—the last three being local residents of whom two were married to Cook Islanders.

By international standards, the sample enterprises were usually

small in size—essentially one- or two-person operations. Gross
sales revenue averaged $100,000 per year with only two compa-
nies exceeding $300,000 while two others reached levels of
between $200,000 and $300,000. Of the remaining enterprises,
gross revenue was mostly below $50,000 with several varying
from $300 to $5,000.

Insofar as the market area was concerned, the majority of enterprises served Rarotonga exclusively. Those that also served other
markets, including some of the outer islands, consisted of commercial farmers and the manufacturers of clothes, crafts, carvings,
and soft drinks. The main outside market was New Zealand, and
the only notable product shipped to the outer islands was soft
drinks.

Business establishment

As shown in Table 4.3, a majority of enterprises had been in operation for a period of between one and ten years. However, the data
were compiled on the basis of current ownership, and in fact many
have had an even longer lifespan under different owners. Among
those enterprises in operation for more than ten years are several
that had been established by a parent and handed down to the
present generation.

Almost all the sample enterprises—23—had been established by
the present owners. The others had been acquired through inheritance from a father or father-in-law (three cases) or had been purchased. In conjunction with Table 4.3, this information suggests
an acceleration in the development of entrepreneurship in the
Cook Islands in recent years. (See ESCAP/SPC 1983:179 for further
observations on this apparent trend.)

Table 4.3. Age of current business

Less than 1 year	2
1–5 years	10
6–10 years	8
11–15 years	3
16–20 years	1
20 years or more	4

The amounts initially invested to set up or acquire the businesses varied widely, but the data revealed that in the majority of cases extremely small amounts were involved. Several of the older businesses were set up with only a few hundred dollars in capital, and in the case of more recent enterprises, amounts of no more than $5–6,000 were involved. Only four businesses invested funds in the order of $15–30,000 while four others outlayed $30,000 or more. In the latter case, the largest outlay totaled $140,000 with $40,000 coming from the owner himself and the remainder being contributions from a local lawyer ($20,000) and an overseas investor ($80,000).

As shown in Table 4.4, most of the businesses were established without outside funds. Loans from the local commercial bank represented the most widely used outside source, but the amounts so obtained were modest, varying from $500 to $21,000 and averaging $10,000. There have not been many loans from the CIDB institution. Small amounts were involved, even with the largest loan, which totaled $24,000. The negligible use of non-bank institutional sources was noteworthy.

The heavy reliance on the owners' savings for starting up a business can be explained partly by deficiencies in the local capital market (e.g., its narrow base) and partly by a failure to secure funds from existing bank facilities. The reticence on the part of some entrepreneurs to approach existing financial institutions also played a part. Whatever the reasons, a consequence is that the entrepreneurs will have had more limited funds at their disposal for establishing a business than they may have preferred. Such an initial disability can prove a serious handicap, causing inferior

Table 4.4. Sources of finance for establishing
and purchasing business

Owner's/manager's savings	17
OS + CBL	7
OS + CIDBL	2
OS + CBL + CIDBL	1
OS + other loans	1
Total	28

OS = Owner's savings
CBL = Commercial bank loan
CIDBL = Cook Islands Development Bank loan

physical facilities, low stock levels, over-reliance on trade credits, and general undercapitalization. These problems are likely to persist so long as access to outside sources of capital funds continues to be limited.

Other aspects

A major characteristic of the sample entrepreneurs interviewed was their extensive participation in other business ventures, wage employment, and/or other forms of work. At least 22 entrepreneurs were involved in this way, including those in subsistence farming (usually combined with commercial farming) and government employment. There were three cases of husbands employed as public servants.

Table 4.5 shows that participation in subsistence and commercial farming was most common while the number of people engaged in trade stores was also noteworthy. There were several instances of participation in two "secondary" activities and, in one case, as many as three. The latter was a restaurant owner who was operating a trade store and a commercial farm while also being employed in government.

An involvement in several business operations is apparently not unique to Rarotonga. Croulet and Sio (1986:36) found a similar pattern among Western Samoa businessmen as has Finney (1987) in the Goroka Highlands of Papua New Guinea. Croulet and Sio suggest that the benefits of being engaged in a number of diverse activities include spreading the risk of failure and obtaining mutual support among different ventures such as sharing trucks, buildings, and other assets.

That the Rarotonga businesses surveyed were essentially family

Table 4.5. Nature of other business
connections

Subsistence and commercial farming	15
Retail shops	4
Motel/hotel	2
Transportation	2
Entertainment	2
Other	5

units was commented upon earlier. This aspect was also apparent in the employment aspect. Eleven of the sample businesses did not employ paid labor but relied solely on the family; ten businesses each employed paid labor totaling between one and three people; and five businesses each employed between four and seven people. Only two enterprises employed eight or more paid workers.

The survey revealed that the Rarotongan entrepreneurs are conscientious in keeping business records. In this respect, they seem to be more advanced than small business owners in other parts of the South Pacific, for example, Western Samoa (see Croulet and Sio 1986:59). The level of education, extensive overseas experience, and the need to pay the turnover tax every month may be the reasons for keeping business records. Many Rarotonga entrepreneurs used the services of private accountants both for keeping business records and for obtaining advice on business operations.

Entrepreneurs

Entrepreneurs have been commonly perceived as those who carry out a variety of functions, both managerial and innovative, that are essential to the establishment and operations of a business. In this chapter, entrepreneurs are assumed to be those who operate and manage businesses whether or not they have played a part in founding these businesses. They are, in effect, "businesspeople," as popularly conceived, who are responsible both for routine managerial functions and for major business initiatives or innovations. This definition is not only useful from a practical viewpoint but also realistic in the context of the South Pacific.

The survey confirmed that the ownership and operation of businesses in Rarotonga is far from being a male preserve. In fact, women play a significant role as evidenced by the fact that nine of the 28 entrepreneurs interviewed were women. They were most prominent in the services: retail stores, restaurants, handicrafts, and motels.

The age group of the entrepreneurs interviewed ranged from 28 to 72 years. Specifically, 11 entrepreneurs were 28–40 years of age; 14 were 41–60 years, and the remaining three were 61–72. All the entrepreneurs were married, and some had large families. The data revealed that five entrepreneurs had family sizes varying from two to four people; 16 entrepreneurs had from five to seven members; the remaining seven had from eight to ten people.

Most of the entrepreneurs were active in church organizations, and some held executive positions in church administration while others served as deacons. Several were also active in community and business organizations such as sports clubs, chamber of commerce and tourism, and education boards.

The educational level of the entrepreneurs was relatively high and based on the available evidence seemed to rank well above the national level (ESCAP/SPC 1983:60). Nine had attended a university, usually in New Zealand, though not all had completed their degrees. Five reported technical college and nine cited secondary school experience as their highest educational level achieved. Only five entrepreneurs had an education limited to elementary school.

Eight of the entrepreneurs had experienced some form of vocational training including teacher and business training. Several others reported that they had benefited directly from training by their fathers, especially those in commercial agriculture.

Insofar as previous work experience was concerned, 50 percent had experience in the same kind of business and 14 percent in a similar type of business. These results confirm a fairly close correlation between previous work experience and present involvement in business. This applied particularly to those who had received vocational skills training (e.g., welding, joinery, and motor mechanic), to those who had received agricultural training at the tertiary level, and to those who had received training from their fathers. However, among the 36 percent of entrepreneurs whose previous work history had been in areas unrelated to their present business interests, several indicated that such experiences had enhanced their business performance and contributed to success.

Overseas exposure was extensive. With only one exception, all entrepreneurs either had worked overseas or had studied at universities or technical institutions in New Zealand, Australia, Fiji, Western Samoa, and one or two other Pacific island locations. Twenty-four entrepreneurs reported work experience in New Zealand alone.

Major areas of experience included commercial farming and government employment either as public servants or as teachers. As reported earlier, the continuing involvement in agriculture as a "secondary" activity is notable. However, the relatively few (about three) respondents who reported farming as part of their previous

Table 4.6. Reasons for going into business

To earn more money/to attain a better standard of living	13
To support family/employment for family members	9
To be independent/one's own boss	6
To continue family traditions	2
To achieve ambitions/interests	7
To take advantage of long-term prospects	2
Other	8

experience is significant. This is particularly so when considered together with the evidence on the occupation of the entrepreneurs' fathers, which showed that at least ten fathers had been "growers."

The various reasons for the sample entrepreneurs entering business are presented in Table 4.6. The data incorporate cases where more than one reason was given, each of which was tabulated separately. The results should be interpreted with caution. A problem arises from possible interconnections between the individual reasons cited by respondents. For example, the desire to earn more money may underlie the wish to achieve financial independence or to be "one's own boss."

Based on Table 4.6, the entrepreneurs appear to be in business to make money, to improve living conditions, and to foster the economic interests of their families. Of secondary importance were "the wish to be one's boss" and personal interests and ambitions. The emphasis on family is of interest because it is not normally a significant motive of entrepreneurs in developed economies such as Australia (see, for example, Johns, Dunlop, and Sheehan 1983:29).

A variety of reasons are encompassed in the "other" category of Table 4.6 and include dissatisfaction with public service pay, efforts to provide competition against a local monopoly, and an attempt to try something different. Professional pride was also evident: for example, one grower responded that he was in business "to set an example for other growers."

Financial aspects

The survey attempted to highlight certain financial aspects of the enterprises based on financial business reports and documents, where they were available, or on estimates provided by respondents. Particular interest centered on changes in the value of fixed assets, profit levels, trade debts, financial reserves, and reinvestment. However, both the detail and the quality of the data proved inadequate for detailed analysis, and thus only several salient features can be highlighted.

The available data showed that many enterprises were realizing large profit margins from revenues. The average (pre-tax) profit margins for retailing and hotel/motel accommodations were over 20 percent. However, the overall performance was highly variable; many respondents reported extremely low profit margins, and at least two incurred losses.

In absolute terms, profit levels were equally varied. For the smallest enterprises, realized profits were typically between a few hundred New Zealand dollars and $6,000. At least ten enterprises reported profits of over $20,000, with one village store reporting a profit of $80,000.

The evidence showed that problems over excessive trade debts were insignificant. A large proportion of the respondents (43 percent) reported having no current trade debts, while those that did have such debts seem to have succeeded in keeping them at low levels—typically from $100 to $5,000. Regarding bad debts, a high proportion (72 percent) reported having no accumulated bad debts at all, and the others who had experienced losses reported that only very small amounts were involved. On the other hand, the use of trade credit with suppliers was fairly extensive with just over two-thirds of the respondents being affected.

A shortage of working capital was common with its resulting adverse effect on operational efficiency. This suggests a weakness in cash management among entrepreneurs, which is possibly due to excessive withdrawal of funds for consumption purposes and/or over-investment in fixed assets.

On the subject of business reserves, just over one-half of the entrepreneurs reported that they kept reserves. These reserves were usually small amounts and varied from $400 to $6,000. There were only two cases where reserves were in excess of $10,000.

Little can be said about the fixed asset positions due to lack of data, but many enterprises apparently had been able to achieve substantial increases in their holdings of fixed assets over time. This seemed to be particularly true for retailing, hotel accommodation, transportation, and construction.

Almost all enterprises (only three exceptions) planned to reinvest part of their profits to expand their operations or to start a new venture. Methods of expansion included the enlargement of premises, the purchase of equipment, and the hiring of specialist workers.

Business problems

A major aim of the survey was to identify and ascertain the seriousness of the various problems faced by businesses. These problems related to areas such as the availability of capital funds, marketing, transportation, competition in the domestic market, and government support. The results can be summarized in order of importance to the businesspeople themselves.

Transportation

Nineteen of the entrepreneurs interviewed indicated that they experienced transportation problems, particularly in commercial agriculture, tourism, and trade sectors.

Shipping was frequently cited with enterprises reporting dissatisfaction with the unreliability and infrequency of shipping services and inadequate cargo space. Damaged goods were reported in one instance. A recurring complaint was the unsatisfactory service from New Zealand—the main source of imports for the Cook Islands. In this case, shipping was affected by limited cargo space because the service also carried cargo destined for Tahiti en route to the Cook Islands. The stop in Tahiti also caused delays. Such shipping problems affected business operations in a variety of ways including the periodic shortage of vital supplies, spare parts, and above-normal stock holdings. All these factors served to raise costs of operation.

Eight entrepreneurs referred to problems over air transportation. The need for more frequent flights was emphasized by four entrepreneurs including commercial growers and one tourist operator. Several with an export interest referred to the high cost of air freight, and a commercial grower expressed annoyance at the occasional off-loading of produce to accommodate passengers.

Since the survey, air transport links with Sydney, Australia, have been inaugurated as the result of a joint venture (Cook Islands International Airline) between government and an Australian company (Ansett). The service to New Zealand has also improved with the addition of a weekly flight to Auckland by the new joint venture.

Insofar as domestic transportation is concerned, the need to improve the local bus service, especially for tourists, was cited on several occasions.

Market factors

Problems connected with the market affected 11 enterprises. These problems related to such factors as local market conditions, marketing arrangements, competition from imported goods, and specific export facilities.

Five entrepreneurs responded that they faced a "weak local market." The enterprises affected were mainly the small domestic market-oriented businesses such as taxis, trade stores, bread makers, and, to some degree, handicraft dealers. Two local producers (in bread making and vegetable growing) felt that the local demand was being weakened by imported substitutes.

Five entrepreneurs (including two commercial farmers and one tourist operator) reported that they were being disadvantaged by weak or poor marketing institutions. According to the farmers, the export of local produce could be increased if research could identify new overseas markets. Another major complaint was poor post-harvest facilities, especially cold storage. A tourist operator felt that the Tourist Board, as the body responsible for the promotion of tourism, favored big companies.

Among the other market-related problems, one enterprise complained about the high prices being charged by the large companies at the wholesale level. Another entrepreneur referred to problems over a failure "to gauge the size of the local market," a market that turned out to be less buoyant than expected.

Responses were sought from the sample enterprises on problems arising from competition in the domestic market. Twelve enterprises responded, of which four felt that competition was either "under control" or "healthy" for the economy. Another reported the absence of competition because he was operating as a monopoly. Areas where competition was considered a threat were transportation (buses and taxis), motor repair, and panel beating, where it was said that there were too many operators in relation to the amount of business available.

Government support

Eighteen entrepreneurs agreed that government was not providing adequate support for their businesses. Eight of these responded in general terms and said that government policies were "wrong" or "non-existent," that they did not provide incentives to the private sector, and that there was too much "bureaucracy."

Most of the criticism, however, was directed at specific areas. Several entrepreneurs thought that the levy on imported vehicles and other major imported items and components was too high, that the price for electricity was excessive, and that the tax system was too complex—all combining to raise the operational costs of doing business. Three other specific points of interest were raised: (1) the failure of government to control competitive imports (e.g., bread), (2) weak marketing organizations, and (3) lack of adequate training facilities including those to promote servicing skills in the tourism sector.

Although ten entrepreneurs did not find government support to be inadequate, several suggested specific areas where some government intervention was warranted. These are discussed at the end of this chapter.

Capital funds

A total of 19 entrepreneurs admitted that they faced problems of capital shortage. With many contemplating expansion through the upgrading of existing facilities or through entry into new lines of activity, the need for supplemental investment funds was not surprising. In other instances, the main motive was to accumulate working capital or to increase stocks.

Many respondents reported dissatisfaction with the services being provided by both the CIDB and the private bank. One claim was that these institutions were "too restrictive" in their loan policies, that their interest rate charges were too high, and that they tended to neglect the small business people.

Criticism of the country's single trading bank was particularly severe, and there was general agreement on the need to review and improve the present situation. Six entrepreneurs thought it was time to establish another bank—an idea that has since been translated into reality (see Chapter 10).

Other problems

Serious personnel problems were encountered by 11 entrepreneurs over the shortage of workers with basic skills, training, or experience. Migration overseas was often said to be the primary cause, and some entrepreneurs themselves sought to remedy the shortage by conducting on-the-job training. The respondents identified other problems in this area, for example, lack of motivation, unpredictability of workers, and difficulty of enlisting workers.

Certain elements of the traditional culture can undermine the efficient operation of a business if they are not remedied. A common manifestation of this is pressure from relatives and neighbors for personal credit, which if not restrained can cause business failure. Evidence suggests that a necessary condition for business success in many parts of the region is an ability to contain those aspects of culture that can debilitate business (see Croulet and Sio 1986:95).

The survey suggests that sociocultural pressures did not significantly undermine the operation of the sample businesses. Only seven entrepreneurs responded that they were exposed to such pressures mainly in the form of "community business" and "family obligations." None of them considered these pressures to be a serious impediment.

Business problems on two outer islands

Surveys were conducted on the islands of Aitutaki and Atiu to highlight aspects of business development and problems on the outer islands, which in comparison with those on Rarotonga, suffer even more intensively from remoteness and smallness, both physical and demographic. (However, because both Aitutaki and Atiu are not more than 260 km away from Rarotonga and are served by regular air and shipping services, they experience less isolation than, say, the more distant islands of the Northern

Group.) Information on entrepreneurship and current business problems was collected from nine enterprises in Aitutaki and six in Atiu, based on the same interview procedures used in Rarotonga.[3]

The survey results showed that the entrepreneurial patterns and business characteristics found in Aitutaki and Atiu tended to conform rather closely to those in Rarotonga. This was true of such major features as ownership structures, motives for going into business, reliance on self-finance at the establishment stage, and the extent of overseas travel as a way of building up business experience (Fairbairn with Pearson (1987:51–64). Where differences were observed, they were largely ones of degree rather than of kind. For example, the size of enterprises on Aitutaki and Atiu were generally smaller than those on Rarotonga, while an involvement in agriculture both as a primary and secondary activity was more pervasive on the two outer islands.

Insofar as business problems were concerned, the most intractable problems were those relating to transportation, market conditions, and finance. On transportation, most entrepreneurs saw the need for improved shipping as a priority. The value of a reliable service was emphasized, on one hand, by growers who needed to send fresh produce to Rarotonga and, on the other, by traders who were concerned about ensuring a regular inflow of stocks and supplies. For Atiu, the particularly heavy dependence on fresh pineapple as a cash crop made adequate shipping a matter of considerable importance.

Complaints over the weak state of local demand were prevalent among those enterprises whose activities are geared to the local market. In several cases, this problem was said to stem from the pressure of competition from other local operators who had cut into individual market shares. For growers, the principal concern was the need for expanded overseas markets for their produce and the securing of attractive prices.

While various aspects of existing financial arrangements were criticized, a major problem was said to be poor access to the loanable funds controlled by the trading and development banks. Local entrepreneurs felt penalized by the failure of these institutions to develop local facilities that could reduce the dependence on Rarotonga. (However, since 1984 Aitutaki has been served by a local branch office of the development bank.) Entrepreneurs saw the need for these institutions, especially the trading bank, to improve their outreach service so that the credit needs of the outer islanders could be better served.

Government's role

Not all the above problems fall within the purview of government for their solution. Many problems, for example, those connected with transportation, originate from outside forces and are largely beyond the capacity of the Cook Islands government to influence. Other problems are properly the responsibility of government and can be corrected by appropriate policy measures as, for example, in the training and credit areas. Others are amenable to remedial action by the enterprises themselves as in the control of trade credit and skills training. In some cases, entrepreneurs mentioned many specific problems that amount to no more than a grievance over some aspect of government policy or action. Closely related matters were cited as "problems" even though on closer examination they appear to be based on an inadequate understanding of the facts. Respondents criticized the level of interest rates charged on loans, but they did not take into account the real rate of interest or the interest rates paid on deposits.

Valid concerns were expressed about the need for remedial government action in the following areas: shipping and air transportation; marketing including the strengthening of basic institutions and post-harvest storage facilities; banking and the promotion of less restrictive credit policies and the need for a new bank; training to build up a reservoir of basic skills at all levels; and policies regarding the cost of electricity, tax system, and the protection of local industries from imported substitutes.

Other responses not already specifically highlighted referred mainly to improving the local business environment. Specific proposals advanced by the entrepreneurs interviewed included the needs for (1) a central coordinating unit to provide essential management and technical assistance to small businesses, and (2) the government to avoid becoming involved in areas that compete directly with, and consequently discourage, the private sector. Also included were suggestions on possible ways of improving administrative performance, for example, in administering the turnover tax and in enforcing business licensing and inspection procedures. Finally, several entrepreneurs voiced the need for the government to gain a better understanding of the problems affecting small businesses and the private sector in general and to improve channels of communication. In the view of one entrepreneur, success in these areas calls for government "to listen more to the views of the business community."

Success factors

Perceptions by the entrepreneurs of how their businesses were doing were highly favorable. Twenty-one entrepreneurs felt satisfied with their present situations and were optimistic about the future. Such confidence appears to be firmly based; for example, many entrepreneurs had been in business for a long time; were making a profit, which, in some cases, was substantial; were keeping trade debts under control; and were able to balance the requirements of business against community obligations.

As an additional indication of business performance, the entrepreneurs were asked to identify and rank in importance the main factors that they perceived as being responsible for success. As a guide, several factors were suggested to the respondents under the general headings of personal qualities, management, market advantage, and government support.

The responses confirmed the overriding importance that the entrepreneurs themselves attach to personal qualities. Certain personal attributes were particularly highlighted: a capacity for hard work, honesty, reliability, and motivation. It was pointed out that success also requires an ability to perceive "good possibilities" and a capacity at times to be "ruthless in pursuing goals." Regarding good management, the entrepreneurs emphasized the need for exercising proper financial control over their operations and the importance of keeping records. Additional management requirements included maintaining good relations with employees, being able "to outsmart your competitors," and "judging what your customers want."

The survey results suggest that several other major factors support the successful performance of the entrepreneurs. One is the unusually high level of education and training exposure experienced by the entrepreneurs, even though some particular areas of educational emphasis and training seemed to be of little relevance to the business. Another is the extensive travel experience of the entrepreneurs, particularly to New Zealand, for purposes of employment, training, education, family visits, and (originally) migration. As Epstein (1968) pointed out in the context of the then territory of New Guinea, such travel can play a vital role in the development of indigenous entrepreneurship by breaking up narrow economic horizons of would-be entrepreneurs, making them more aware of new business opportunities, and engendering more diversified patterns of entrepreneurial activity.

Finally, entrepreneurial success can also be partly attributed to the common practice of being involved in more than one business or economic activity. Among other benefits, such an involvement can be of value in reducing the risk of failure and in spreading management skills to achieve certain economies of scale.

Concluding comments

A major focus of the original study of the Cook Islands was to identify salient characteristics of indigenous entrepreneurship, which is dominated by Cook Islanders of mixed Maori-European ancestry who operate small family businesses. Typically, entrepreneurs are mature individuals, predominantly male, and well educated with extensive travel experience, especially to New Zealand. Supported by family members, they start the business, utilizing their own funds (usually small amounts), and remain involved in other "secondary" activities particularly farming, both subsistence and commercial. The motives for entering business are essentially economic—to earn more money, to improve living standards, and to support the family.

Among the operational problems, the responses of entrepreneurs affirmed that the most difficult areas relate to transportation —especially the lack of reliable shipping services—weak market conditions, both domestic and overseas; inadequate government support in *certain* areas; and paucity of capital funds. A variety of views was presented on what government can do to overcome these problems or at least to mitigate them.

Regarding the various factors contributing to success, the respondents emphasized the importance of personal qualities and good management. But other factors—some closely reflecting management attributes—were also relevant. Prominent among these factors were educational and training background, travel experience, involvement in other forms of economic activity, and control over debts.

Many areas need to be addressed by the Cook Islands government if indigenous entrepreneurship—and indeed the private sector as a whole—is to make further progress. The major areas for improvement are shipping and air services, both overseas and interisland; marketing, including the development of new overseas outlets; commercial and development banking; business training and advisory facilities; and communication between government and the private sector.

NOTES

1. Values in this chapter are expressed in New Zealand dollars, which is the official currency of the Cook Islands. At the time of the field surveys (May–June 1985), the rate of exchange was NZ$1.00 = US$0.50 (approximately); at the time of writing (March 1987), it was NZ$1.00 = US$0.57.

2. Foreign aid and other external influences have served to transform the Cook Islands economy into what Watters and Bertram (1985:3) call a MIRAB economy—a shorthand term for migration, remittances, aid, and bureaucracy. Such economies are driven, not by export earnings, but rather by "external rent income" derived from budgetary support, remittances from overseas relatives, and the marketing of identity in the form of tourism and philatelic sales.

3. In Aitutaki, the sample enterprises included two manufacturers, three retail traders, three commercial growers, and one transport operator (for tourists); in Atiu they included two manufacturers, two retail traders, two commercial growers, and one motel operator.

REFERENCES

Croulet, C. R. and L. Sio
  1986 *Indigenous Entrepreneurship in Western Samoa,* Pacific Islands Development Program, East-West Center, Honolulu.

Epstein, T. Scarlet
  1968 *Capitalism, Primitive, and Modern—Some Aspects of Tolai Economic Growth,* Michigan State University Press, East Lansing.

ESCAP/SPC
  1983 *Population of the Cook Islands,* Country Monograph Series, No. 7.3, P.K. Printing Ltd., Bangkok.

Fairbairn, Te'o I. J. with J. M. Pearson
   1987 *Entrepreneurship in the Cook Islands,* Pacific Islands Development Program, East-West Center, Honolulu.

Finney, B. R.
   1987 *Business Development in the Highlands of Papua New Guinea,* Research Report Series No. 6, Pacific Islands Development Program, East-West Center, Honolulu.

Government of the Cook Islands
   1984 *Cook Islands Development Plan 1982–1985,* Government Printing Office, Rarotonga.
   1985 *Cook Islands Quarterly Statistical Bulletin* (June), Statistics Office, Rarotonga, Cook Islands.

Johns, B. L., W. C. Dunlop, and W. J. Sheehan
   1983 *Small Business in Australia: Problems and Prospects* (2nd edn), George Allen & Unwin, Sydney.

Watters, R. F. and G. Bertram
   1985 Comments in unpublished summary record of workshop on the subject: *New Zealand and its Small Island Neighbours,* held at Victoria University of Wellington, Wellington, under the auspices of Institute of Policy Studies.

Chapter 5

Indigenous Entrepreneurship in Western Samoa

C. Ross Croulet

This chapter examines indigenous business development in Western Samoa based on the results of a larger study conducted in 1985 by the author and Laki Sio (Croulet and Sio 1986) under the auspices of the Pacific Islands Development Program (PIDP). As with the other country studies in this book, this chapter focuses on major characteristics of indigenous entrepreneurship, business problems, reasons for success (or failure), and policy recommendations.

Fieldwork for the study was undertaken in October–November 1985 when a sample of 70 indigenous entrepreneurs were interviewed. A detailed questionnaire was used to collect basic data, and these results were supplemented by information collected from an "institutional" survey of 26 representatives of government, the private sector, and voluntary organizations (see Appendix A). Data analysis and preparation of the final report on Western Samoa were conducted at the East-West Center, Honolulu (see Appendix B).

Background

Western Samoa is located in the central Pacific, approximately 2,900 km northwest of New Zealand and 4,300 km northeast of Sydney. It comprises four inhabited islands and five other small islands with a total land area of 2,935 sq km. Two islands—Upolu, the group's political and administrative center, and Savai'i

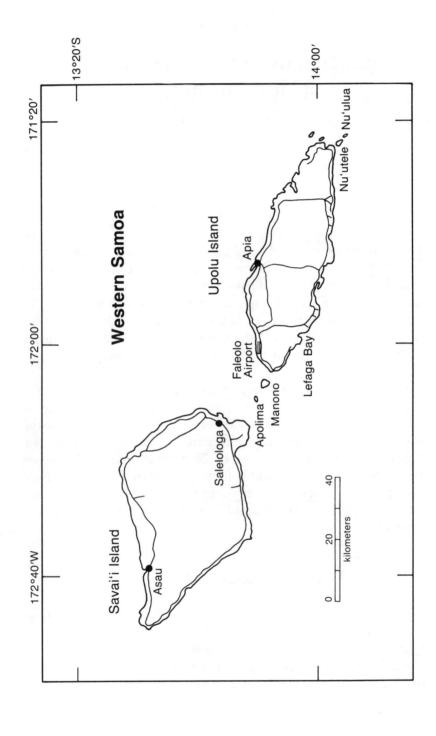

Western Samoa

Savai'i Island

Asau

Salelologa

Apolima
Manono

Faleolo
Airport

Upolu Island

Apia

Lefaga Bay

Nu'utele Nu'ulua

172°40'W   172°00'   171°20'

13°20'S

14°00'

0   20   40
kilometers

—dominate, together accounting for approximately 98 percent of the total land area. The population totals approximately 164,000, and although the natural rate of population increase is high, the actual annual rate is about 0.8 percent because of heavy emigration. Historically, the country first made effective contact, via missionaries, with the outside world in the 1830s, and this was followed by periods of successive colonization by Germany (1899) and by New Zealand (1914), which also administered the country under the League of Nations and later the United Nations. Independence was gained in 1962—the first Pacific island country to do so.

The economy is characterized by a thriving subsistence sector coexisting with the modern cash sector. Subsistence activities are organized under large extended families headed by a *matai* or family chief. The subsistence sector accounts for a large proportion of food production including taro, bananas, fish, and coconuts. The cash economy revolves around the production for export of copra, cocoa, taro, and several manufactured products in exchange for a wide range of imported commodities. Local manufacturing is dominated by the production of coconut oil, beer, and cigarettes. International trade has been characterized by a substantial surplus in the value of imports over exports, which has been largely offset by foreign aid receipts and cash remittances from relatives living overseas.

Development objectives emphasize economic growth through the development of available physical and human resources (Government of Western Samoa 1984). The private sector, including small businesses, is to be encouraged as a vital strategy for achieving economic growth. Practical support for such a strategy is represented by government assistance in the areas of tax incentives, development finance, and training.

Racial homogeneity is strong, with about 90 percent of the population being pure Polynesian. Socially, Samoans have maintained their traditional family system based on the extended family under the *pule* or authority of a *matai*. The *matai,* as the head of a family, directs the activities of the group and exercises his authority over land. Nationally, there are about 13,000 *matai*. The *matai* and the extended kinship unit are an integral part of the *fa'asamoa* or "the Samoan way of life."

Profile of the Western Samoan entrepreneur

If an entrepreneur in Western Samoa can be described from the
PIDP survey, then the following profile may be considered typical.
He or she (much more likely to be a he) is in the upper 20 to 30
percentile of the general population in age. The entrepreneur has
nine dependents, which is average for the general population. The
business usually concerns trade, service, manufacturing, or agrobusiness. The entrepreneur's business is likely to be located in a
rural area near Apia, the only major town. Ethnically, the entrepreneur is much more likely to be a Samoan, although if he or she
is part-European, success and growth are more likely. The business probably does not have more than five employees; it is usually
one or none. Annual turnover is less than T50,000.[1] The business
is usually a sole proprietorship. He or she is likely to have been in
business for fewer than ten years. The entrepreneur has probably
obtained his or her capital to start the business from family
sources and the original investment is likely to be less than
T10,000. The most likely reason for the entrepreneur to enter into
business is because no other money-earning employment opportunities were available. The entrepreneur has more formal education
than the average Samoan, is married, and has the traditional
chiefly status of *matai*. The entrepreneur is likely to have less than
five years' work experience and is not likely to have relevant technical training. The typical entrepreneur has had limited overseas
exposure, and his parents could be farmers or government employees. The entrepreneur usually has another business or income-
generating activity and generally views the government as the biggest obstacle to the progress of the business.

Business problems

The following problem areas were individually analyzed in terms
of their effects on business.

Government

The 70 entrepreneurs surveyed characterized the government as
the biggest obstacle to the success of their businesses. The reasons

are varied, with some entrepreneurs indicating five or more areas where the government has actively or passively worked against private sector initiative. The survey of 26 institutional officials (many of whom were government officials) acknowledged the government as ranking second—behind the lack of business management skills—as the most serious obstacle to private sector initiative.

An analysis of the complaints about government by those surveyed include

- High tariffs on imported inputs such as stocks for trade stores, machines for manufacturers, and motors for fishermen;
- Little or no capital assistance from the government-owned Development Bank of Western Samoa or the other commercial lending institutions;
- Lack of infrastructure or programs such as business advisory assistance or, in the case of transport operators, poor roads;
- Overall cost of goods, which, if the goods are imported, have their costs raised by duties and taxes;
- High taxes, especially income, excise, and export levies;
- Unfair competition from government-owned enterprises such as the Western Samoa Trust Estates Corporation (WSTEC);
- Government red-tape and cumbersome procedures for loan applications and approvals;
- Lack or non-enforcement of price controls on inputs;
- Discontinuation of subsidies; and
- Lack of overseas export market development by government.

Management and technical skills

Next to government, the entrepreneurs' own lack of managerial skills rated as the most serious problem affecting business performance. Institution officials ranked the lack of managerial skills as the most serious problem hindering both the private sector and indigenous Samoan entrepreneurship. From the survey, specific indicators of ineffective managerial abilities included an inability to organize or associate with others to secure benefits from purchasing in bulk from wholesalers and importers and an incapacity to keep financial records.

The entrepreneurs interviewed characterized themselves as well as their workers as deficient in technical skills. Businesses that were affected the most by the lack of technical skills included transport operators (bus, taxi, and truck), hotel and restaurant operators, mechanics, carpenters, and electricians. Due to low technical skill levels, the entrepreneurs themselves did some of their employees' work. In having to substitute for underqualified employees, the entrepreneur had less time for the overall marketing and management tasks necessary to run the firm efficiently. Other consequences were lower quality, and, as a result, lower profits. Those entrepreneurs who possessed higher levels of skills were those who were trained or had received experience overseas. Only two institutions in Western Samoa offer rudimentary vocational/technical skills training.

Capital access and availability

The provision of sufficient working and investment capital is crucial for the operation and success of a business. According to the businessmen surveyed, the problem of capital availability and access ranked third in the nine problem areas assessed. Over two-thirds of the firms surveyed began with less than T4,000. Availability of capital per se should not, however, be viewed as the main problem. The survey of the institutions and a review of the government statistics indicate that the supply of capital for private investment need not be a problem if small businesses had easier access to it.

The problems over access to capital funds can be attributed to the fact that a large proportion of capital funds are used by the government and the large public sector corporations to the disadvantage of small business. In addition, on the basis of strict commercial criteria, commercial banks tend to perceive small businesses as "too risky" borrowers. Moreover, whereas small businesses need loans on a longer-term basis, the commercial banks are usually prepared to lend only on shorter seasonal terms.

Markets and competition

The problem of markets was described as that of the limited wealth and size of the domestic market. With a population of only 160,000 and a gross domestic product (GDP) of almost T600 per capita, firms that compete with one another in the sale of similar products or services in the same areas experienced poor sales performance. This was especially true of trade stores, where entry is easy and many sellers are thereby created for too few people. Those firms that specialized in products or services not offered elsewhere ranked the problem of markets as very minor.

The nature of the problem of competition was defined in terms of (1) the number of other firms involved in the same kind of business activity, (2) whether government or a public enterprise produced a similar good or service, and (3) whether similar goods were imported from overseas. Entrepreneurs producing products such as meat, soft drinks, transportation, and furniture felt that the government-owned WSTEC and other government agencies should tender bids to the private sector rather than produce these goods in competition.

Supplies

The problem of supplies was characterized as the inability of a business to receive a steady supply of raw materials or other goods at consistent qualities, quantities, and prices. Rural trade stores, for instance, characterized the supply problem as one of monopolistic behavior on the part of the few wholesalers that operate in Apia. Those entrepreneurs working with or selling technical products complained about the periodic shortage or non-availability of spare parts and raw materials.

The analysis of the survey data for Savai'i indicated that the problem of supplies was naturally more serious for businesses located there than for those located in the Apia urban area. Surprisingly, the problem of supplies for Savai'i was only slightly less in degree than that for businesses located in rural Upolu. Although rural Upolu is contiguous to Apia, Savai'i is relatively close to Upolua and is regularly served by ferries that can carry goods-ladened trucks and by domestic cargo ships between Apia and Savai'i.

Transportation

Entrepreneurs interviewed felt that transportation was the least serious of their problems. Geographically, Western Samoa is a compact nation with a good system of urban and rural roads and ample access to passenger and cargo vehicles. Another factor bearing on the ranking of this problem is that the survey sample included many transport operators; thus the problem of transportation did not apply.

Nonetheless, the data do indicate that Savai'i-located businesses are more adversely affected by the lack of transportation. The distance across the ocean channel by ferry from Upolu to Savai'i is 24 km and implies greater costs and less frequency of transportation to and from Apia.

Tradition and culture

From their own perspective, Samoan entrepreneurs characterized their own culture and traditions as not seriously affecting the performance of their businesses. In fact, more than one entrepreneur characterized a successful Samoan entrepreneur as one who can effectively know about and take commercial advantage of the *matai* traditions to increase business. At worst, the bulk of the entrepreneurs interviewed characterized traditions as having no effect on business performance, either negative or positive. Rural trade stores felt most adversely affected by traditions. This was because trade stores were mainly patronized by extended family members who would buy on credit but almost never repay.

Sector perspectives of problems

The survey of indigenous Western Samoan business activity focused on four different sectors of private business activity: merchandising, agrobusinesses, services, and manufacturing. A sector-by-sector perspective on the main problems is provided in the following summary.

1. *Merchandising:* Problems significantly affecting this sector include the fact that trading is an easy profession to enter, and it is subject to having to supply goods directly without payment for traditional purposes and to suffer from too much competition. Suggestions for rendering the sector more productive include targeting trade store owners for special training and assistance in management, incorporating the stores so that procurement of goods by non-paying relatives for traditional purposes can be reduced, licensing the stores to reduce over-competition, encouraging transport operators to serve the rural areas more frequently, and using selective incentives for stores to stock locally made goods.

2. *Agrobusinesses:* The most significant problem affecting agrobusinesses is that of capital. Rural areas are more subject to traditional practices, which, as already stated, adversely affect a firm's ability to retain or accumulate capital. Excessive demands for traditional contributions for weddings and funerals are more prevalent in the rural areas where agrobusinesses are located than in the Apia urban area. A major recommendation with regard to agriculture is for the government to view farms and other agriculture ventures as profit-making businesses. This will help render more uniform and consistent the policy and program treatment that the government gives to all business sectors. Forming any agricultural enterprise will also cause the farmers concerned to plan their agricultural ventures in improved financial and administrative management terms.

3. *Services:* The most significant problems affecting the service sector include the need for higher degrees of technical skills among workers (e.g., electronics and motor repairs), problems with government regulations and program support, and deficiencies in management skills. Specific recommendations to help the sector become more productive include stricter prohibitions against those who claim to have professional technical skills but who are not licensed. Also needed are increased levels of technical training for workers to gain the skills necessary to perform complicated technical tasks such as motor repair and electronics.

4. *Manufacturing:* Although manufacturers performed best among the four sectors surveyed, the sector is especially sensitive to taxes and tariffs. Specific recommendations for its improvement include resurrection of the Enterprise Incentives Act of 1984, which provides selective tax holidays and duty-free privileges for manufacturers in growth-potential areas, technical training and consultation among those most qualified in the relevant fields of manufacturing, and advisory/extension services to assist administrative and financial management.

Assessment of results, policy guidelines, and recommendations

This section highlights major results and presents recommendations on ways to improve the performance of the small indigenous business sector.

Overseas experience

The survey and subsequent analysis indicated that those entrepreneurs who had worked, trained, and/or traveled extensively outside Western Samoa were more likely to succeed in their own businesses than those entrepreneurs who either had never been outside Western Samoa or had been outside for only brief holidays or religious purposes. Many entrepreneurs with extensive overseas experience spent considerable time in New Zealand, Australia, and the United States being trained and apprenticed in technical skill areas. They were also more likely to have higher levels of formal education and to be exposed to the modern practices of operating a business.

A considerable brain drain from the country occurs through emigration. It therefore follows that the government, if it wants to encourage indigenously run businesses, has a relatively simple way to entice skilled emigrants to return home. Thus the development bank and other development agencies can identify products or services that can be produced and economically sold by indigenous entrepreneurs. If the domestic pool of talent cannot provide the individuals for such services, inducements for those suitably skilled expatriate Samoans can be made for them to return to establish businesses. Inducements can include tax incentives, easier access to credit, and management advisory assistance.

Those Samoans who have extensive skills can also be used to provide training in skills and management areas to indigenous entrepreneurs through institutions such as the Technical Training Institute and the Development Bank of Western Samoa. Another means of acquiring business skills is to sponsor visits by Samoan entrepreneurs overseas.

Location

A characteristic considered important for success is that of location, that is, whether an entrepreneur is in Apia (urban), around Apia (peri-urban), or on Savai'i and distant parts of Upolu (rural). The survey indicated that the group of entrepreneurs most likely to succeed were those located in Apia. Factors adversely affecting entrepreneurs located in the rural areas, especially in the more remote Savai'i, mainly focused on the government and its fiscal policies affecting the cost of goods, small market size, difficulty of access to urban markets, lower levels of management skills, *fa'asamoa* traditions, and transportation.

To equalize the opportunities for entrepreneurs and to encourage businesses in the rural areas, the government should take specific initiatives to improve the climate for rural businesses. The rural businesses surveyed especially complained about price controls; as applied to retailers, they could charge only one price imposed by a price control board. This price, say, for rice, was uniform throughout the country and did not compensate rurally located entrepreneurs for additional storage and transportation costs incurred by more distant rural locations. At the same time, retailers alleged that wholesalers, inherently monopolistic due to their small number, often impose unrealistically high prices upon retailers. This situation allows no profit for rural retailers. Another entrepreneur surveyed, whose business is construction on Savai'i, complained about the policy on tendering for contracts. This entrepreneur felt that for construction jobs on Savai'i, preference should be given to those contractors located on Savai'i who are licensed and can bid competitively.

Their recommendations to the government are that it should (1) adjust, if not eliminate, price controls so that retailers in rural areas are able to charge prices that compensate for higher costs while regulating the prices that wholesalers charge due to inherent monopolistic practices; (2) grant preference to and encourage indigenous businesses, especially those in rural areas, when tendering for government contracts; and (3) grant incentives for businesses such as manufacturers to locate in rural areas. Incentives can include the provision or improvement of infrastructure such as electricity, water, and roads as well as tax incentives such as tax holidays if certain kinds of businesses will locate in designated rural areas.

To equalize the access to banking and business advisory services, the government is encouraged to consider upgrading the banking and advisory services that the Development Bank of Western Samoa and the commercial banks provide in Savai'i. For transportation, the government should consider making the port of Asau on Savai'i an international one. This would give Savai'i direct international shipping access, thereby allowing more direct and economical export and import opportunities.

Formal education

The analysis of the survey data strongly indicates a direct correlation between levels of formal education and business performance. Over the past several years, the government has made significant strides to improve the educational status of the Samoan population.

In recommendations to the government concerning the use of education in improving the performance of the business and enhancement of entrepreneurship, the study recommends adjustments to the primary and secondary school curricula. Exercises in creative thought, even at an early age, can foster entrepreneurship. Original, creative thinking is the essence of successful, dynamic entrepreneurship. Also in primary school, projects such as school gardens can be encouraged and taught so that children can learn the basics of earning and managing money. Even though only a small number of children may eventually become entrepreneurs, the exposure to business will assist students in understanding how to be more informed consumers.

At the secondary level, special curricula to teach basic accounting, management, marketing, and other business skills can be provided to those students demonstrating an active interest in pursuing business on their own after graduating. Coupled with technical training in appropriate areas, basic business training for the primary and secondary school leavers would help create and educate entrepreneurs, as well as enlighten the consuming public.

Religion

Although a sensitive area of discussion, the significant role of religion in Western Samoan society requires that recommendations be made concerning its role in the economy. Almost one-half of the general population as well as one-half of the entrepreneurs interviewed belongs to the indigenous Congregational Christian Church of Samoa (CCCS). As an indigenous body, the CCCS tends to demand a higher level of contribution from its members due to its non-affiliation (such as with the Catholics) with a large international church body. The result is that substantial transfers of capital and other resources are made to the CCCS that might otherwise be invested for productive purposes.

In relation to the significant concentration of investable resources in the churches, especially the CCCS, the study recommends that the churches consider the reinvestment of some of these resources for productive purposes. This would include the possible investment of monies as debentured securities into such institutions as the Development Bank of Western Samoa. Monies could then be on-lent to indigenous entrepreneurs. The churches could also establish programs to educate and train Samoans in business and technical skills.

Technical skills

The degree to which an entrepreneur has training relevant to his or her business will largely determine whether or not a business is successful. This relationship is strongly borne out by the survey. Technical training opportunities in Western Samoa are limited to one technical training institute, the YMCA, and the Women's Advisory Council.

In addition to increasing the amount and quality of technical training provided in various vocational areas through existing institutions, the government should take increased advantage of low-cost consultancies. Countries such as the United States have programs available to developing countries that provide low-cost consultancies by retired executives. The U.S. Agency for International Development (USAID) funds the International Executive Service Corps. This corps is composed of retired U.S. business executives who consult in developing countries (USAID 1987:36). Australia also has a similar program from which one of the Samoan entrepreneurs surveyed benefited. Also, relative to the technical skills of entrepreneurs, the government is recommended to implement standards of skill certification. Entrepreneurs who are certified as to minimum technical competency in their relevant skill areas can assure the public that it is receiving competent service from reputable entrepreneurs.

Length of time in business

According to the survey results, the correlation between length of time in business and business success resembles a bell curve (see Figure 5.1) where the vertical axis of the graph is the degree of suc-

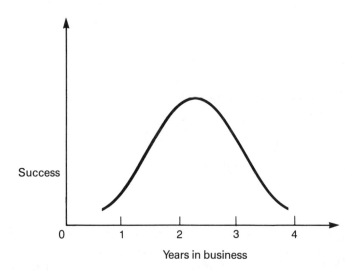

Figure 5.1. Success levels in relation to the age of the business

cess and the horizontal axis is the number of years in business. Those surveyed who were in business for three or four years performed better in business than their counterparts who had been in business for fewer than three years and more than five years. For those who were in business for only a relatively short time, the explanation may be because the enterprise usually suffered losses during the first three years of operation before it would earn profits.

For businesses with five or more years in operation, the explanations become more speculative about performance declines. A likely explanation, supported by general theories of business and product life cycles, is that if an entrepreneur does not produce new and innovative products and services, the appeal and demand for products will decline unless they are improved. People tire of the same product. After five years, competitors come in with new products and services, or variations thereof, rendering the existing ones unattractive.

To counteract these cycles and to maintain the dynamism necessary for older businesses to succeed, the study recommends continuing education and training, selected overseas visits, and provision of venture capital for new business ideas. Continuing education for existing entrepreneurs in subjects such as new product and service designs will stimulate new products and services. Overseas exposure to businesses similar to their own will stimulate innovativeness. In addition, greater availability of funds for venture capital can generate new products and services.

Samoan traditional status

The majority of the entrepreneurs interviewed held *matai* titles, but in business performance those without such titles performed better. The responsibilities of the *matai* are considerable, and their influence extends over approximately 90 percent of the general population.

The study does not suggest changes to the existing system of traditional authority. But the study does recommend that businessmen be trained in how to deal with the realities of the system so that business performance is not adversely affected. This can include training for businessmen to plan and budget for those traditional responsibilities involving the handling of funds. Businessmen should also be trained to separate business from personal obligations and to budget accordingly.

One of the most critical aspects to the *matai* system—one that needs adjustment if business is to grow—is that of land tenure. Over 80 percent of the land is held under traditional authority. If a system could be devised whereby businessmen and their lenders are assured of fixed tenurage on the land businesses occupy, less expensive and more secure business finance can be obtained.

Years of prior work experience

There was no direct link between improved business performance and the number of years of experience an entrepreneur had in prior relevant work. The only relationship noted in the analysis was that the longer the prior experience, the fewer management problems experienced by entrepreneurs.

This finding suggests a possible way to foster entrepreneurship through providing incentives for those with ample work experience in strategic skill areas (such as plumbing, agrobusiness, or carpentry) to form their own businesses. Incentives can include access to credit and advisory assistance. In this way, those with the skills can then go into business to employ and train others. The study also recommends that people who have many years of management experience and who may not want to go into business for themselves should be used as management advisers and trainers for those struggling in business.

Finance

A common cause of business failure is that businessmen often begin with less than a sufficient amount of investment capital. The provision of adequate capital is vital for those businesses that, when starting, often make losses before they earn profits.

In the analysis of the survey data, no direct correlation could be identified between the initial amount invested in a business and its success. Overall, those businesses with an initial investment of T2,000 or less performed the worst while those with initial amounts of T30,000 or more performed the best. Although the study did not distinguish whether a business was in manufacturing, services, trade, or agriculture, a general conclusion is that the availability and amounts of capital for small businesses need to be increased. Recommendations about how more capital can be made available to small businesses can be considered in seven areas.

1. *Loan source diversification:* In most instances, the only institution that small businesses have for capital is the development bank of Western Samoa so that there is an urgent need to develop alternative sources. It is crucial that the other commercial lending institutions, especially commercial banks, should be encouraged to make more loan capital available to small businesses. In the event that the loans are perceived as too risky, guarantee arrangements through the development bank should be considered.

2. *Loan approval process:* Because the development bank will remain the primary source of loan capital for small businesses, it should continue to seek ways of improving its procedures in approving and disbursing loans. This would probably entail increasing the number of staff and their level of training, raising the approval limit for loans for the general manager, and processing the smallest loans through other institutions such as credit unions.

3. *Interest rates:* The disparity of lending rates among business

sectors should be narrowed so that every business is charged a rate that is roughly uniform.

4. *Equity:* It is recommended that the government encourage and provide equity financing to small businesses as a means of capital source diversification.

5. *Expansion of the development bank into commercial lending activities:* This would allow small businesses a one-stop means of gaining both working capital and longer-term capital loans.

6. *Lending ceiling:* The development bank has lent up to T400,000 each to individual businesses. One business that qualified for such a loan could not be considered small in Western Samoa. The government might consider restricting the development bank from making exceptionally large loans to individual companies to the detriment of small enterprises. For loans that exceed T50,000 a percentage should be syndicated with other lending institutions.

7. *Capital retention:* Of course, once profits are being generated, the business is faced with the possibility of retaining the money for reinvestment. In this regard, counseling on the use of profit can be valuable and could include advisory sessions and workshops to teach businessmen the importance of capital retention for the survival of a business.

Conclusion

Collectively and individually, entrepreneurs in Western Samoa have the capacity and the background necessary to improve their performance. Historically, Samoans are socially well disposed to the attributes of saving, hard work, specialization, and upward motivation, all of which are necessary for entrepreneurship to succeed. However, a pervasive orientation to the traditional *matai* system, a strong religious orientation, limited access to monetary capital, poor technical skills, and a government still entrenched in the legacy of a colonial system obstruct the ability of entrepreneurship in Western Samoa to perform better. This study has identified those groups of entrepreneurs who need special help. The study has also highlighted alternative solutions and approaches that the government should consider if it is serious about improving the country's economic performance. Among these solutions are (1) enticing back and helping to set up in business technically skilled expatriate Samoans, (2) encouraging and training children in school through business studies to go into business, (3) reinvesting monies of the cccs through the development bank for on-lending to Samoan businesses, and (4) encouraging businesses to locate in rural areas through infrastructure improvements and incentives.

APPENDIX A. SURVEY APPROACH

In selecting the survey sample, the following four factors were taken into account:

1. *Size:* Gross revenue is T200,000 or less, and ten or fewer people are employed.

2. *Ethnicity:* The survey team sought as many "pure" ethnic Samoans as possible; however, for the evaluative purposes, 39 percent of the sample interviewed were not pure ethnic Samoans.

3. *Manufacturing:* A third parameter was interviewing a large proportion of firms whose activities included value-added goods manufacture.

4. *Rural location:* Historically, and even today, economic development has tended to favor urban versus rural development. This bias was an important influence in the decision to select one-half the survey sample from rural locations.

As for a suitable questionnaire, the survey team found the survey form already being used by PIDP in other country studies to be quite adequate. With a few minor modifications, the essential features of the form covered questions concerning the background of the entrepreneur and features of the business itself. Specific areas covered by the questionnaire included (1) the general background of the business, (2) financial structure of the business, (3) business performance, (4) problems affecting the survival and performance of the business, (5) factors contributing to the success of the business, and (6) a page for interviewer comments or analysis. (The final page was completed at the end of each day by the survey team while memories of the day's interviews were still fresh.)

The 70 sample enterprises covered by the survey included 20 in manufacturing, 30 in services, 12 in trading, and 8 in agrobusiness and fishing (see Appendix C). Racially, the sample comprised 43 full Samoan entrepreneurs, 26 part-Samoans, and one full-European. A total of 35 enterprises were located in urban (Apia) or peri-urban locations, and the remaining 35 were rural including Savai'i. The majority of enterprises (71 percent) recorded an annual turnover in sales below T50,000 of which at least one-half fell below the T25,000 level. Annual sales of over T100,000 were experienced by just under one-fourth of the enterprises.

APPENDIX B. CHARACTERISTICS OF SAMOAN ENTREPRENEURSHIP

The original survey revealed much about the characteristics of entrepreneurship and business operations, which are discussed below by subhead.

Age

The entrepreneurs interviewed were mostly in the middle- to advanced-age groups. None was younger than 26 years of age while 77 percent was over the age of 35. The tendency for older ages in the sector significantly correlates with the fact that (1) greater respect and patronage are accorded to people who are older in Western Samoa, and (2) many who go into business have retired or resigned from positions in government or large business and have accumulated sufficient capital and experience to start a business. With respect to the correlation of advanced age, respect, and going into business, those interviewed who were at least in their 40s indicated this correlation to be an incentive for going into business. They felt customers would tend to patronize their businesses because of the confidence that customers would have in those businesses owned and operated by people of older age who were traditionally worthy of respect and confidence.

Another reason why older persons pursue business is due to the nature of the *matai* system. It necessarily takes a long time to achieve rank and status in the *matai* system. The pursuit of business becomes more necessary as one gets older so as to provide the material means to achieve greater rank. Wage or salary labor often cannot support the material demands that the traditional system places on Samoans who seek ever higher traditional status. In this increasing effort to seek higher status, an older entrepreneur is inspired to seek alternative economic opportunities by pursuing business.

Gender/family size

Although women traditionally play a major role socially and economically in Samoan society, the correlation of their numbers as entrepreneurs is quite low. Nineteen percent of the entrepreneurs surveyed were women, although roughly one-half of the population is female. In family size, the average of 9.23 members per family unit in the general population correlated with that of the entrepreneurs surveyed. This contrasts with average family sizes of three or fewer in the United States or Europe. Such high averages in Western Samoa imply high dependency ratios that can be an important factor in making fewer family resources available for productive business investment.

Ethnicity

Whereas 89 percent of the general population is considered fully ethnic Samoan or Polynesian, 61 percent of those surveyed were of such ethnicity; it was difficult to find more due to their underrepresentation in business. This situation correlates with other developing countries whose indigenous populations have only recently had access to political, economic, and social development opportunities since independence. The higher proportion of non-ethnic Samoans in business indicates that they or their ancestors came to the islands with skills and attitudes that enabled them to succeed in business, especially given the limited access to village lands. What is different in Western Samoa as compared with other countries such as Fiji or Indonesia (where ethnic non-indigenous groups tend to be more isolated from the indigenous population) is that the distinctions between ethnic and non-ethnic Samoans are blurred. A certain degree of integration exists among all ethnic groups allowing non-ethnic Samoans to achieve rank and status within the traditional *matai* hierarchy.

Traditional status

Although *matai* comprise only 8 percent of the general population, 63 percent of those surveyed are *matai*. As already noted, the *matai* have a strong need to gain material wealth to fulfill traditional responsibilities. The survey data strongly confirm that the pursuit of gainful business is viewed by entrepreneurs as an important vehicle for the acquisition of the resources necessary to fulfill *matai* responsibilities and to achieve status.

Religion

The percentage distribution of entrepreneurs surveyed according to church affiliation roughly matches that of the general population. The church that has the highest membership is the Congregational Christian Church of Samoa (CCCS) at 47 percent in 1981 (South Pacific Commission 1985:57). A slight variation is that a slightly lower percentage of the entrepreneurs surveyed belong to the indigenous CCCS than a similar percentage of the population. What is significant about religion is not so much the percentage distribution according to affiliation. Rather, it is the intensity to which Samoans believe in and support their churches. This intensity of affiliation translates, especially for entrepreneurs who are members of the cccs, into high contributions of resources that could be otherwise reinvested in business growth and productivity.

Training and experience

Compared with the general population, the entrepreneurs surveyed achieved superior levels of formal education. According to the data, 81 percent of the entrepreneurs surveyed had at least attended secondary school as compared with only 42 percent of the general population of adult age (Government of Western Samoa 1981). It is widely accepted that the higher the level of education, the greater the chances of success in business. The study strongly supports this relationship.

For the purposes of analysis, the survey team defined training in terms of its relevancy to the business and the length of the training received. Such training should have lasted for at least one month and should have created or improved a technical or business skill that the entrepreneur could use directly in the business.

According to the survey, entrepreneurs who had received training relevant to their business showed better results and performed more successfully than those who had not been trained. The analysis of the survey data, which related the technical training factor to business performance, suggested that those who received relevant training were 1.6 times more likely to succeed in business than those who had not received training.

Overseas experience

Fifty-seven percent of the entrepreneurs had overseas experience (experience is defined as work, training, and/or travel outside Western Samoa for more than three weeks). In business performance, the results indicate that entrepreneurs with extensive overseas experience were far more likely to succeed in business than those who had no such experience. Many had lived and worked in New Zealand or Australia and upon returning to Western Samoa were able to start businesses and apply the practical training and knowledge they acquired while away. Interestingly, those surveyed who had limited holiday-type experiences overseas performed the worst relative to those who had never gone overseas and those who had lived overseas for long periods. One plausible explanation offered by more than one official indicated that many of those who travel for holiday purposes use for airfares what little financial resources they have—resources that otherwise could be used for productive business pursuits.

Family background and reasons for going into business

In contrast to the 75 percent of the country's households involved in agriculture, 50 percent of the entrepreneurs surveyed came from families whose backgrounds were in non-agricultural fields. Family background seems to influence whether one pursues business and whether one succeeds in business (Nafziger 1978:53).

Evidence from the survey, however, suggests that family background does not strongly correlate with business success. Other factors such as relevant training, overseas exposure, formal education, and amount of initial finance appear to be more important in determining success.

Contemporary American and other western literature indicate that most people do not go into business because of money. Rather they want to be independent and be free from a boss and an institution (Smilar and Kuhn 1984:53–62). However, the survey indicated that the reasons most people pursue business in Western Samoa, as in other developing countries, is that few other money-earning employment opportunities exist. Lack of employment opportunities in formal sectors forces those who want to avoid a subsistence existence to opt for the only alternative— pursuit of a business. Indeed, only 13 percent of the entrepreneurs surveyed began their businesses for reasons of independence and personal satisfaction; the majority pursued business because there were no other alternatives to make money.

The study did not analyze whether the reason for going into business could influence success.

How the capital to start the business was acquired

Lack of access to or the actual lack of capital supply is the main reason why 63 percent of the entrepreneurs surveyed relied entirely on their own resources to start their business ventures. Such resources include personal savings contributed by family members, remittances, and earnings from other sources. The survey analysis indicates that the amount of capital funds initially invested is an important factor in determining whether a business will eventually succeed. Those businesses with an initial investment of over T20,000 were 1.6 times more likely to succeed than those who began with T1,000 or less. A rule of thumb in business is that the greater the amount of capital invested into a business, the greater the capacity to take risks and to succeed.

Other business activities

No direct analysis was made as to the extent that diversification in other business activities influenced the performance of a business. Statistically, 64 percent of those surveyed did engage or had an interest in other business ventures. For 36 percent the business for which entrepreneurs were surveyed was their sole means of support. The kinds of alternative income-generating activities ranged from plantations, to trade stores, to government service.

APPENDIX C. TYPES OF BUSINESSES SURVEYED

1. Manufacturers: 20 (29%)
   • Furniture makers 5
   • Bakeries 3
   • Copra driers 3
   • Soft drink makers 1
   • Tailors/seamstresses 1
   • Artisans/handicrafters 1
   • Banana/taro/breadfruit chip maker 1
   • Butchery 1
   • Timber processing 1
   • Upholsterer/foam mattress maker 1
   • Axe handle maker 1
   • Water tank maker 1
2. Services 30 (43%)
   • Bus owners/operators 7
   • Trucking services 4
   • Mechanical workshops 4
   • Hotel/tourist accommodations 4
   • Restaurants/foodstalls 3
   • Typing school 1
   • Newspaper 1
   • Electronic repair 1
   • Real estate broker 1
   • Ferry service interisland 1
   • Building contractor 1
   • Electrician 1
   • Taxi operator 1
3. Merchants 12 (17%)
   • Small trade stores 11
   • Import/export wholesaler 1
4. Agrobusiness/fisheries 8 (11%)
   • Fishermen 5
   • Farmer/taro exporter 1
   • Poultry/piggery 2

NOTE

1. At the time of the survey in 1984, one tala (T) was worth approximately US$0.48.

REFERENCES

Croulet, C. R. and L. Sio
  1986 *Indigenous Entrepreneurship in Western Samoa,* Pacific Islands Development Program, East-West Center, Honolulu.

Government of Western Samoa
  1981 *Western Samoa Census,* Department of Statistics, Apia.
  1984 *Fifth Development Plan 1985–1987,* Department of Economic Development, Apia.

Nafziger, E. W.
  1978 *Class, Caste and Entrepreneurship: A Study of Indian Industrialists,* University of Hawaii Press, Honolulu.

Smilar, R. W. and R. L. Kuhn (eds.)
  1984 *Corporate Creativity,* Praeger, New York.

South Pacific Commission
  1985 *Population 1983,* Statistical Bulletin No. 26, Noumea.

U.S. Agency for International Development
  1987 *Economic Growth and the Third World,* Washington, D.C.

Woman washing ginger in Fiji. (Photo by Andrew McGregor)

A Tonga-based joint venture (between a New Zealand company and a Pacific island woman) makes soccer balls for local and international markets. (Photo by S. Deacon Ritterbush)

Because carriers provide such a vital link between rural and urban areas, they are often purchased collectively by villagers. (Photo by John M. Hailey)

A commercial farmer sorts vanilla beans—Tonga's leading cash crop in the early 1980s. (Photo by S. Deacon Ritterbush)

A shop clerk in American Samoa points to a variety of canned goods. (Photo by S. Deacon Ritterbush)

A Tongan woman displays fabrics for sale in a local store. (Photo by S. Deacon Ritterbush)

Dalo (taro) and yagona (kava) are sold at Suva, Fiji, market. (Photo by John M. Hailey)

Government business advisers in Fiji discuss business operations with store owners. (Photo by John M. Hailey)

Young entrepreneurs sell fish daily from their family boats. (Photo by John M. Hailey)

A guest house on an outer island of Fiji is the only tourism accommodation on Vanua Balavu. (Photo by John M. Hailey)

Copra processing (smoke-heat) in Tonga remains a source of income for rural families. (Photo by S. Deacon Ritterbush)

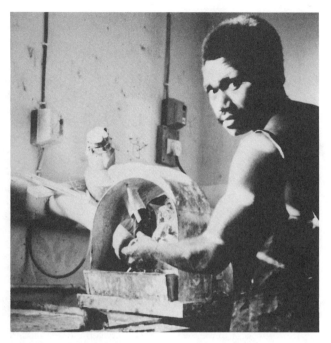

Ni-Vanuatu employee manufactures buttons from trochus shells for export to the Paris fashion industry. (Photo by John M. Hailey)

Port Vila woman sells vegetables at Saturday street market. (Photo by John M. Hailey)

A joint venture to process timber was formed between indigenous interests and Japanese investors in Western Samoa. (Photo by S. Deacon Ritterbush)

The first regional workshop on Indigenous Business in the Pacific, held in Apia, Western Samoa, in 1986, was attended by participants from 20 Pacific nations. (Photo by Forrest g. Hooper)

CHAPTER 6

Obstacles to Success: Entrepreneurship in the Marshall Islands

John J. Carroll

THE ADVANCEMENT of Pacific island economies depends on improving the productive capabilities of their respective private sectors. Enhancing private sector capabilities has often been cited by political leaders and planners as vital to achieving greater economic independence. Yet the private sectors of many Pacific island nations have not become the backbones of economic growth that they had anticipated. In an effort to understand the factors that may be inhibiting the process, the Pacific Islands Development Program (PIDP) undertook a series of research studies aimed at identifying obstacles to business success. Attention was focused on the people who are believed to be the heart and future of private sector growth, the indigenous entrepreneurs.

The fieldwork for this study of indigenous entrepreneurs in the Republic of the Marshall Islands was conducted from November 1984 to late January 1985. Most interviews were done on Majuro Atoll, site of the nation's capitol and the business center. In order to capture some sense of the conditions and problems affecting outer atoll entrepreneurs, additional survey work was done on Ebeye, Arno, and Kili islands.

The survey strategy was to select a representative sample of indigenous businesses, interview the major decision makers of those businesses, and interview government officials, bankers, and educators familiar with private sector growth problems and issues. These data—as well as information gathered from government records, public documents, local publications, informed citizens, and scholarly works—constituted the sources used to produce this report. The analytic strategy was to view the entrepreneur and the entrepreneur's environment as the two major sources of obstacles to business success.

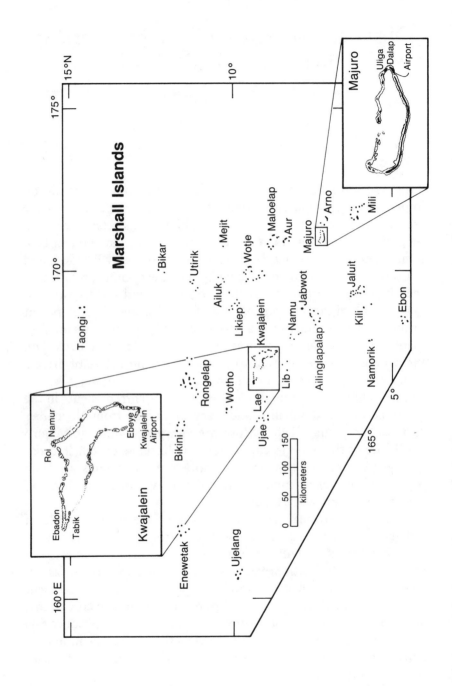

Marshall Islands

Taongi

Bikar

Utirik

Ailuk

Mejit

Likiep

Wotje

Maloelap

Aur

Kwajalein

Namu

Jabwot

Majuro

Arno

Mili

Ailinglapalap

Jaluit

Kili

Namorik

Ebon

Rongelap

Wotho

Lae

Lib

Ujae

Bikini

Enewetak

Ujelang

Kwajalein

Ebadon

Tabik

Roi Namur

Ebeye

Kwajalein
Airport

Majuro

Uliga
Dalap

Airport

0   50   100   150
kilometers

160° E

165°

170°

175°

5°

10°

15°N

Land and people

The Republic of the Marshall Islands is an archipelago in Eastern Micronesia of 29 atolls and five coral islands forming two roughly parallel chains that stretch northwesterly from just above the equator through 910,000 sq km of mid-Pacific waters. Known as the Ratak (sunrise) and Ralik (sunset) chains, it is not uncommon for islands to stretch for 15 or 30 km along a reef. The islands total only 192 sq km (74 square miles) of not particularly fertile land.

The population of the Marshall Islands has almost tripled since the mid-1930s and continues to grow at an alarming rate. Based on the 1980 census, 52.5 percent of the population is under the age of 16, the highest proportion found among Pacific island countries (Connell 1983:13). The census reported the population at 30,873 with 11,791 people living on Majuro, the administrative center and the most heavily populated atoll. Almost 7,000 people live on Ebeye, a 30-hectare (75-acre) island, located within sight of the Kwajalein Missile Range. Ebeye is the most densely populated island in the Pacific owing to employment opportunities on the missile range, which attract outer islanders and their families. This migration of outer islanders to Ebeye and Majuro in search of employment opportunities and new lifestyles has resulted in the urbanization of almost two-thirds of the total population on approximately 10 percent of the land (Alexander 1978:65).

Traditions and entrepreneurship

The Marshallese have been experiencing change in traditional lifestyles since shortly after the Carolinians sailed eastward to inhabit the islands. The change process has been hastened over the past 100 years by the culture-modifying exploits of German, Japanese, and American colonizers. The effect among the Marshallese appears to be an ambivalence with respect to the old and new ways of life, which may partially explain the troubles faced by some indigenous entrepreneurs. It is not uncommon for an indigenous entrepreneur to encounter conflicting obligations that arise when striving to honor traditions while at the same time pursuing business growth. It is likely that in today's business environment, where western-style practices are common, the Marshallese who seek business success will need to overcome the contradictions of ambivalence and exhibit a certainty that enables them to function effectively at the cutting edge of the change process, whether for traditional or business reasons. The challenge is to minimize the contradictions. Potential for conflict lies at the crossroads of traditional authority, land tenure, economic, and sociocultural structures of Marshallese society and the profit requirements of business success.

Traditional authority

The traditional ascription-based authority system operates to perpetuate feudalistic relationships that are founded on the privileges of land ownership and class distinctions. The introduction of a democratic-based, secret ballot election procedure has not noticeably altered the authority structure. The coexistence of the traditional feudalistic system and a modern democratic system has been referred to by one U.S. congressman as "traditional oligarchy operating under the facade of constitutionality" (Marshall Islands Journal, 20 September 1985).

As long as traditional leadership heads the government, as is the case today, or is heavily represented in government, efforts to foster either feudalistic or democratic relationships will be of vital importance to indigenous entrepreneurs of commoner-class status. That is, from a traditional point of view, the leadership can be expected to regard increased economic power in the hands of the people as a potential threat to its control and therefore generally be opposed to measures designed to widely distribute wealth and opportunities. In emphasizing the nation's democratic constitution, the leadership can be expected to promote the inalienable rights of its citizens, including more equal distribution of wealth and access to economic opportunities. The positions taken by traditional leadership with respect to these extremes will largely determine business success.

The success of commoner-class indigenous entrepreneurs depends on reasonable access to two extremely important resources —land and money. The traditional authority system places nearly absolute control over land in the hands of traditional chiefs, a situation described by anthropologists as tantamount to control over life itself, as long as no alternatives are available to provide for life's necessities (Alexander 1978:99).

In the past there was no alternative; today money provides an alternative as is suggested in Kiste's description of the Marshallese who had spent time working as laborers on Kwajalein. "As they earned their livelihood outside the traditional economy, they were no longer inclined to accept a status subservient to that of the chiefs, and they questioned the traditional social order which divided islanders into privileged and commoner classes" (Kiste 1974:90). Access to money threatened traditional controls over people's lives.

The issue of traditional leadership members seeking to control access to money as a safeguard of their authority has been covered in a study by Alexander (1978) on wage labor, urbanization, and culture change. He found that traditional leaders had taken the initiative to control access to money as well as land.

> In the change from the traditional economic system to a wage labor system, it might be expected that a new power and prestige system would develop related to the source of money. To some extent, the traditional leadership structure has maintained its position. A son of the present paramount chief has firm control over Mid-Atoll Corridor negotiations and division of the funds. A nephew of the paramount chief holds a key position in the Global Associates Micronesian IRO (personnel) Office, thus potentially controlling who is able to get jobs (Alexander 1978:76).

Although both these people work in new capacities, they are active in controlling the distribution of millions of dollars received by payments of Kwajalein land owners for the U.S. military's use of their lands and lagoon. Since 1984 the Marshall Islands' court system has been trying a family dispute between traditional leaders over the title to Kwajalein lands. At stake in the dispute is the right to distribute the payments and to claim the *iroij*'s (traditional chief's) share of the fortune (Marshall Islands Journal, 12 November 1984, and 3 January 1985).

The desire to control suggested above is not just a characteristic of the traditional leadership, but of the entire population.

> Marshallese attitudes and behavior reveal a generalized concern over the distribution and acquisition of power, influence, privilege, and control, not only of land but of all resources which they deem

of substantial worth. The system of landholding and land rights was integrally related to the islanders' lineage and kinship system, and it was the rights to land that defined the most important political and economic relations among individuals and groups. Social statuses entailing authority over land were the supreme prizes in the competitive arena of Marshallese life. Authority over land provided power and influence over others and entitled those who possessed it with special privileges. The statuses were few relative to the aspirants to them, and as a consequence, they were the objects in a never ending rivalry (Kiste 1974:5).

In the pre-contact era, control over the land meant control over people and hence power. Over the years, the formula for power has changed to include control over access to money because control over land alone was no longer sufficient to guarantee traditional loyalty. As such, as long as traditional rivalries continue, there will be persistent attempts to control the most important determinants of power—land and money. Thus access to these two necessary requirements of indigenous business success will be difficult to achieve, particularly among the Marshallese who are not from the highest traditional social class.

Land tenure

The entrepreneur who uses family land for a business must obtain approval from the land manager, or *alab*, because "land is not individually owned, but rather held in trust for future generations by a lineage" (Alexander 1978:82). Obtaining the *alab*'s blessing is not always easy, particularly because many family members have worker rights to a single parcel of land. At the worst, it requires making promises that are contrary to business interests. When a nonfamily member is involved, more uncertainty shrouds any land use agreement. Generally, agreements are oral and not backed up in writing, a requisite that could be perceived as insulting to the person giving land use authorization.

The tribute system requires that a percentage of copra and other agricultural yields be given to the landowner. This practice is observed in the more traditional rural villages and to a lesser extent in the urban areas. People who operate businesses situated on land belonging to another family are typically expected to follow this customary practice. Although the family head, *alab,* may have little control over the way the land is used, he or she is still able to demand some type of "rent" payment for its use. This tribute becomes a problem in many situations because of its variable nature. The retail store owner, for example, is sometimes expected to give money, sometimes merchandise. The time at which these payments are made is not set, and the amounts can vary dramatically.

At least one business manager interviewed suggested that the amount expected was directly related to the perceived success of the business. In other words, if the business showed signs of growth, a larger rent payment would be expected. In the extreme case, this could include eviction; that is, the landowners decide that they want to take control of the business and do so by reclaiming the land. In any event, it becomes exceedingly difficult for the businessperson to plan effectively because of the variable nature of this expense; rent is a cost that should remain fixed over a reasonably long period of time.

Traditional economy

The subsistence affluence that was once a reality is no longer possible because of increases in population and consumer demands (Schwalbenberg 1984; Fisk 1982; Sahlins 1971). The replacement of the traditional economic system with a monetized system finds some Marshallese reacting adversely. Among workers, high wage levels are needed to attract them. Among entrepreneurs there is a tendency to expect greater returns than the business can withstand. Interviews are replete with tales of indigenous businesspeople who spent cash received from business transactions as if it were pocket money until the business was in financial ruin.

Social relationships

A system of reciprocity pervades the society that is equivalent to communal ownership among family members. This customary practice makes it extraordinarily difficult for a businessperson to withhold goods or services for monetary reasons. Responding to this cultural norm has crippled many businesses by creating cash flow problems due to overextension of credit, particularly to family members. As individuals and families become more autonomous (due to migration, urbanization, a greater reliance on wage employment, and the gradual extinction of the traditional economic system), such customary practices are expected to wane. In the meantime, stiff competition will continue between the profit requirements of the market economy and the reciprocity obligations of the traditional system for the indigenous entrepreneurs' loyalty.

Colonization and entrepreneurship

The Marshallese experience with foreigners began with navigators bartering pieces of metal for provisions and information. Colonial domination by Spain, Germany, Japan, and the United States followed in succession. Spain's influence was centralized in the Mariana Islands and never reached the Marshall Islands. Real outside interests in the Marshall Islands began with missionaries and German trading companies in the mid-1800s. During this era, commercial interest in copra set the stage for the adoption of a monetized economic system to satisfy growing consumer demands.

The German control lasted until the outbreak of World War I when Japan occupied much of Micronesia. The often referred to "economic miracle" that the Japanese performed in Micronesia during their occupation involved the Marshall Islands only as a bit player. Copra trade and other commercial activities continued to flourish although restricted somewhat by administrative regulations. World War II brought devastation and confusion that put Micronesia's burgeoning economy into a tailspin. The new administrators, the United States, were unable to articulate any meaningful development strategy early on, and hence the economy languished for years. Partially revived by the infusion of huge sums of money and access to u.s. federal programs during the past 25 years, the economy has remained underdeveloped.

The colonial periods of Germany, Japan, and the United States have an important characteristic in common. Each country made an initial effort to accomplish its objectives by working with the traditional system rather than against it. Later, each country also challenged the system because it became an obstacle to achieving colonial objectives. In general, each of the colonial administrations attempted to introduce structures similar to its own for the purposes of advancing change and meeting its policy objectives. To facilitate these objectives they consistently attacked traditional structures as being counterproductive to achieving what they prescribed as improved standards of living. This prolonged pressure has probably contributed to the ambivalence, referred to earlier, that complicates decision making among indigenous business people.

The u.s. period of administration was the most recent and probably has had the most profound impact on indigenous entrepreneurship in Micronesia. The United States as administrating authority under a u.n. Trust Territory agreement has been accused of spending lavishly in the islands while allowing the economy to languish in order to ensure a continued relationship that would preserve its military control and privileges. The intensity of the u.s. relationship with Micronesians may have been greatest among the Marshallese because of u.s. determination to conduct a nuclear testing program and operate a missile range on Kwajalein Atoll. These military objectives were accomplished through forced migration or other separation of many Marshallese from their most valuable assets, their lands and lagoons. This tactic left them without traditional means of support and almost totally dependent on compensation monies, u.s. federal programs, and other forms of social services.

The considerable sums of money received in rent payments for use of Kwajalein Atoll and the compensations paid to the nuclear-affected people served as a two-edged sword. On the one hand, it made wage labor less attractive, contributed to the artificiality of the economy, undermined traditional self-sufficiency, and reinforced people's dependency on external sources of assistance. On the other, it put a significant amount of buying power into the hands of consumers and businesspeople.

u.s. involvement through educational programs and other social services has raised people's expectations to high levels, which serve as an additional hindrance to realistic and objective assessments of economic worth. The employment experience of most wage laborers has been in government service, where there is little relationship between quantity and quality of output and wage levels. Indigenous entrepreneurs operating in the private sector have the difficult task of trying to establish an economically sound relationship between wages and worker productivity.

Government and commercial development

The level of indigenous participation and performance in the private sector can be influenced by government efforts to create a
favorable commercial environment. The potential impact in this
regard is related to the government's development strategies,
incentive programs, legislation, and the quality of the infrastructure created.

The overall economic development strategy, as expressed in the
First Five Year Development Plan 1985–1989 and confirmed by
government officials, relies heavily on foreign investment through
joint partnerships between the government and foreign companies
and on businesses owned and operated exclusively by the government. Although this strategy recognizes the importance of private
sector growth to the development goals of the nation, it is
expected that private sector entrepreneurs will capitalize on the
opportunities that occur as a result of government-sponsored
businesses. Effectively, indigenous entrepreneurs are relegated to
the "spin-off" commercial activities that arise if these primary
efforts are successful.

If the government is to promote private sector development by
participating in business ventures, then it is fair to expect government to demonstrate competency. A general appraisal of the government's performance by the auditor general in three semi-annual
reports is that the government suffers from serious financial management problems including the inability to bill and collect
amounts for utilities and other services, as well as from a major
lack of control and guidance throughout the government (Republic of the Marshall Islands, Office of the Auditor General 1985:9).
It appears that prior to the second report the government "has
never prepared comprehensive financial statements, and consequently, has never known to any degree its overall financial position" (Republic of the Marshall Islands, Office of the Auditor
General 1985:25). The first two reports cite numerous cases of
irregularities that have resulted in waste, unnecessary expendi-
tures, and even cases of embezzlement and fraud that have been
referred to the Attorney General's Office. The third auditor general's report again disclosed numerous cases of misuses of government funds and abuses of government policies (Marshall Islands
Journal, 23 August 1985).

The process by which projects were approved was also a subject of serious criticism. As described by one cabinet member, the government's planning is best characterized as reactive. There is reportedly little well-thought out, long-term detailed analysis of projects. Legislators have been known to vote without benefit of any written analysis of a project's financial (or any other) impact. Although the Marshall Islands government has involved itself in a shipping company, an airline, a milk factory, off-shore banking, a copra-processing plant, and a fuel farm among other ventures, no official interviewed was aware of a cost-benefit analysis or any other research on these projects.

Evidence shows that the government has enacted some legislation directed at encouraging entrepreneurial efforts. However, little noticeable implementation exists of the program constituted to provide such assistance. Some tax requirements appear to present appreciable constraints on small-scale indigenous entrepreneurs, and no evidence has been shown of any concessionary rates that might promote local production or import substitution.

Improvements have been made in the quantity and quality of the infrastructure needed to support commercial ventures. Improved electrical power and communication systems have benefited entrepreneurial activities, and improved air and sea transportation systems are planned. The unreliability of these services and utilities has hampered indigenous business success in the past.

The private sector

A major force behind business creation has been the profits to be made from servicing the spending power created through government wages, rents paid to Kwajalein landowners by the U.S. government, wages paid to Kwajalein workers by U.S. contractors, and compensation paid to the nuclear-affected people. The result has been a proliferation of small retail stores, restaurants, and other service-related businesses. A survey restricted to Majuro Atoll identified 127 service-type businesses, 122 trade stores, 25 industrial enterprises, and only a few extractive-type businesses, extractive referring to businesses that depend on the land or ocean for their products (e.g., agriculture, aquaculture, and fishing).

In addition to the government-sponsored copra processing mill, the industrial sector includes a machine shop, a few construction companies, some small boat-building operations, some handicrafts production, a print shop, a few bakeries, and several tailor shops. The extractive sector contributes a few small-scale agriculture, aquaculture, and fishing businesses. Although the government has plans to invigorate these two areas through its policy of government-owned businesses, the prognosis for greater industrialization must be tempered by the realization that natural resources are limited, infrastructure remains inadequate, domestic wage levels are high, domestic markets are small, and venture capital is difficult to find.

The private sector's contribution to the economy's strength can be seen as a percentage of the nation's gross domestic product (GDP). In 1977 private enterprise accounted for only 5 percent of the GDP (Connell 1983:7), and it has probably not changed much since then. The total value of all goods and services produced adjusted for price level changes (real GDP) did not increase between 1975 and 1981. Because the population is growing at over 3 percent a year, the per capita real income (real GDP/population) declined at an even faster rate (Republic of the Marshall Islands 1985:21).

The development plan claims that to achieve an increase in production and income, the efforts of "the formal business organizations, subsistence and semi-subsistence producers, self-employed, and the non-formal small business entrepreneurs" are critical (Republic of the Marshall Islands 1985:32). The plan also acknowledges that the "productive base of the economy is very weak . . . [which] implies the need to exploit the economy's natural resources more extensively and more efficiently . . . [and] the need to start to expand the secondary and tertiary activities which can be built around the primary sector" (Republic of the Marshall Islands 1985:28).

One of the most pressing problems faced by the indigenous entrepreneur was meeting the capital requirements to run even a small business, which was also a finding in similar studies conducted in Western Samoa (Croulet 1986) and the Cook Islands (Fairbairn with Pearson 1987). Many of the indigenous-owned small retail trade stores found in Majuro and Ebeye are totally dependent on the few large retail-wholesale outlets from which they buy their merchandise, usually on some type of wholesale credit arrangement. In fact, several small merchants reported that this relationship is so important that without it they could not have started a business or would no longer be in business.

As might be imagined, merchants who struggle to operate small retail stores in the outer islands must endure additional difficulties and greater expenses. Except for one or two businesses on Ebeye, those that do exist on outer islands rely heavily on the wholesale distribution channels of one or more larger stores. They must assume, however, the added shipping costs and the risks associated with the unreliable shipping service to the outer islands. The lack of private or government financial services in the outer islands further stifles entrepreneurial efforts by making credit inaccessible.

The inability of indigenous businesspeople to gain access to needed capital is exacerbated by two unfortunate realities: the propensity among business owners to spend earnings on personal consumption rather than to reinvest them in the business, and the insufficiency of the financial services available. A business failure scenario offered by several representatives from the financial and government sectors interviewed went as follows: a person borrows as much money as possible from family, friends, bank, or credit union; the person stocks a small store with merchandise purchased with cash borrowed; when cash flows into the business as a result of sales the person fails to put aside enough cash to restock the store and pay off past debts; when the stock is depleted the store closes.

The major problems leading to the insufficiency of financial services are the cost and questionable practices that typify most of the financial services available to indigenous entrepreneurs. Financial services available in the Marshall Islands are limited to three commercial banks, the development bank, four credit unions, and two insurance companies.

At least two different Taiwanese groups have operated one of the commercial banks in the past; both have been plagued by loan delinquencies and management problems. During an interview, one bank manager cited the government's rather sudden increase in its licensing fee from $500 to $5,000 a year and its attempt to collect the increase on a retroactive basis as indicative of the uncertainty that makes business in the Marshall Islands less attractive to legitimate foreign investors.[1] He likened the government's action to a decision to "kill the goose to get the egg," which he felt was an appropriate metaphor to explain why the government has failed to stimulate real private sector growth. He went on to remark that the high loan delinquency rates and low deposit levels made it necessary to charge interest rates in excess of 20 percent on commercial loans. According to the bank manager, loan delinquency is at least as common among highly paid government employees as it is among those at the low income levels. The net effect is that the cost of borrowing to the businessperson is high because of the growing demand for money, a history of credit irresponsibility, and deposit levels that generate little income for the bank.

The Marshall Islands Development Bank has yet to become a force in support of the efforts of indigenous entrepreneurs. The information gathered during the fieldwork exercise strongly suggests that the development bank offers financial services that are limited and hence of marginal benefit to most indigenous entrepreneurs in search of financial or other assistance.

The enterprises

Eighty-six entrepreneurs were interviewed, 71 indigenous and 15 non-indigenous. Because many of them operated more than one venture, the number of businesses represented in their response totaled 150. Because entrepreneurs were generally unable to distinguish between their various commercial activities in their responses, the term enterprise is used to mean the "basket" of economic ventures controlled by a single entrepreneur, while business refers to a single commercial activity.

Indigenous entrepreneurs were most heavily represented in the

Table 6.1. Non-indigenous and indigenous enterprises by sector

Sector	Non-indigenous (%)	Indigenous (%)	Total (%)
Trade	26	60	53
Service	58	38	42
Industrial	16	0	3
Extractive	0	2	2
Total	100	100	100
Number of responses	$N=31$	$N=119$	$N=150$

Table 6.2. Non-indigenous and indigenous enterprises by market value

Market value ($000)	Non-indigenous (%)	Indigenous (%)	Total (%)
$0–10	13	34	30
$10–50	27	32	32
$50–100	20	13	14
$100–500	20	17	17
over $500	20	4	7
Total	100	100	100
Number of cases	N=15	N=71	N=86

trade and service sectors (Table 6.1). Only a few indigenous entrepreneurs were engaged in enterprises in the extractive sector, that is, agriculture, aquaculture, or fishing. By comparison, the non-indigenous entrepreneurs favored service-type businesses over trade and were active in the industrial sector.

Based on an estimate of each enterprise's market value, over one-half of those surveyed were worth less than $50,000 (Table 6.2). Over two-thirds of the indigenous enterprises and approximately 40 percent of the non-indigenous enterprises fell into this grouping. The non-indigenous enterprises were better represented in the higher market value categories.

A sense of variation in complexity is gained from the many business combinations that were evident. The enterprises surveyed included from one to as many as 12 business activities, but most operated no more than three. Indigenous entrepreneurs were primarily engaged in a single activity at one location, although some were involved in single and multiple activities at one or more locations. The non-indigenous entrepreneurs appeared to be slightly more involved in multiple ventures at one or more locations.

Most enterprises were staffed by family members, many of whom did not receive wages. Out of the 63 indigenous enterprises that reported, 56 percent indicated that family workers were not paid. Owners claimed that family members either were expected to work as part of their family responsibility or were occasionally given money or merchandise in lieu of wages. The degree of reliance on family workers was further substantiated when only 39 percent of the indigenous entrepreneurs and a smaller percentage of non-indigenous entrepreneurs were willing or able to state a dollar amount. The claim among indigenous entrepreneurs was

Table 6.3. Non-indigenous and indigenous businesses by age

Years in business	Non-indigenous (%)	Indigenous (%)	Total (%)
0–5	77	62	65
6–10	13	21	19
11–15	7	5	6
16–40	3	12	10
Total	100	100	100
Number of responses	$N=30$	$N=117$	$N=147$

that they paid an average of $50 per week in wages, which was comparable to weekly government employment.

The number of years in business indicates that more than three-fourths of the non-indigenous businesses surveyed were five years old or less (Table 6.3). Among indigenous businesses over 80 percent were 10 years old or less. Within the indigenous group only a few businesses reported being in existence for more than 15 years. What is noteworthy is that there were so few of these mature businesses and that most had remained small.

Although the sampling technique used was not perfect, the information from those interviewed provided a description of indigenous enterprises that is believed to reasonably depict the private sector. Enterprises were typically small, young, single-owner service or trade types engaged in one, or perhaps two, economic activities that relied on family members as workers. The non-indigenous enterprises differed modestly in a few areas. They tended to be slightly larger, involved in more than one economic activity, and engaged more in industry.

The entrepreneurs

Of the 71 indigenous entrepreneurs interviewed, 65 were males and six were females. In the non-indigenous group all but one were males, which included Filipinos, Americans, Taiwanese, Japanese, and several Pacific islanders. The lack of female representation may not reflect the true extent of their involvement as private sector entrepreneurs. In several cases, husbands chose to answer questions about businesses that were probably controlled almost entirely by their wives.

The average age of all entrepreneurs interviewed was 43. The average formal education attained by the two groups was about 12 years, with a slight edge going to the non-indigenous entrepreneurs. The amount of nonformal, or out-of-school, education experienced by the entrepreneurs was limited. About one-half of each group reported participating in short courses or training sessions.

Entrepreneurs in both groups reported approximately the same number of years of work experience, 27. Their experiences were generally similar: a few years of self-employment and a modest amount of private sector work experience. In general, indigenous entrepreneurs reported more public sector work experience than did non-indigenous entrepreneurs. The data seem to indicate that while non-indigenous entrepreneurs were typically not involved in government service, indigenous entrepreneurs often maintained dual participation. For many indigenous entrepreneurs their public sector income was likely to be used for financing their businesses to some extent.

Another area of questioning focused on the start-up of the enterprise. Over 80 percent of the indigenous enterprises were begun by the entrepreneur interviewed, with 50 percent claiming an initial business investment of $1,000 or less. The non-indigenous entrepreneurs reported initial business investments at closer to $2,000. Family members of the indigenous group, the government, and foreign investors were also mentioned as responsible for starting some businesses.

A few indigenous entrepreneurs claimed to have begun their businesses with no money. One such person purchased goods on credit from a friend who was one of the larger wholesalers. He sold the goods, paid his debts, and restocked his store again with credit help from his friend. The process continued, each time the entrepreneur becoming a bit more solvent. His approach stood in rather stark contrast to a few other indigenous entrepreneurs who claimed to require large sums of money to survive the competition. He expressed his start-up philosophy best perhaps when he remarked that "a man should not begin with more than he can lift."

In both groups, personal savings or family resources were the most frequently reported sources of initial investment. For most indigenous entrepreneurs this meant that the money received as wages from government employment, as rent money received by landowners on Kwajalein or as compensation paid to the nuclear-affected people, was contributed by one or more family members for the purpose of beginning a business. Only a few people in each group reported loans from commercial banks as the source of their start-up capital; even fewer cited the development bank.

Entrepreneurs were asked if they had received any non-monetary assistance in establishing their businesses and, if so, the kind of assistance received. In close to three-fourths of the non-indigenous and one-half of the indigenous cases, entrepreneurs claimed that additional assistance was not received. Those that admitted to receiving help cited family and friends as the most frequent sources. The assistance typically consisted of donations of building materials, equipment, other goods, or labor. None of the interviewees reported receiving any consultative, legal, or other assistance from the commercial banks or the government.

The general picture painted is that the entrepreneurs started new businesses themselves with small investments that came from personal or family savings or from whatever help family and friends could offer. The non-indigenous entrepreneurs tended to be divided between very large and very small investors who did not always begin their own businesses and were somewhat more self-reliant in establishing them.

Information was also gathered about how the entrepreneurs managed to keep their businesses going. Among the non-indigenous entrepreneurs, reinvestment of profits was the most frequently cited source of subsequent investments in the business. Only one-fourth of the indigenous entrepreneurs reported reinvesting profits as the source of subsequent investment, while almost one-half said that subsequent investments were not made. Again there was no evidence cited from either group that commercial banks or the development bank provided any assistance.

In dealing with the day-to-day chores of business management, it appears that indigenous entrepreneurs were more reluctant to seek advice from an external source than were non-indigenous entrepreneurs. This tendency may reflect the near absence of advisory services available to indigenous entrepreneurs or a preference to keep matters within the family.

Non-indigenous entrepreneurs kept more sophisticated business records than indigenous entrepreneurs. Almost one-third of the indigenous group admitted to having no record keeping system at all. The lack of record keeping appeared to be most common among the smallest-scale businesspeople who often claimed that it was a waste of time and was needed only by larger businesses.

Some evidence suggested that record keeping was more strongly associated with the negative image of the tax person rather than with the positive image of a valuable decision-making tool. Whatever the correct inference, being equipped with information or advice needed to plan effectively was not important. Management decisions in indigenous enterprises were made almost exclusively by the entrepreneurs themselves without such aid. The non-indigenous group relied somewhat on business managers in contrast to the indigenous entrepreneurs who tended to regard decision making strictly as an internal matter.

The entrepreneurs on problems

The entrepreneurs were given several opportunities to express their views about the commercial environment and obstacles to business success. An overwhelming majority was impressed with the private sector's growth over the last decade. Some, however, expressed reservations that included concern over who benefited the most, the necessity for foreign competition, the relationship with government, and the negative influence of business growth on Marshallese traditions. All those who responded did insist, however, that private sector growth was essential to economic development and greater self-sufficiency. Most were convinced that the private sector should take responsibility for providing employment opportunities, rather than relying on the government, and that local business, rather than the government, should become the backbone of the nation's economy.

When asked about changes that had occurred over the past ten years to make business success easier, nearly one-half of the indigenous entrepreneurs cited the increase in money from external sources. A little more than one-fourth referred to various infrastructure improvements. Mention was made of the new power plant, the airline, the new dock, and improved international trans-

portation and communication networks. The remaining one-
fourth cited factors such as increased employment, population
growth, and government assistance.

Concerning personal characteristics that entrepreneurs felt were
possessed by successful local businesspeople, just over one-half
talked about the importance of management know-how and other
business skills. The most often repeated Marshallese term used
was *tiljok*. No direct English translation was possible, but informants offered many variations. The terms most commonly used
were diligent, careful, and cautious, which are presumed to
embrace the word's true meaning. Ethnic background was also
mentioned by a few who insisted that part-Marshallese stood a
better chance of being successful. Ostensibly, they felt that people
of mixed ancestry were less tied to the demands of the culture and
were socialized in such a way that better disposed them to busi-
ness-style competitive behavior.

The entrepreneurs also commented on contributions that the
educational system, the banks, and the government had made to
help local businesspeople. About 90 percent were unable to identify any link between programs offered through the Ministry of
Education and business success. A few, however, made reference
to the Marshall's Community Action Agency program, courses
offered through the College of Micronesia, and the occasional
internationally sponsored training programs.

Many entrepreneurs felt that the banks were of some help to
them, but most insisted the assistance offered was inadequate. The
banks were accused of offering only high-interest loans with short
pay-back periods, typically 23 percent with an 18-month limit.
The bank's lending policies were described by some as discriminatory, based on a claim that only government employees or "well-
established" people could borrow money. In addition, the banks
were perceived to be more profit motivated than service oriented.
That few banks and no banking laws exist were given as reasons
for their failure to service the Marshallese better.

Finally, the government was viewed as being of no help by
about two-thirds of the entrepreneurs who commented. Those
who expressed dissatisfaction with government efforts mentioned
high taxes, questionable foreign investment policies, lack of legislation supporting local businesses, no signs of privatization, and
discriminatory practices. The entrepreneurs who viewed govern-

ment as aiding local businesses favored foreign partnerships and hailed infrastructure improvements as important contributions. They also mentioned the direct benefits realized when the government makes purchases from local businesses and when the established u.s. federal programs buy from local merchants, as well as create jobs.

In addition to the questions discussed above, entrepreneurs were given four other opportunities to identify obstacles to business success (Table 6.4). Factors related to social and cultural conditions were identified as the most serious source of problems by both groups of entrepreneurs, a finding similar to those of studies done in Tonga (Ritterbush 1986), Western Samoa (Croulet and Sio 1986), and Fiji (Hailey 1985).

Entrepreneurs frequently reported strained relationships with family members of landowners because of contradictory responsibilities between them and the business. Most businesspeople claimed it was practically impossible to control the credit levels of family members and friends. As such, credit abuse was cited as the single most likely reason for business failures. Extended family relationships and perhaps a cultural aversion to self-aggrandizement forced many entrepreneurs to operate with high levels of accounts receivable. Those who have attempted to control credit, by either limiting or eliminating it, reported loss of customers and increased family problems.

The entrepreneurs' concern over relationships with landowners dealt particularly with lease arrangements. Entrepreneurs report-

Table 6.4. Problems cited by non-indigenous and indigenous entrepreneurs

Problem areas	Non-indigenous (%)	Indigenous (%)	Total (%)
Social/cultural	27	35	34
Market	22	15	16
Government	22	13	14
Capital	4	13	12
Infrastructure	5	12	10
Competition	9	7	8
Management	2	3	3
Personnel	9	2	3
Total	100	100	100
Number of responses	$N=45$	$N=206$	$N=251$

ed that some landowners would not permit long-term leases and insisted on month-to-month arrangements. Such arrangements proved to be fraught with problems of uncertainty concerning duration at the location and the time and amount of periodic rental payments.

Another major problem area identified by the entrepreneurs was the market. Most of the comments, however, were restricted to a concern about the number of potential customers and their purchasing power. Entrepreneurs felt that wages had remained constant over the years while prices had climbed, thus weakening consumer buying power.

The difficulty in gaining access to venture capital, discussed earlier, was also cited as a problem. The indigenous entrepreneurs felt that they were hampered by its relative scarcity and high cost. Non-indigenous entrepreneurs were not nearly as bothered by this area.

The government was again cited as an obstacle to business success by both groups of entrepreneurs. In general, they remarked that the relationship between the private sector and government was not good. Many felt that the government was too involved in business itself and had hurt local businesspeople through its policies rather than helped them.

Finally, entrepreneurs were asked what could be done to overcome these problems. Almost one-half felt that the primary responsibility rested with the individual entrepreneur, and about 40 percent felt that the government should bear at least some responsibility. Some entrepreneurs suggested that businesses hire non-Marshallese to act as buffers between them and their relatives. Others thought that the government should enact laws to help them control credit abuses, lower taxes, and raise salaries to provide people with more buying money.

Conclusions and policy guidelines

Obstacles to indigenous business success were found in traditional structures, historical experiences, government policies and procedures, and private sector conditions. Conflicts between traditional systems and the demands of western-style business were identified as one source of problems. The way in which traditional leaders, particularly those in public office, chose to fulfill their obligations was claimed to affect entrepreneurial opportunities. Adherence to the land tenure system often entitled the entrepreneur to only limited control over the land and subjected him to the changing demands of the landowner. Traditional practices made controlling credit difficult, while residual subsistence affluence may have prompted workers and businesspeople to expect high wages and better-than-justifiable profits.

The islanders' colonial experiences brought alternatives to the old ways that engendered ambivalence and hampered decision making. Removing people from their traditional lands and lagoons deprived them of valuable assets, and compensations made may have vitiated latent entrepreneurial spirit while at the same time glamorized dependency status.

Government policy favored foreign investment and government-foreign joint ventures. Interested indigenous entrepreneurs were expected to take advantage of the secondary opportunities that might result. Records indicate that the government, however, suffered from poor financial management and did not conduct project analysis. In addition, the government has yet to use old legislation or pass new legislation that either protected Marshallese businesspeople or enhanced their position in the market place relative to non-indigenous competition.

Opportunities in the private sector were curtailed by economic conditions: limited natural resources, less than adequate infrastructure, relatively high wage levels, a small domestic market, and a capital shortage. Entrepreneurs found financial services inadequate, interest rates high, and government tax and import regulations obstructive.

By focusing on the problems and issues raised and by following up with decisive action, the Marshall Islands government could create a more fertile environment for indigenous entrepreneurship to flourish. Policy directives that more specifically define the role of the private sector in economic development would be helpful, particularly if the contributions of indigenous entrepreneurs were proposed and if the mechanisms for achieving such were clearly identified. A complement to private sector policy directives would be a comprehensive policy on foreign investment enabling a fairly precise determination of government expectations from and commitments to foreign and indigenous businesses. The development plan could benefit from any such policy decisions if they were incorporated into the strategy and project planning for stimulating private sector growth.

The government might also consider making improvements by exercising its influence over certain domestic programs and seeking the assistance of competent international organizations. The elementary and secondary school curriculums may be appropriate places to introduce business concepts in a context that attenuates disparities between old and newly acquired values. Support is also encouraged for entrepreneurship and other business courses that could be offered through the College of Micronesia's Continuing Education Center in Majuro. In addition, promoting closer ties with the Chamber of Commerce could help to improve conditions, particularly if it was allowed to participate more actively in private sector planning.

Finally, in addition to efforts aimed at improving its own efficiency, if the government was to enact legislation that more favorably regulated the banking industry, revitalized the development bank, and generally provided greater business incentives, indigenous entrepreneurs might find themselves with greater opportunities to become more dynamic participants in shaping the economic future of their country.

NOTE

1. U.S. dollars are used in the Marshall Islands.

REFERENCES

Alexander, William J.
  1978 *Wage Labor, Urbanization and Culture Change in the Marshall Islands: The Ebeye Case,* Ph.D. thesis, The New School for Social Research, New York.
Bryan, E. H.
  1972 *Life in the Marshall Islands,* Pacific Science Information Center, Bernice P. Bishop Museum, Honolulu.
Connell, John
  1983 *Migration, Employment and Development in the South Pacific: Country Report No. 8 Marshall Islands,* South Pacific Commission, Noumea, New Caledonia.

Croulet, Ross C. and Laki Sio
1986 *Indigenous Entrepreneurship in Western Samoa,* Pacific Islands Development Program, East-West Center, Honolulu.

Fairbairn, Te'o with Janice M. Pearson
1987 *Entrepreneurship in the Cook Islands,* Pacific Islands Development Program, East-West Center, Honolulu.

Fisk, E. K.
1982 "Subsistence Affluence and Development Policy," *Regional Development Dialogue,* Special Issue, United Nations Centre for Regional Development, Nagoya, Japan.

Hailey, John M.
1985 *Indigenous Business in Fiji,* Pacific Islands Development Program, East-West Center, Honolulu.

Kiste, Robert C.
1974 *The Bikinians: A Study in Forced Migration,* Cummings Publishing Co., Menlo Park.

Mason, Leonard E.
1947 *The Economic Organization of the Marshall Islanders.* Economic Survey of Micronesia, u.s. Commercial Company, Vol. 8, Washington, D.C.

McHenry, Donald F.
1975 *Micronesia: Trust Betrayed,* Carnegie Endowment for International Peace, New York.

Nevin, David
1977 *The American Touch in Micronesia,* W. W. Norton and Company, Inc., New York.

Nufer, Harold
1978 *Micronesia Under American Rule: An Evaluation of the Strategic Trusteeship,* Exposition Press, New York.

Peoples, James G.
1985 *Island in Trust: Culture Change and Dependence in a Micronesian Society,* Westview Press, Boulder.

Republic of the Marshall Islands
1985 *First Five Year Development Plan 1985–1989,* Majuro, Marshall Islands, Office of Planning and Statistics, Majuro.

Republic of the Marshall Islands, Office of the Auditor General
1984 *First Semi-annual Report to Nitijela,* Report of the Functions and Activities of the Office of the Auditor General, January 1 to June 30, 1984, Majuro.
1985 *Second Semi-annual Report to Nitijela,* Report of the Functions and Activities of the Office of the Auditor General, July 1 to December 30, 1984, Majuro.

Ritterbush, S. Deacon
1986 *Entrepreneurship and Business Venture Development in the Kingdom of*

Tonga, Pacific Islands Development Program, East-West Center, Honolulu.

Sahlins, Marshall
  1971 "Tribal Economics," in George Dalton, ed., *Economic Development
     and Social Change: The Modernization of Village Communities,* Amer-
     ican Museum of Natural History, Garden City, New York.

Schwalbenberg, Henry M.
  1984 "Traditional Economic Systems and their Response to Westernization,"
     in *Past Achievements and Future Responsibilities: A Conference on
     Economic Development in Micronesia,* Majuro.

Spoehr, Alexander
  1949 *Majuro: A Village in the Marshall Islands,* Chicago Natural History
     Museum, Chicago.

CHAPTER 7

Entrepreneurship in an Ascribed Status Society: The Kingdom of Tonga

S. Deacon Ritterbush

TONGA is a small Polynesian Kingdom located in the central South Pacific. Consisting of 150 islands with a total land area of 699 sq km, Tonga's population is about 100,000. Recent archaeological evidence indicates that the Tongans were associated with a *lapita* (a type of pottery) tradition originating out of Southeast Asia. Slowly migrating eastward through Melanesia, these peoples settled in Tonga around 1000 B.C. and established an elaborate, highly stratified social system long before European contact in the 18th century.

Contemporary Tonga, often characterized as a deeply religious and traditionally conservative society, is largely composed of semi-subsistent farmers and noble elite. Approximately 95 percent of the people are practicing Christians and 65 percent obtain their livelihood from farming. As in all Polynesian cultures, kinship and collectivism predominate. Even today groups based on kinship are often formed to carry out activities. Similarly, many valued possessions are still collectively owned.

Fertile soils and adequate but not excessive rainfall provide Tonga with good conditions for crop production throughout the country (Maude 1973). This situation coupled with a lack of significant mineral resources indicates why land has been, and still is, the basis of the Tongan economy. One-half of the total gross national product (GNP) and over 70 percent of the active wage labor force originates in this sector. Although tourism and a smattering of small industries are beginning to have some input into the national economy, agriculture accounts for about 90 percent of Tonga's total export earnings. In addition, rural-to-urban as well as overseas migration has been steadily increasing since the mid-

137

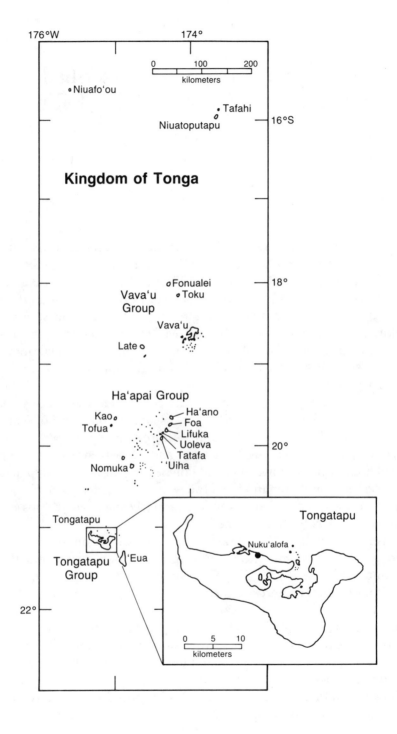

176°W   174°

0   100   200
kilometers

∘ Niuafo'ou

• Tafahi
∘
Niuatoputapu   16°S

Kingdom of Tonga

∘ Fonualei   18°
Vava'u   ∘ Toku
Group

Vava'u

Late ∘

Ha'apai Group

Kao ∘   Ha'ano
Tofua •   Foa
            Lifuka
            Uoleva   20°
            Tatafa
Nomuka ∘   'Uiha

Tongatapu

                 Tongatapu
Tongatapu   'Eua
Group   Nuku'alofa •

22°   0   5   10
                    kilometers

1960s, and the money derived from remittances is a leading source of income both for individual Tongans and for the government.

Despite the existence of local and export markets, a large segment of the population still survives primarily on a subsistence basis, particularly in the rural and outer island areas. Furthermore, even though capitalist principles and practices were introduced well over a century ago by foreign missionaries, indigenous private sector growth has been a slow process. Changes are occurring due to population pressures, urbanization, education, land acquisition problems, and the low esteem of agriculture (Walsh 1980). But some theorists, most notably Parsons (1956) and Finney (1973, 1976), suggest ascribed-status societies such as Tonga are not culturally pre-adapted to entrepreneurship. Finney's work in particular highlights the entrepreneurial differences between achievement-oriented Melanesians and ascribed-status Polynesian societies, concluding that within different social constructs are forces that tend to encourage or discourage entrepreneurial initiative.

Under the sponsorship of the Pacific Islands Development Program (PIDP), I conducted research from 1983 to 1984 on those factors that facilitate or obstruct business development. The data collected indicate that Finney's hypothesis, though partially correct, may be too simplistic; that Tonga's traditional social structure may be only one of the factors that constrain indigenous attempts at business venture development in contemporary Tongan society. This chapter attempts to provide a comprehensive analysis of the complex and varied factors that have traditionally affected and are presently affecting indigenous entrepreneurship and private sector growth.

Theoretical background

Although basic principles of entrepreneurs and their activities do exist, definitions of entrepreneurs are essentially location- and culture-specific. Thus in some societies an entrepreneur can be one who marshals and redistributes resources (Belshaw 1955), who innovates (Schumpeter 1971), or who aggrandizes business and is profit-oriented (Smith 1967). At the most fundamental level, an entrepreneur can be characterized as someone who marshals and redistributes resources (Belshaw 1955:5). Even Schumpeter, who initially viewed entrepreneurship as synonymous with technological innovation, took a broader view of the concept in later years, defining entrepreneurs as "the people who take the ruling decisions in life" (Cole 1959:180).

For the last 30 years, however, most theorists have tended to examine the importance of entrepreneurship only in terms of its casual significance to economic development. This interpretation views entrepreneurs as "transformers" or "generators" to the extent that they have an independent additive influence on economic development. This desire to place entrepreneurship in the context of generating economic activity rather than initiating or controlling it stems from the experiences of post-industrial nations and is based on the idea of an individual who is primarily responsible for gathering together the necessary resources to start a business (Cole 1959). The inherent assumption is that such a person will then aggrandize that business because he is profit oriented. Usually this person is someone who is willing to take risks, innovate, plan, reinvest, and look toward the future. Such a person obviously is oriented toward business expansion, involving the accumulation of capital, increased consumption derived from greater use of existing resources (previously used below potential), and increased velocity of circulation of working capital (Belshaw 1955).

The important variable in this conception of "entrepreneur" seems to be the concept of "expansion."[1] Yet in many traditional or non-western societies, this type of "aggrandizing" entrepreneur does not appear to be as obvious or as frequent as in post-industrial nations. Instead, entrepreneurial styles appear to be more static, less oriented toward expanding business and maximizing profits than with satisfying subsistence requirements.

One of the first attempts to identify and examine the contextual factors associated with the observable differences between entrepreneurial types in different cultural contexts was made by Alexander (as cited in Finney 1976). Based on Parson's (1956) assertions that capitalist societies are characterized by a prevalence of achievement norms and that underdeveloped societies are characterized by a prevalence of ascriptive norms, Alexander singled out a segment of Parsonian theory that was relevant to the question of entrepreneurship. This was developed into a pattern variable that he labeled "ascriptive/achievement" and was based on the belief that "in societies where ascription is the rule, the entrepreneurial class is liable to be small and lack dynamism" because economic activity is not a status-conferring variable (Parsons and Smelser 1956:5–6). Subsequent studies by Finney (1976) and LeVine (1966) support this hypothesis.

Finney's research, in particular, concluded that ascribed-status Polynesian societies, unlike the more achievement-oriented Melanesian societies, were traditionally anti-enterprise because a person's status was recognized through blood and kinship affiliation rather than through individual economic achievement. In contemporary Polynesian societies, Finney asserts that apparently few enterprise-generating forces or personal incentives exist to encourage people to adopt a more dynamic orientation toward business development. Instead, most Polynesians tend to practice a relaxed or static business style. Conversely, culture groups and societies in which status is derived from personal achievement rather than from birth or kinship affiliations appear to be more supportive of entrepreneurial endeavors.

This hypothesis suggests two ideas. First, a society can achieve economic efficiency only if its social structure bestows a high degree of social recognition on the achievement of occupational success (Dusenberry in Cole 1959). Second, the operation and understanding of entrepreneurial systems must take into account the social ideas that are congruent with entrepreneurial aspirations, as well as those social structures that are respondent to entrepreneurial success. Thus in traditional societies the non-entrepreneurial stimuli to entrepreneurial achievement are a potentially important variable in the emergence and manner of indigenous entrepreneurship.

When economic incentives arise from the need to fulfill kinship or ceremonial obligations, entrepreneurs will be more motivated to accumulate capital than people from societies in which such incentives are weak. Thus we have the concept of "economic man" seeking to maximize profits, not for the sake of profit, but rather to achieve specific sociopsychological goals via the accumulation of money.

Although this framework is useful in identifying and comparing different entrepreneurial styles and motivations, Belshaw (1955) notes that it can encounter problems in its assumption that all societies are customary and static. It also eliminates the possibility of social change, discounts the potentially influential role wielded by traditional leaders, and infers that within all traditionally ascribed-status societies, no upward mobility channels exist whatsoever for the common classes.

Pre-contact Tongan society

In pre-contact Tongan society where status was "fixed" and immutable, the social system was composed of three distinct classes: the chiefs *(hou'eiki)*, the chiefs' attendants *(matāpule)* whose rank was hereditary, and the commoners *(tu'a)*. The most powerful person in the country was the high chief, *Tu'i Tonga,* who, together with two other high chiefs *(hau),*[2] held ultimate authority over the life, liberty, and property of all other Tongans. Each chief headed a branch of the entire island group, and all of the land within this branch nominally belonged to each of them. As owners of the land, it was the chiefs' job to distribute it to those beneath them, which they did via the secondary chiefs, who in turn parceled out portions of the land to family members. *Matāpule* and *mu'a*[3] (the highest strata of *tu'a*) were given their own plantations to work, but peasants and slaves were responsible for cultivating land both for their own subsistence needs and for the kings and chiefs above them.

Although evidence shows occasional status mobility for *tu'a* who possessed an excellence in social or technical skills (e.g., farming, fighting, oratory), the structure of pre-contact Tongan society largely restricted personal ambition. But the social structure was not entirely inflexible, especially for the chiefly classes. For instance, although status was inherited, upon the death of a chief, elections were often conducted to choose a successor. Sometimes the new chief would be one who, according to his blood rank, was in an inferior position, but his superior prowess on the battlefield was such that he demonstrated more able and chiefly leadership. In addition, in the 18th and 19th centuries, extensive trade with Fiji and Samoa was commonplace and included the bartering of Tongan sails, bark cloth, pearl shells, and whales' teeth for Fijian hardwood, sandalwood, pottery, and Samoan fine mats (Bollard 1974:137). As noted by Lātūkefu:

Such exploits became extremely popular among young chiefs in Tonga who were thirsty for excitement and renown. They only had to join a party going to Fiji for canoes to place themselves in the way of gaining honor and fame enough to satisfy the most ambitious (Bollard 1974:11).

But Tonga's rigid social structure and economic system, where a limited number of chiefs controlled the resources and monopolized trade between subjects, provided few opportunities to the masses in which to better their economic and social standing.

Business development in post-contact Tonga

This state of affairs changed, however, soon after the arrival in 1822 of the first missionaries, who introduced not only Christianity but also the principles of western capitalism via the establishment of blacksmith and carpentry shops. Succeeding missionaries stressed the Protestant work ethic and initiated the first cash cropping, manufacturing coconut oil for export. During the next 30 years, foreign immigrants established several manufacturing and trading companies. By 1875 a total of 236 Europeans were residing in Tonga, many of whom were merchants, traders, bakers, boat builders, fishermen, carpenters, and planters (Bollard 1974). Even though a variety of export crops was being produced, most were grown by the European *pālangi* (white foreigner) populations (Maude 1965). In fact, foreigners dominated the small business sector.

By the late 1890s, European commercial interests dwindled due to economic depressions in New Zealand and later in Australia, crop diseases, and expired land leases that were not renewed (Bollard 1974:45). But the withdrawal of these commercial interests had negligible effects on the lifestyles of the Tongan people because most European commerce occurred outside the non-monetized sector. Moreover, because Tongans did not yet use money in commercial exchange, they had little need for it except to pay for fines, taxes, and church tithes and to occasionally purchase commercial goods such as tinned meat.

Most Tongans displayed a lukewarm reaction to the prospect of wage labor, preferring subsistence farming instead. When they did participate in the wage economy, their efforts tended to be short-lived and sporadic. This ambivalence was due to a number of factors including the provisions in Tonga's Constitution of 1875, enabling Tongan males to obtain land for subsistence farming; the influence of Tonga's traditional barter economy, negating the need for a wage income; and the sociocultural ethos of the time. In brief, money had little value in providing for the material necessities of life, nor was it especially useful in gaining status mobility.

On the contrary, upward mobility for the *tu'a* revolved around the traditional elite system or the religious domain; of the two, the church proved to be a particularly effective medium in which to increase an individual's social standing. This trend began shortly after the conversion of Chief Taufa'ahau (who later became King Tupou I) in 1834. Soon thousands of Tongans followed suit. The adoption of a new set of religious beliefs by influential chiefs and commoners alike rapidly undermined the traditional religious system and with it the political, social, and economic structures that had been so closely woven around it. By the end of the century, the church took on such paramount importance, second only to the King, that a new elite class emerged, composed mostly of commoners who were church leaders. From then on, the teachings of the church, solidly backed by the government and noble elite, were instrumental in molding and influencing people's attitudes and behaviors.

The influence exerted by the church became especially evident during the first half of the 20th century. Although foreign commercial interests were again on the rise, the Tongan people's desire or need for a wage income increased little. Apart from a widespread lack of exposure to different socioeconomic lifestyles, this indifference to money was also due to the promotion of the traditional Tongan way of life by the government and the churches. These institutions, in reaction to the expatriates' increasing demands for land and the Tongan people's growing indebtedness to the church and foreign traders, adopted new legislation to protect Tongan citizens from future attempts by speculators to exploit native resources. Both the church and the ruling monarch, Queen Salote, emphasized the importance of respecting and adhering to traditional customs and stressed values such as selflessness, humility, poverty, and generosity. Because of this emphasis, the Kingdom again encountered little structural or systemic change during this second withdrawal of foreign business involvement.

Events during and after World War II, however, began to change the traditional way of Tongan life forever. Engendered first by the widespread introduction of modern medicine, which reduced Tonga's previously high infant mortality rate, by the early 1960s the increasing population pressures on limited land resources soon made it impossible for many to practice the still ideal but no longer feasible subsistence or semisubsistent lifestyle. Moreover, an education system modeled after New Zealand's, influenced both a receptiveness to change and a desire to move away from farming into business and industry. Tongans, above all, were a practical people: being humble and materially impoverished was fine up to a point, but not if it meant starving.

By the time the present King, Tupou IV, was crowned in the late 1960s, indigenous participation in the wage economy was on the increase. But because Tonga's private sector was small and largely undynamic, the government faced an economic impasse. Lacking lending institutions, it had neither the capital to lend to aspiring businesspersons nor did it have the land resources to provide all of them with a viable economic alternative. In an attempt to rectify this situation, the Tongan and New Zealand governments established an emigration act that allowed Tongan citizens to travel to New Zealand on "working holidays" for up to one year. Many jumped at the chance to earn wages abroad, but the repercussions from this act affected every facet of Tongan life. Remittances heightened local consumption and the desire for western goods at the expense of decreased local productivity. Seeking greater economic opportunity, many of Tonga's brightest, best educated, and technically skilled citizens emigrated overseas. Some, who found the prospects more advantageous, never returned. The extended family became nucleated and was soon replaced by many single female heads of households, many of whom were unskilled and often without land resources at their disposal. Conversely, remittances provided some aspiring indigenous entrepreneurs with the financial wherewithal to begin small ventures. And returning migrants, many of whom had been highly successful or whose ambitions had been whetted by the greater socioeconomic leverage abroad, began their own business undertakings, often drawing on the invaluable business skills mastered overseas.

Although emigration had the potential to greatly assist locally based business venture development, it was not until the mid-

1970s that a public campaign was adopted to encourage citizens to save, invest, and re-invest income. Business development was promoted, and two banking institutions, the Bank of Tonga and the Tongan Development Bank, were established. Finally, now aware that many Tongans were handicapped by their lack of business acumen as well as by their limited access to markets, sophisticated technology, and equipment, the government embarked on large-scale infrastructure projects and actively began to pursue foreign investors and advisers to assist in the development of the Kingdom's industrial sector.

By 1980 many citizens—not only persons from the *hou'eiki* and *matāpule* classes—had responded with enthusiasm to these measures. Because the *hou'eiki* were traditionally conditioned to decision making, generally had greater access to land and financial resources, and had been accustomed to power and position, most of them were apparently less ambitious to seek them in the new and highly different ways that monetization required.[4] Not surprisingly, most commoners, who usually had fewer socioeconomic options open to them, have more often been urged to try new means of achieving success. Christianity was one vehicle in which the *tu'a* could heighten their status. Upward mobility in the past 40 years can also be seen in the quest for higher education and academic degrees or in Tongans who have excelled in business and professional endeavors abroad and are now attempting to achieve the same success at home.

Survey findings

By the time I arrived in Tonga in 1983, a record number of manufacturing, retail, service, tourism-related, and commercial farming ventures had been established by local and expatriate residents alike. Some of these were prospering. However, despite their enthusiasm, the failure rate of indigenous-owned businesses was comparatively quite high. In an effort to determine the reasons—financial, infrastructure, sociocultural, or technical—a PIDP survey was conducted on the problems associated with business venture development in the Kingdom. With the assistance of Alipate Tu'itavake, my Tongan counterpart, 185 interviews were conducted with a variety of businesspersons from all business sectors.

The survey questionnaire contained in-depth questions on personal background, type of business owned, business operations, leading business problems, and strategies used (if any) to overcome these problems. Although the majority of informants were indigenous Tongan businesspersons (131), 20 expatriate and 34 mixed-race Tongans were also included for comparison. In addition, a concerted effort was made to determine the specific business problems faced by female and rural-based businesspeople.[5]

Also included was an examination of the effects of Tonga's sociocultural customs on business ventures, especially indigenous businesses. Areas of emphasis included Tonga's system of customary obligations and status hierarchy, the land tenure system, and the nation's religiosity, unparalleled in the Pacific islands region even today, with its well-entrenched system of tithings, religious hierarchy, and code of moral and church ethics.

Characteristics of indigenous entrepreneurs

Of the survey sample, 70.8 percent claimed to be indigenous Tongans or those who had no foreign blood that they could remember (usually four or more generations). This diverse group included both the least and most educated and the least and most financially successful businesspersons in the country. On the average, however, indigenous entrepreneurs had less formal education and fewer business management skills, and their businesses were generally more undercapitalized and less financially stable than those of expatriate or part-Tongan entrepreneurs.

Most ventures had initially begun with financing from personal savings or money derived from various sources, including salaries and sales of firewood, coconuts, handicrafts, or farm produce. Some of the more successful indigenous entrepreneurs had inherited their businesses, had been or were government employees, were closely related by marriage or blood to government employees, had been trained in accounting (or rudimentary bookkeeping), or had worked closely with a relative or trusted friend who had received such training. But the majority lacked the government, business, or social contacts of their more successful counterparts. Many were inadequately informed about government business policies or programs. Those who were aware of them were often hesitant to use them because they felt that "they lacked the status needed" to do so.

Another characteristic of indigenous entrepreneurs was their tendency to be "poor innovators but good imitators" in the types of businesses they established. This was due to several factors including the smallness of local markets, limited exposure to the multifarious services and products offered in western societies, limited local resources, expensive or unreliable overseas transportation networks, limited capital, lack of imagination, or simply the fact that the same type of enterprise that was successful in Tonga was located right down the street. Indigenous businesspersons tended to copy those businesses that they perceived as successful. This tendency led to an overabundance of certain types of businesses, culminating in the success of few and the downfall of many.

Accordingly, most indigenous entrepreneurs also lacked "business scope"—the ability and/or confidence to articulate their business dreams and set appropriate goals to reach these dreams. Instead, although many were regarded as highly ambitious and hard working, their progress was severely hampered by a lack of confidence; a frustration over their lack of "business savvy," experience, and training; and a fatalism over their lot in life. In brief, this lack of confidence, coupled with poor business skills and business contacts, constrained their attempts to establish dynamic or even stable commercial ventures.

Several indigenous entrepreneurs practiced a socialistic, rather than capitalistic, business style in terms of goals and personal motivations. They cared less about making profits and expanding business than about wanting to "help the Tongan people and the country" via training Tongans in specific work skills or bartering the goods and services for pigs, food, or whatever their customers could afford. Entrepreneurs such as these readily and willingly contributed a large percentage of their business profit to churches or to family obligations. Although many such businesses were not prospering, they were neither declining nor nearing bankruptcy, perhaps because the services and products offered were highly valued or the business was favorably situated. It could be conjectured that this orientation to business was highly traditional in its more communalistic (as opposed to individualistic) orientation.

Most of the entrepreneurs in this category were, on the average, older (40 years of age or over) and hence could have been influenced during Queen Salote's reign, when both the government and Tonga's religious institutions encouraged such attitudes. However, the highly protective and often paternalistic influence that was also exerted during that era appeared to foster expectations of entrepreneurs toward the public sector, as well as heighten their dependency. Entrepreneurs asserted that the government should further encourage indigenous attempts at business development by adopting additional business incentives and financial aid programs.

The churches also played a crucial role in either facilitating or constraining indigenous attempts at business venture development. Members of the Wesleyan Church and Free Church of Tonga, whose constant rounds of obligations and frenzied tithings *(misonali),* were generally among the most impoverished or frustrated informants sampled. Even those businesspersons, who viewed church obligations as personally rewarding and not overly detrimental to the financial stability of their enterprises, asserted that the constant tithings were at times overwhelming. Mormons, on the other hand, seemed to benefit from their religious affiliation. Although at least 10 percent of their yearly income was devoted to the church, most entrepreneurs affiliated with the Mormon Church had received vigorous in-church financial management training such as bookkeeping, which was helpful in managing their businesses.

Factors affecting indigenous business development

The survey data confirmed that indigenous entrepreneurs shared the same technical difficulties with expatriate and part-Tongan entrepreneurs and indeed with businesspersons throughout the Pacific islands region. These difficulties, which greatly handicapped their efforts, included generating adequate capital to expand or up-grade existing businesses, marketing products locally or overseas, transporting products abroad, obtaining equipment or having access to adequate repair services, and finding skilled labor and middle-management staff (Table 7.1).

Regardless of ethnicity, many entrepreneurs were affected by Tongan social customs even though indigenous entrepreneurs

Table 7.1. Leading business problems

	Business type and number of informants													
	Commercial farming		Animal husbandry		Business manufacturing		Retail services and tourism		Commercial fishing		Outer island businesses		Cumulative	
	%	(94)	%	(6)	%	(51)	%	(25)	%	(5)	%	(4)	%	(185)
Markets	26.6	25	0.0	0	34.0	17	24.0	6	0.0	0	0.0	0	25.9	48
Management	2.1	2	0.0	0	4.0	2	8.0	2	0.0	0	25.0	1	3.8	7
Transportation	5.3	5	16.6	1	2.0	1	4.0	1	60.0	3	0.0	0	6.0	11
Equipment	10.6	10	50.0	3	14.0	7	12.0	3	20.0	1	25.0	1	13.5	25
Land	2.1	2	0.0	0	2.0	1	4.0	1	0.0	0	0.0	0	2.2	4
Financing	41.5	39	16.7	1	18.0	9	20.0	5	20.0	1	25.0	1	30.3	56
Thieving	0.0	0	0.0	0	6.0	3	8.0	2	0.0	0	0.0	0	2.7	5
Government policies	1.1	1	16.7	1	12.0	6	0.0	0	0.0	0	25.0	1	4.9	9
No problems	2.1	2	0.0	0	0.0	0	0.0	0	0.0	0	0.0	0	1.0	2
Other, including customary obligations	8.6	8	0.0	0	8.0	5	20.0	5	0.0	0	0.0	0	9.7	18

SOURCE: Ritterbush, *Entrepreneurship and Business Venture Development in Tonga*, 1986.

more readily felt the potentially adverse effects (see Table 7.2). *Fua kavenga,* or the obligatory contribution in connection with the Tongan family, the church, and the government, affected nearly all indigenous entrepreneurs as well as some foreigners with Tongan spouses. Some entrepreneurs did not consider their obligations to be a liability to their businesses ("by giving more, you naturally receive more"). Others admitted that such obligations posed an enormous financial burden on them ("without *fua kavenga,* I would be a millionaire by now"). Although the survey sample included a few indigenous businesspersons who had entirely abandoned the practice of *fua kavenga,* thus engendering anger, disrespect, or ostracism from their family and local community, others had adopted a more pragmatic view—neglecting one's social obligations could be as harmful to their businesses as could excessive spending. The more savvy and successful indigenous businesspersons tended to regard their obligations as a motivating force that pushed them to work harder and therefore to earn more money. Hence, they attempted, some quite skillfully, to devise financial strategies that enabled them to simultaneously fulfill their customary obligations and generate a business profit as well.

The dual issues of selflessness and communalism (of working for the good of the family, the village, the church, and the King), were also problematic for many indigenous entrepreneurs. In a business context, a communal (traditional) orientation often clashed with the more individualistic (western) approach adopted by some businesspersons. Perhaps this latter approach often engendered jealousy, greed, and competition, which were subtle but recurrent themes in the Tongan business community. Those entrepreneurs who were perceived as successful often found themselves in the contradictory position of being greatly admired and respected for their business savvy yet condemned for their apparent "individualism," "ruthlessness," and "selfishness" that may have contributed to that success.

It seemed to annoy Tongans if an individual Tongan was more successful than the group as a whole. This irritation often led to an attempt to undermine the successful entrepreneur's business via gossip, theft, or outright competition. Meanwhile, successful businesspersons were also held responsible for providing jobs for relatives and friends (qualified or not), for hiring children during school breaks, and for extending credit or giving loans or hand-

Table 7.2. Effects of social obligations on business operation and profits (%)

	Commercial farmers (94)	Animal husbandry (6)	Business manufacturers (51)	Retail services and tourism (25)	Commercial fishermen (5)	Outer island (4)	Cumulative (185)
				Business type and number of informants			
No social obligation	–	–	21.6	8.0	–	–	7.0
Very adversely	9.6	16.7	17.6	20.0	60.0	75.0	16.0
Adversely	24.5	–	19.6	16.0	–	25.0	20.3
Neutral	30.8	50.0	33.4	48.0	40.0	–	34.3
Beneficial	35.1	33.3	7.8	8.0	–	–	22.4

SOURCE: Ritterbush, *Entrepreneurship and Business Venture Development in Tonga*, 1986.

outs to various members of the local village and church community.

At the same time, well-warranted speculation has noted that the Polynesian extended family can cripple individual entrepreneurial aspirations and successes. The survey data confirmed that, in some cases, family enterprises were more stable in terms of profit, employee turnover, expansion, and diversification. In fact, if family members could be trusted or had a vested interest in the financial health of the business, they usually worked harder to ensure its success. Problems tended to arise after the death of the original founder when the business was dissolved in order to serve the different interests of individual family members. These kinds of developments may partly explain why Tonga still has few dynastic indigenously owned and operated enterprises.

The social convention of reciprocity was another area of potential conflict for indigenous entrepreneurs. Reciprocal social and financial arrangements permeate the daily interactions among Tongans and act as a means not only of sharing goods communally but also of ensuring a balance of material possessions among groups of people.

Within this context, there are several forms of reciprocity. These include *kole* (to make a request, to ask, or to borrow), *fatongia* (a duty or obligation), and *takitaki* (a social obligation with ulterior motives). Reciprocal arrangements are usually practiced between individuals who have a social relationship with each other (such as family members or with the village noble) and incorporate the tacit understanding that one person is then mutually obligated at some time.

But reciprocal transactions often spill over into the business domain where favors are exchanged between business associates for business gain. Such favors run the gamut from small gifts of food to financial pay-offs. Although the latter form of reciprocity might be considered bribery in other societies, under-the-table financial transactions between business associates is neither uncommon in Tongan society nor entirely unaccepted. The ethic of "I'll help you and then you help me" is still strong, having filtered down through years of traditional social obligations and reciprocity.

Such transactions, however, conducted both by businesspersons and civil servants, are gradually gaining disfavor, especially among the more western-oriented entrepreneurs and those who are unable to financially compete with their business counterparts. Both groups stated that, in the business world, reciprocity often fostered favoritism, slowed efficiency, and encouraged a black market ethic for goods and services that should be provided to all.

Successful indigenous entrepreneurs

A logical assumption, given the constraints articulated, is that successful Tongan entrepreneurs were aberrant, were in some fundamental way different from their fellow countrymen. Or, were they successful simply because they were better equipped to manage a business due to their educational and technical background, past business experience, and personal characteristics?

Generally, the most successful entrepreneurs were better educated, better traveled, and more worldly than their less successful counterparts. However, this was not always the case, especially among commercial farmers, most of whom had received some business training. In addition, most possessed a fierce determination and a surprising tenacity to get the job done in spite (or because) of existing constraints. Finally, most were disciplined and worked hard at their jobs, not as much for status mobility as for improving their families' standard of living. Others had few other economic options; others simply enjoyed the work.

Essentially, successful indigenous entrepreneurs were masters at manipulating the environment to suit their own needs. If this meant fulfilling traditional customs or participating in traditional rituals to further their business interests, they did so because they instinctively realized that community support in such a closed environment was crucial to the success of their ventures. Moreover, the financial price exacted was probably far less debilitating than if social obligations were neglected or ignored. Thus the ability to synthesize and incorporate various aspects of the traditional culture with modern business practices was an essential difference between successful and unsuccessful indigenous entrepreneurs. By devising specific strategies to meet the traditional demands and expectations placed on them, they turned potential obstructions into positive forces. Customary obligations motivated them to work harder to earn more.

Some entrepreneurs held three or more bank accounts earmarked specifically for business, household, and social obligations. Others designated specific acreage for growing the produce used to fulfill certain obligations. One businessperson accepted pigs as payment for services rendered and began a piggery, the stock of which was used for wedding feasts, funeral offerings, or special church events. Another established a cultural center staffed by family, friends, and members of her church, thus serving the dual purpose of assisting the Tongan community and simultaneously attracting tourists to her motel complex. Most supported scores of relatives with food, income, or employment, but their generosity to others and their adherence to tradition rewarded them tenfold with loyalty, goodwill, and assistance in times of emergency.

Successful entrepreneurs also made communalism work in their favor. For instance, groups of farmers banded together to purchase large quantities of fertilizer and seed in bulk. Many formed work groups and credit unions so that they could have affordable labor to work their plantations or could secure ready cash at lower interest rates whenever necessary. Family businesses, rather than using more expensive or less dependable outside expertise, invested in themselves, sending junior members overseas for training in bookkeeping, commerce, and vocational skills. Female entrepreneurs who operated in a largely male domain, instead of cutting themselves off from their menfolk, used them to full advantage for business advice, emotional support, and assistance in securing bank loans or land leases.

Thus, in the Tongan context, the ability to devise effective strategies that incorporate important aspects of both a socialist and a capitalist orientation was fundamental to the success of indigenous—and often non-indigenous—owned enterprises. This synthesis could not have been accomplished without first identifying the specific cultural expectations that might affect business performance, despite the extent of training, education, experience, or financial support. In other words, these factors equipped indigenous businesspersons with a more effective ability and confidence to work within the system, thus potentially saving them from making the costly errors or tacit assumptions that often caused the downfall of many of their less successful counterparts.

Structural impacts

Unlike other eras, the present emphasis on and participation in capitalist ventures is not only increasing but also beginning to make decided structural impacts on Tongan society. In particular, Tonga's deeply entrenched system of status hierarchy based on birth, its traditional land tenure system, and the role of Tongan women in contemporary society are all undergoing enormous changes. Most Tongans readily admit that their society is still status conscious. Previously, aside from the noble elite and their relatives, those persons generally regarded as having status and hence accorded the respect and requisite prerogatives were church elders, educated or wealthy foreigners, part-Tongans, and those "who work with their minds, not their hands" (teachers, government personnel, and the owners of large, successful businesses). Farmers, fishermen, small businesspersons, and builders, such as cart makers, were and often are still regarded as having inferior status unless they are affiliated with persons of high status or are themselves highly successful in their profession.[6]

However, the emblems of status are slowly changing. As the Kingdom becomes more monetized and people's livelihoods become more dependent on ready cash (or the access to ready cash), persons regardless of their profession or genealogy who can afford goods and also pay their creditors on time are slowly being accorded a respect that had previously been denied them. This may be partly responsible for the decline in status of Tonga's land-rich but usually cash-poor nobility, at least insofar as the business community is concerned. One informant noted that close relations to a noble are now considered a business liability rather than an asset. Also, where traditionally the brightest Tongan youths sought high-status positions with the government, many are now opting for work in the private business and commercial farming sectors where, as one university-educated youth said, "Profits are better and one can lead a more individualistic lifestyle." In fact, Tonga's farmers now claim that they are beginning to enjoy greater prestige and respect as a result of Hurricane Isaac in 1982. The sudden disruption in Tonga's food supply, coupled with the higher earning power derived from the increase in food prices, made Tonga's farmers some of the most sought after people in the Kingdom. As Tongans are fond of saying, "You cannot eat money."

Traditionally, origin of birth has also been a source of prestige. District center residents tend to look down on rural villagers and outer islanders. Yet, aside from the fact that many government positions are held by outer islanders, immigrant businesspersons also appear to do better than average in the market place. One reason is that with fewer resources such as land, they are less complacent and are forced to work harder and more diligently at their business endeavors.

The status system, however, is still a strong force in Tonga, often encouraging preferential treatment to the well connected rather than the well deserving. In the business sphere, the system tends to discourage "low status" businesspersons who need assistance from seeking it and to encourage the granting of favors to others who may be unworthy of them. This system has been a source of frustration for many of those surveyed, often hampering their attempts to obtain loans or receive information. As a result, many disillusioned entrepreneurs have severed all business relationships with the government.

Tonga's land tenure system is also under challenge, as it has been for the last 25 years. But now, instead of simply talking about land reform and waiting another decade or two before the government is finally forced to take action, citizens are taking land reform into their own hands via the informal leasing of land or the illegal purchase of land leases. Tonga's present land distribution system dates back to 1875 when the Tongan Land Tenure Law decreed that all male commoners were allowed to become independent landholders at age 16. From then on, for a small yearly poll tax, they were entitled to apply for and receive a bush allotment (*'api'uta*) of 8.25 acres and 0.16 hectares of townsite. Although all land was still the ultimate property of the Crown, large estates were divided among the 33 nobles who then granted *'api* allotments, subject to their approval, to those applicants living under their jurisdiction. Ultimately, Tonga's land tenure system afforded the majority of its citizens the opportunity to pursue a more independent subsistence lifestyle unencumbered by the demands of the chiefly classes, kept Tonga's most important resource in the hands of the indigenous population, and, as a social service to the people, provided them with the means to ensure that their subsistence needs could be met (Fonua 1975, Lātūkefu 1974).

However, given the country's population problems, the validity of Tonga's land tenure system has come increasingly under attack. Four factors have been particularly influential, including (1) the present inability of many Tongan citizens to obtain farmland, (2) inequitable land inheritance rights favoring firstborn males over their younger male siblings and brothers over sisters, (3) absentee landlords (due to overseas emigration and expatriation), and (4) the purchase of land leases by those not otherwise entitled to it.

This fourth factor has been on the increase since the early 1970s when returning emigrants used their overseas earnings to buy leases from the village noble or from a growing nucleus of private real estate brokers.[7] Eventually, land values increased until nobles began to accept cash payments for an *'api'uta* rather than freely distribute allotments as dictated by Tongan law.[8] Sometimes two, three, and four allotments were purchased by one individual even when persons who were legally entitled to an *'api'uta* were unable to obtain their own rightful allocation.

Another popular practice that is becoming more prevalent is the informal leasing of land. A recent survey by Tonga's Central Planning Department (1985) of 367 commercial farmers revealed that one-half of the allotments in the survey were not owned by the user but rather had been informally leased. This procedure effectively enabled considerable land amalgamation and the development of commercial enterprises. Unfortunately, however, informal land leasing also resulted in the owners' reneging on contracts (usually around harvest time), requesting escalating lease payments (in cash or food), or not allowing the commercial farmers to obtain binding long-term lease agreements that would enable them to cultivate long-term crops such as kava, vanilla, and coffee.

By 1983 the government passed an act that had some effect on landholdings and that established formal subleasing contracts between allotment owners and anyone of their choosing for periods of up to 20 years for an *'api'uta* and 99 years for a town allotment. Today a person can now legally sublease up to 10 *'api'uta* or 80 acres (although some farmers acquire even more acreage but register it under relatives' names). Also, by law, no one is allowed to buy more then one *'api'uta,* although some persons purchase several (again registering them under relatives' names).

In addition, the role of women in Tongan society has undergone enormous change in the last 20 years. Traditionally, the women's role revolved around childcare and domestic activities. Subsistence needs were largely provided by males with women acting as support labor. Even though this situation continues today, especially in commercial farming ventures where women assist their husbands in weeding, harvesting, produce marketing, and cooking for work crews, the changes now sweeping across Tonga have resulted in a female wage labor force in the modern wage sector that is larger than initial government estimates (Kingdom of Tonga 1980; Fifita 1975). Greater educational opportunities, the impact of male emigration, and the necessity to find new income-earning opportunities outside the home have motivated women, as sole heads of households, to provide for their children's well-being or to supplement their husbands' income. Because their demand for work could not be met through the traditionally male-dominated agricultural sector and because there were few well-paying opportunities available to them in the private sector, more and more Tongan women began to establish sole proprietorships or joint ventures in their own right. Of the 185 businesses surveyed, 29 (16.7 percent) were owned exclusively by women. Of 166 spouses interviewed, 124 (74.3 percent) acted as business partners or assisted their husbands in their businesses at least 51 percent of the time, including business management, bookkeeping, inventory, and marketing goods and services. If present trends indicated by this data continue, female participation in the business sector will increase significantly over the next several decades.

Summary

Although Tonga's traditional social system has been influential in changing indigenous entrepreneurial styles and attitudes toward business, other factors have been influential in depressing, and later encouraging, entrepreneurial initiative. Prior to World War II, Tongans appeared less "anti-enterprise" than they did "anti-inclined." Land resources were plentiful and food was abundant; Tonga's monarchs were respected and trusted; and widespread contact with other foreign socioeconomic systems was limited. Furthermore, for the masses, the church provided an affordable and acceptable avenue for status mobility. Hence, the need or the desire to radically alter the traditional Tongan lifestyle was not urgent.

Once land resources became scarce and people's livelihoods

were threatened, however, the drive to find alternative means to
survive overrode social constraints and individual inertia. This
event—coupled with a greater sophistication derived from education, emigration, and the purchasing power of remittances—irre-
vocably changed people's attitudes toward wage labor and business enterprise. That many indigenous attempts at business
venture development were not successful during the last 30 years
has to do less with the specific cultural predisposition of the
Tongan people than with infrastructure, financial, and geographic
limitations and with the general lack of business training, acumen,
and experience.

Finally, the fact that successful business ventures are being
established, however difficult, in a society that still practices vir-
tues antithetical to the principles of capitalism, indicates that non-
western cultures need not entirely revamp their societies to mirror
those of the west to establish a healthy private sector. On the contrary, to be a business success in Tonga, an entrepreneur cannot
run roughshod over the customs that bind a culture together and
that the majority of the population respect. Above all, indigenous
business in nations such as Tonga, where the disbursement of business profits among many individuals is commonplace, means that
the well-being of the people still rests with the people, not with the
government or foreign nations.

NOTES

1. Belshaw (1955) defines expansion as a situation "that may or may not
involve the accumulation of capital, but can also involve consumption derived
from more intensive effort, greater use of existing resources that previously have
been used below potential or from increased velocity of circulation of working
capital so that a surplus can be generated."

2. The *Tu'i Ha'atakalaua* and *Tu'i Kanokupolu.*

3. Although there is some disagreement among historians, the *tu'a* class consists of three levels. The highest strata, or *mu'a,* probably consisted of younger
brothers or sons of the *matāpule* and hence either acted as their righthand men or
were the chiefs' warriors. The majority of *tu'a* were peasants, whose job was to
cultivate the land. The lowest strata of *tu'a* consisted of the *pōpula* or *tamaio'eiki*
(Williamson 1924). These people were the slaves who had forfeited their liberty
by crime or who had been taken captive in war.

4. This fact correlates with Hagen's assertion that "Typically, the elite in traditional societies feels that his innate superiority consists in being more refined

than simple folk. One evidence of his greater refinement is that he does not like the grubby attention to the material details of life which is one of their more distinguishing characteristics" (in Kilby 1971:127).

5. Women comprised 12 percent (or 29) of the total survey sample and nearly 30 percent (or 29 out of 91 informants) of the non-commercial farming sample.

6. As one well-educated and wealthy farmer stated, "Most Tongans are still too concerned with style and show over substance and productivity. Because of this, farmers are not highly respected because our clothes are dirty and our hands are rough. But although we might look dirty, most of us pay our bills on time, which is more than can be said for a lot of wealthy looking individuals in this country" (pers. comm. 1984).

7. A number of informants noted that, unable to amass the appropriate savings in Tonga, their main motivation to work overseas was to enable them to acquire enough cash to purchase farmland upon their return. This strategy worked for several growers who have since established large and successful farming businesses. Others have returned to a life of semisubsistence.

8. In 1984 a large percentage of informants confirmed that the average land lease could be purchased for about T$3,000 to T$5,000 and that good quality, well-situated farmland was selling upwards to T$10,000. In 1984, T$1.00 = US$0.68.

References

Belshaw, Cyril S.
1955 "The Cultural Milieu of the Entrepreneur: A Critical Essay," *Explorations in Entrepreneurial History*, Vol. 3, pp. 146–163.

Bollard, A. E.
1974 *The Impact of Monetization on Tonga*, Dissertation, University of Auckland, New Zealand.

Central Planning Department.
1985 *Mid-term Review of Development Plan IV 1980–1982*, Government Printing Office, Nuku'alofa.

Cochran, Thomas C.
1971 "The Entrepreneur in Economic Change," in *Entrepreneurship and Economic Development*, edited by Peter Kilby, The Free Press, New York.

Cole, Arthur H.
1959 *Business Enterprise in its Social Setting*, Harvard University Press, Cambridge, Massachusetts.

Faletau, Meleseini
1983 "Changing Roles for Tonga's Women," *Pacific Perspectives*, Vol. 2, No. 2, pp. 45–55.

Fifita, S. Laitia
1975 "Problems of the Land: People's View," in *Land and Migration*, edited by Siosiua H. Fonua, Tongan Council of Churches, Nuku'alofa.

Finney, Ben
  1973 *Big-Men and Business: Entrepreneurship and Economic Growth in the New Guinea Highlands,* University of Hawaii Press, Honolulu.
  1973 *Polynesian Peasants and Proletarians,* Schenkman Publishing Company, Cambridge, Massachusetts.
  1976 *Big-Men, Half-Men and Trader Chiefs: Entrepreneurial Styles in New Guinea and Polynesia,* Technology and Development Institute, East-West Center, Honolulu.

Fonua, Siosiua, ed.
  1975 *Land and Migration,* Tonga Council of Churches, Nuku'alofa.

Gifford, E. W.
  1929 *Tongan Society,* Bishop Museum Press, Honolulu.

Hagen, Everett E.
  1971 "How Economic Change Begins: A Theory of Social Change," in *Entrepreneurship and Economic Development,* edited by Peter Kilby, The Free Press, New York.

Hau'ofa, Epeli
  1977 *Our Crowded Islands,* Institute of Pacific Studies, University of the South Pacific, Suva.
  1978 "Tonga in Transition Part I," transcription of a lecture delivered at Atenisi University, Tonga, Nuku'alofa.
  1979 "Tonga in Transition Part II," transcription of a lecture delivered at Atenisi University, Tonga, Nuku'alofa.

Hoselitz, Bert F.
  1963 "Entrepreneurship and Traditional Elites," in *Explorations in Entrepreneurial History,* Vol. 1, No. 1, pp. 36–49.

Kilby, Peter
  1971 *Entrepreneurship and Economic Development,* The Free Press, New York.

Lātūkefu, Sione
  1974 *Church and State in Tonga: The Wesleyan Methodist Missionaries and Political Development, 1822–1875,* University of Hawaii Press, Honolulu.

LeVine, R. A.
  1966 *Dreams and Deeds: Achievement Motivation in Nigeria,* University of Chicago Press, Chicago.

Macdonald, Ronan
  1971 "Schumpeter and Max Weber: Central Visions and Social Theories," in *Entrepreneurship and Economic Development,* edited by Peter Kilby, The Free Press, New York.

Maude, Alaric
  1965 *Population, Land and Livelihood in Tonga,* Australian National University, Canberra.
  1973 "Land Shortage and Population Pressure in Tonga," in *The Pacific in Transition,* edited by Harold Brookfield, St. Martin's Press, New York.

McClelland, David C. and David G. Winter
1971 *Motivating Economic Achievement,* The Free Press, New York.

Moore, Wilbur E.
1963 *Social Change,* Prentice-Hall, Inc, Englewood Cliffs, New Jersey.

Parsons, Talcott and Neil J. Smelser
1956 *Economy and Society,* The Free Press, Glencoe, Illinois.

Ritterbush, S. Deacon
1985 *The Effects of the Constitutional Monarchy on Development Trends in the Kingdom of Tonga,* thesis, University of Hawaii, Honolulu.
1986 *Entrepreneurship and Business Venture Development in the Kingdom of Tonga,* Pacific Islands Development Program, East-West Center, Honolulu.

Schumpeter, J. A.
1971 "The Fundamental Phenomenon of Economic Development," in *Entrepreneurship and Economic Development,* edited by Peter Kilby, The Free Press, New York.

Smith, Norman R.
1967 *The Entrepreneur and His Firm: The Relationship Between the Type of Man and His Company,* an occasional paper for the Bureau of Business and Economic Research, Michigan State University, East Lansing.

Tonga, Kingdom of
1980 *Mid-term Review—3rd Five Year Development Plan, 1975–1977,* Central Planning Department, Nuku'alofa.
1985 *Mid-term Review—4th Five Year Development Plan, 1980–1982,* Central Planning Department, Nuku'alofa.

Tonga Council of Churches
1975 *Land and Migration,* A collection of papers presented at the Tongan Council of Churches Seminar, Nuku'alofa.

Von der Ohe, R.
1981 "Women Entrepreneurs: Access to Capital and Credit," in *Women's Economic Development,* edited by Barbara Reno, World Council of Credit Unions, Inc., in collaboration with OED, Washington, D.C.

Walsh, A. C.
1981 "Some Questions on the Effects of Migration in the Pacific Islands," paper presented to the Conference on the Consequences of Migration, East-West Center, Honolulu.

Wilkens, Paul
1979 *Entrepreneurship: A Comparative and Historical Study,* Ablex Publishing Corporation, Norwood, New Jersey.

Williamson, R. W.
1924 *The Social and Political Systems of Central Polynesia,* Vol. I and III, Cambridge University Press, Cambridge, Massachusetts.

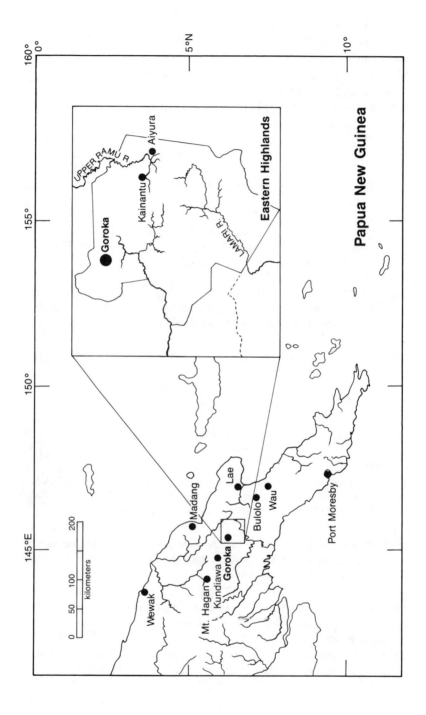

Papua New Guinea

CHAPTER 8

Culture and Entrepreneurship in the Highlands of Papua New Guinea

Ben R. Finney

THIS CHAPTER examines the development of entrepreneurship in the Goroka District of the Eastern Highlands Province of Papua New Guinea in relation to the culture of the people. Compared with the pace of development in most other areas of the Pacific, the growth of indigenous entrepreneurship in Goroka has been rapid. The Gorokan people were not contacted by the outside world until the early 1930s, and they did not begin to be involved significantly in the cash economy until the 1960s. Yet, today they dominate the thriving coffee industry in Goroka and play a major role in other sectors of the local economy.

The rapid efflorescence of indigenous entrepreneurship in Goroka can be explained partly by the late and relatively benign extension of the colonial frontier to Goroka, by the development of a vigorous local economy based on coffee, and by government efforts, particularly since independence, to promote indigenous commercial development. The crucial ingredient, however, has been the entrepreneurial bent of the Gorokan people themselves because they have actively sought out opportunities and have mobilized whatever resources they could master to take advantage of those opportunities.

That Gorokans, or any other Papua New Guineans, had any significant entrepreneurial talents was an issue in 1966, when I was asked to undertake research in Papua New Guinea. The then recently released report of the World Bank mission to Papua New Guinea virtually ignored indigenous entrepreneurship. The focus was on the continued efforts of European planters and businessmen as being essential to the development of the territory's economy, and Papua New Guineans were typically discussed under

165

such terms as "indigenous unskilled labor." That reservoirs of entrepreneurial drive and energy might exist among the people was scarcely considered in the report (International Bank for Reconstruction and Development 1965).

Yet, at that time the press reports on indigenous enterprise indicated that some Papua New Guineans were enthusiastically attempting large-scale cash cropping and other commercial ventures. As the first Fulbright Fellow to be assigned to Papua New Guinea, I was given the task of investigating the nature of indigenous entrepreneurship there. When I arrived in Papua New Guinea in 1967, I elected not to attempt to survey entrepreneurship throughout the entire country, but instead to focus on one region where indigenous business development was accelerating. Hence, I chose Goroka, which was then becoming known as a rapidly developing coffee growing region where the people had a reputation as being "business minded." I was able to spend six months in 1967 and another three months in 1968 undertaking field research on Gorokan entrepreneurship.

In mid-1986, under the sponsorship of the Pacific Islands Development Program (PIDP), I returned to Goroka for two weeks to survey the course of indigenous business enterprise during the nearly 20 years since my first visit to the region. This chapter synthesizes my original research and the results of my 1986 visit to provide an overview of the development of entrepreneurship in Goroka from the very beginnings of its cash economy to 1986 (Finney 1968, 1969, 1970, 1973, 1987).

The development of coffee industry

When I first visited Goroka in the late 1960s, it was a prosperous Australian colonial outpost. Goroka, then a sub-district of the Eastern Highlands District, included some 1,770 sq km of valley and mountain lands, ranging from 1,365 m to over 3,340 m in elevation. Virtually all the 60,000 inhabitants lived in rural areas, and the sole township, also named Goroka, was primarily inhabited by Europeans—administration employees, businessmen, missionaries, clerks, typists, bank tellers, etc.

The basis for the growing prosperity of Goroka was arabica coffee. A number of Australians, some of whom were the same gold miners and patrol officers who had opened the area to the outside world in the early 1930s, had started coffee plantations on land that the administration purchased from local clan groups and leased to the planters. Once these first plantations began to produce high quality coffee that fetched a good price on the world market, a minor land rush ensued as Australians and other Europeans flocked to Goroka to make their fortunes. Many Gorokan groups sought to sell what they considered the least usable portions of their land holdings in order to obtain some ready cash, and also to have an expatriate planter in their midst who would provide employment and purchase produce from them. This land rush was stopped in the late 1950s when the administration, sensitive to criticism about allowing the continued alienation of indigenous lands, banned the further sale of land for coffee plantations.

Sufficient land had already been alienated by then, however, to provide the basis for a local coffee industry, the future of which was assured when the Highlands Highway linking Goroka with the coastal port of Lae was opened and when Australia joined, on behalf of Papua New Guinea, the International Coffee Agreement. With easy access to the coast and an export quota to be filled, the coffee industry started booming in the 1960s.

The Gorokans were not content, however, to stand by and watch the expatriate planters make their fortunes. They judged the small amounts of money received for their lands, as well as for their labor and produce, to be insufficient. The Gorokans wanted to share more directly in the wealth of this new industry by growing and selling their own coffee. Many started experimenting with this new crop, some with the aid of friendly planters and enthusiastic agricultural officers, and others on their own. Although many mistakes were made during the first few years of experimentation, by the late 1960s the Gorokans were producing more coffee than the expatriate planters were, and their production accounted for over 12 percent of all the coffee grown in Papua New Guinea.

Neither were the Gorokans content just to grow coffee. They considered that coffee growing was, what they called in Pidgin English, a *bisnis* and that most of the cash produced should be reinvested in other commercial ventures. Thus, instead of spending the bulk of their coffee money on consumer goods, they used it to build small trade stores, to purchase trucks to haul passengers and freight, and to develop cattle projects and other ventures. Because the per capita cash income at that time was less than A$20[1] and because few Gorokans could obtain bank loans, many of their investments required a high degree of informal pooling of money. The relative ease with which the Gorokans were able to pool their meager funds and also organize labor and obtain land for their ventures is just one reason why the Gorokans came to be considered among the most "business-minded" people in Papua New Guinea.

The first Gorokan entrepreneurs

Leading the Gorokan entry into the commercial world were several indigenous entrepreneurs. Although these men had all had more contact with the outside world—through schooling, work, or other experiences—than the average Gorokan, they were not at all marginal men divorced from their own culture. In fact, in their hard work and their commercial success they seemed to embody much of what was thought ideal in Gorokan culture.

Gorokan culture stressed individual achievement. There were no hereditary classes or chiefs. Men came to be known as leaders or "big men" through their own deeds—in warfare, in oratory, and particularly in the indigenous economy involving the exchange of pigs, shells, and other "valuables." If a man could manipulate this complex system to his advantage, it could bring him considerable wealth and social status as a "big man." In a sense, this cultural emphasis on status mobility through individual economic achievement preadapted the Gorokans for entrepreneurship.

The Gorokans were proud of those who took a leading role in the commercial economy and referred to them as *bikpela man belong business,* a term that literally means "big men of business," but one that I render simply as "business leaders." The case histories of Bimai Noimbano, Sinake Giregire, and Hari Gotoha, three of the most outstanding of these early entrepreneurs, illustrate how these new big men started their business careers, and how they related to their clansmen and others who helped them build up their enterprises.

Bimai Noimbano was one of the first Gorokans to grow coffee on a large scale. Bimai first became interested in cash crops in

1949 when he worked on Manus Island as a plantation laborer. From Manus he moved back to the Eastern Highlands to work as a trainee at the agricultural station located at Aiyura at the eastern end of the province. When he left Aiyura he took with him some coffee seedlings and seed to plant in a remote area of his home located at the western end of Goroka. When these failed to grow he switched his attention to raising chickens and soon had a thriving business selling chickens to expatriates and those few Gorokans who had saved money from government service. He then sent some boys to Aiyura for more seedlings and seed, planted these, and failed again. At this point an Australian agricultural extension officer stationed in Goroka happened by, and Bimai asked him for help. Following his instructions, Bimai set out a model nursery to grow seedlings and then transplanted these into a carefully laid out plantation that started bearing after several years.

A key element in Bimai's commercial success was his ability to mobilize the resources of his clansmen and others. For example, Bimai needed land for his plantation, but as an adoptive member of this clan he had no secure land rights. Similarly, he needed labor —to lay out the nursery, care for the seedlings, and then plant and maintain the plantation—but he did not have the money to pay for workers. Bimai overcame his lack of resources by successfully appealing to his clansmen for help. Although at the time he was a relatively unimportant man, and certainly was not a big man in the traditional sense, the people were nonetheless willing to support him with grants of land, contributions of their labor, and even cash donations because he seemed to know something about the workings of the cash economy and was willing to initiate coffee growing and other commercial ventures that could benefit everyone.

By the early 1960s Bimai was well established. His plantation was thriving, he had purchased several trucks and was buying coffee from small producers and selling it to the processing factories, and he was operating several other small enterprises. Bimai had, in effect, made himself into a prominent "big man of business."

Sinake Giregire was one of the younger business leaders operating in Goroka during the late 1960s. Whereas Bimai and many of the other early business leaders had literally been born in the Stone Age, Sinake had been born in the mid-1930s, several years after initial European contact. He was one of the few boys in his village to enroll in the nearby Lutheran Mission School, and after two years he was sent to the coast to continue his schooling at the Lutheran mission headquarters. At age 13, however, a near-fatal attack of malaria forced him to leave school and to return to the healthier and malaria-free Eastern Highlands. Instead of returning to school, he spent several years recuperating at home and then went to work as a mechanic's helper for a small airline operating out of Goroka. He worked there for three years, following which he briefly held a job at the Aiyura agricultural experiment station. Then, at age 20, he decided it was time to go into business for himself.

While working in Goroka, Sinake had tried to start a coffee plantation in his village, but his youth and lack of accomplishment meant that he could obtain only enough land and workers to plant a small plot of coffee. Thus, to build up his capital and demonstrate his business ability, Sinake turned to lumbering. Noticing the demand for timber for building administration facilities, Sinake took his meager savings, purchased a hand-operated pit saw, and hired some local boys as laborers. He could not, however, compete with the sawmills owned by expatriates, so he abandoned this enterprise to try his hand at panning gold. With a crew of about six laborers, he worked streams from one end of the district to the other until 1958, when he returned to his home village with some A$1,800 in savings.

Although at the time Sinake was just a young and unimportant man, his clansmen were impressed by his accomplishments, and by the amount of money he had accumulated, and were therefore willing to overlook his youth and to accede to his request for land. Accordingly, they allocated a large tract of land to him for planting coffee, and many volunteered their assistance and even contributed to his capital. Sinake used the money to purchase tools and planting materials and hired a crew of laborers from the adjacent Chimbu Province to help him and his clansmen clear the ground, set up a nursery, then plant the seedlings, and care for the maturing coffee trees. The resulting plantation, which in the late 1960s had about 24,000 bearing coffee trees, was the largest coffee property owned by any Gorokan and probably was the largest then owned by any Papua New Guinean.

Like many of the other business leaders who had got their start in coffee, Sinake invested some of his profits in trade stores and trucks. His ambition, however, was to have his own coffee factory for processing the ripe coffee berries into "green coffee," the unroasted beans from which the pulp and husk have been removed. He planned to process his own coffee in the factory, as well as to buy and process coffee grown by other Gorokans. That way he calculated that he could make a substantial profit by selling the processed green beans directly to exporters. During 1969–70 Sinake was able, with the aid of one of the first major bank loans given to a Gorokan, to erect his own coffee factory, the first to be built by a Papua New Guinean, and to start buying and processing coffee on a large scale.

"It all started with thirty cents of self-rising flour," began Hari Gotoha's story of his start in business. Hari was only around 30 years old in 1967 and thus was the youngest of the business leaders prominent then. Unlike Sinake Giregire and the other major business leaders, Hari was not able to start out with a large coffee holding because his clan had sold much of its land to the administration for the founding of the Goroka township. Instead of following the coffee route to success, Hari was forced to build up his business holdings by catering to the nascent market among Gorokans for goods and services in the new economy.

Continuing his story, Hari told me that one day in 1959, when he was a young man employed in Goroka township as a personal servant for an expatriate administration employee, he went shopping and bought some flour. Using his employer's stove while she was at work, he baked some scones, which he sold at the local market. He then reinvested his profits into buying more flour, sold more scones, and so on until he had a flourishing business—so flourishing, in fact, that his employer suggested that he quit working for her and devote himself full-time to baking and selling scones. This he did, earning some A$600 in his first year, which he used to put up a small bush restaurant on his land that was located directly across the road from the Goroka market, an ideal site to attract Gorokans with a desire to taste scones and the other European-style foods that he sold there.

From his profits, he built a trade store on his property, the first one in the town to be owned by a Gorokan. Then, a few years later, he put A$5,000 of his savings into a new restaurant built with modern materials and equipped with running water, electricity, a modern stove, and a refrigerator-freezer. Later, as profits grew from his combined enterprises (which by then included an interest in a small coffee property and a small herd of cattle), Hari started a trucking business to haul freight between Goroka and the coastal port of Lae along the newly opened Highlands Highway. In 1968 he built a large retail store costing some A$25,000 at the site of his old store across from the market, and was earning a good profit on goods that he trucked up from Lae and sold at a healthy mark-up to Gorokans who preferred to trade at his store rather than shop at any other town stores, which then were all owned by expatriate businessmen.

Because Hari dressed like a local Australian businessman, wearing knee-length white socks, a pair of dress shorts, and a white shirt, and because he tended to stress his own individualistic accomplishments when he told expatriates about his success, many outside observers were convinced that Hari represented a new type of Gorokan entrepreneur, a modern businessman who was less entangled with customary obligations and practices than the typical Gorokan business leader of the time. However, behind the individualistic stories that Hari liked to tell curious expatriates, I found a history of major contributions of land, labor, and capital made by clansmen to Hari's enterprises. In addition, upon getting to know Hari, I realized that of all the business leaders he was perhaps the most sensitive to the needs of his fellow Gorokans for economic advancement. He told me repeatedly that his ambition was that all the people, not just he himself, could participate in the new economy.

The high degree to which clansmen contributed to the business ventures of Bimai, Sinake, Hari, and other business leaders does not mean, however, that the coffee plantations, stores, and trucking ventures should be considered primarily as group enterprises. Although group support was vital, entrepreneurial drive was crucial to these enterprises and indeed to the whole Gorokan effort to participate in the cash economy. In soliciting cash and other contributions from their clansmen, for example, business leaders were tapping the only source of capital then available to them. Gorokans were then virtually barred from obtaining bank loans because, lacking clear title to their land or other assets, they were judged by the bankers to have no collateral. While the clan milieu in which these business leaders were operating might seem exotic, they were fulfilling the basic entrepreneurial function: the recognition of new opportunities and the mobilization of resources to exploit those opportunities.

To some expatriate observers this garnering of local resources by the business leaders amounted to exploitation. Yet, clansmen willingly lent support to a business leader so that he could build up his business enterprise and achieve a level of affluence far beyond their own. To understand why the ordinary man did not keep these resources for his own use instead of giving some to a business leader, we need to look at the motivation behind investment.

While aspiring business leaders were certainly interested in acquiring prestige and viewed commercial activity as the main way to do so in the new socioeconomic order, it must be remembered that they were still members of traditional social groups, and that whatever prestige they might acquire from commercial success would be at least partially shared by the other members of the group. In traditional times, men of minimal ambition or skill were willing to support the pig raising and wealth exchange activities of a big man. Similarly, in this first stage of economic transformation such men were willing to support a business leader in his drive for commercial success and status. In both cases, the performance of the leader was also seen as the performance of the whole group.

In addition, clansmen also gained materially by supporting one of their number as a business leader. Some hoped for a share in the profits of the business, or access to credit in the business leader's store, or simply rides in his truck. Others felt, perhaps more realistically, that they stood to gain simply by having a business leader in their midst in that the leader could show them how to plant coffee and undertake other projects in the cash economy. In addition, clansmen expected that their business leader would contribute significantly in money as well as pigs and other traditional goods to feasts, bridewealth payments, and inter-group exchanges, which still dominated the social life in the 1960s, and that he would also help them pay school fees for their children, as well as the annual head tax.

These expectations tested an entrepreneur's skill at balancing the demands of his clansmen with the prerequisites of sound business practice. During this first stage of experimenting with business, many a Gorokan enterprise, and aspiring business leader, foundered because the coffee profits were squandered, or because too much credit was extended at the store, or because the truck was used more for joy riding than hauling paying passengers and freight. The successful business leaders with whom I discussed this issue agreed that how to limit their largesse to a level compatible with good business practices was one of their main problems. Hari Gotoha, for example, explained to me that he could not refuse store credit to his clansmen, particularly those who had helped him get started. But he added that when they sold their coffee he was right there on the spot to collect the amount owed to him.

Economic outlook for Goroka in the late 1960s

Despite the considerable economic progress achieved by the Gorokans during the 1960s, many observers at that time were pessimistic about long-term Gorokan economic prospects. Although Gorokans had enthusiastically planted coffee and enjoyed handsome profits from the first harvests, after a few years many Gorokan yields began to diminish because of lack of proper pruning, fertilizer, and maintenance of shade trees. In addition, many trade stores were foundering because of mismanagement, including the too liberal granting of credit to clansmen. Above all, many trucking ventures were disasters, primarily because of the atrocious state of the roads and the general Gorokan ignorance about proper driving and vehicle maintenance, in addition to careless business practices.

Moreover, in the late 1960s Gorokans were still subordinate participants in an economy controlled by expatriate planters and businessmen. Although Gorokans were producing more coffee than expatriate planters, the latter processed virtually all the Gorokan coffee and sold it to expatriate-owned exporting firms. Similarly, the Gorokans were virtually absent from urban business activities. All the main retail and wholesale stores in town, the automobile distributorships, the lumber yards, the hotels, and all other major businesses were owned by expatriates.

How could Gorokans enter the coffee industry at the processing and exporting level, much less take over the expatriate plantations? This question was hardly discussed in Goroka during the late 1960s. Similarly, it was inconceivable to most people, expatriates and Gorokans alike, that Gorokans could ever become prominent in urban-based enterprises. According to Howlett (1973), a geographer who had studied Goroka throughout the 1960s, the Gorokans were doomed to the fate of other third world peoples dependent upon tropical commodities. She forecast a faltering coffee industry that, combined with population growth and consequent land shortages, was leading the Gorokans into "terminal development." An "infinite pause" in development was settling over Goroka, she claimed, adding that the Gorokans would stagnate at the level of a dependent peasantry.

Goroka in 1986

Some pauses have occurred in Gorokan development during the last two decades, but they have reflected periodic dips in the world market price of coffee. In fact, Goroka and, above all, the Gorokans have prospered since the late 1960s. Coffee production has significantly increased. The amount of coffee produced by the Gorokan people has increased fourfold, while their population has increased by only about 50 percent. Even more impressive has been the successful takeover by Gorokans of virtually all the expatriate plantations. Gorokans also now control most of the coffee buying and processing and recently have gained a stake in coffee exporting. Even in town, where before Gorokans had virtually no share in commerce, they now are major players. Gorokans own and operate a wide range of urban wholesale and retail stores, they own most of the new commercial buildings, and they have equity holdings in some of the remaining expatriate trading firms. While the Gorokans do not totally control commercial activity in their region, their commercial progress over the last two decades has been outstanding.

The new Gorokan business climate

With self-government in 1973 and then independence in 1975, the business climate in Goroka has been greatly transformed. This change was brought about primarily by new government programs and the expansion of previous efforts.

For example, new government programs were inaugurated to aid Gorokans and other Papua New Guineans to expand their coffee holdings. The most prominent of these was the Plantation Redistribution Scheme, whereby the government undertook to buy out expatriate plantations and return them to local ownership. In another important scheme, the government undertook to aid Gorokans to establish small coffee plantations, known locally as "coffee blocks." Funds were made available for these and other Gorokan commercial ventures through the two government-owned banks, the Papua New Guinean Development Bank (now called the Agricultural Bank) and the Papua New Guinea Banking Corporation, as well as private banks. Under these schemes Gorokans have been able to buy up virtually all of the plantations started by expatriates and to start a large number of coffee blocks that are, in effect, mini-plantations.

To enable a traditional group such as a clan to develop a coffee block, to participate in the purchase of an existing plantation, or to engage in other commercial activities, the government passed legislation in 1974 that authorized a new corporate form called a "business group." A business group is a simplified corporation that enables a clan or other group to borrow money and have limited liability, but does not require extensive documentation or record keeping. To aid Gorokans in forming business groups, as well as to provide general business advice, an Office of Business Development was established in Goroka township.

Because it was felt that most Gorokans (and other Papua New Guineans) did not have the skills to manage efficiently the plantations they purchased or the coffee blocks they developed, the government required that they contract with professional plantation managers to oversee the projects. As this was a national problem, a statutory body, the National Plantation Management Agency, was set up to handle the required management functions. The Goroka office of this agency, plus several private firms (all with some degree of Gorokan ownership) and individuals, has continued to provide management services in Goroka under this system.

In addition, Gorokans and other Papua New Guineans who were interested in buying out small retail stores owned by expatriate merchants were aided by the government's "straight fashion store" scheme, whereby promising candidates were trained in retailing practices, placed in a store purchased by the government from an expatriate merchant, and then given a loan to purchase and operate that store.

Two Gorokan "tribal" enterprises

These policies and programs have resulted in many new Gorokan enterprises, most of which are small and undiversified. There are, however, two main exceptions: the Gouna Development Corporation and the Eastern Highlands Development Corporation, the two largest Gorokan-owned enterprises that were organized during the mid-1970s in direct response to the new business opportunities and institutions inaugurated in that decade. These might be called "tribal" enterprises in that they are owned by individuals and business groups drawn from a large number of clans.

By far the biggest and most impressive building in Goroka township is a sprawling, two-story structure called the Gouna Centre. Gouna is one of the largest and most diversified corporations owned by Papua New Guineans and is even more distinctive in that it was organized to give the general populace a stake in the modern economy.

As talk of independence and the takeover of expatriate plantations began to develop during the early 1970s, Hari Gotoha, Auwo Kitauwo, and several other Gorokan business leaders began to discuss ways in which Gorokans could take over expatriate plantations and develop new plantations and other enterprises. Although each of these businessmen was prominent in his own right, they all felt that the need was for a broadly based organization involving all Gorokans, not just themselves. Indicative of their group orientation is the name chosen for the organization. Gouna means "united" in one of the local languages; it also stands for, and is composed of letters from the three geographical areas from which its members are drawn *(Goroka* township, *Unggai, and Bena).*

In 1975, after approximately K100,000[2] was raised from thousands of Gorokan subscribers, the Gouna Development Corporation was formally organized with the aid of the local Office of Business Development. At first it was structured as a proprietary company owned by seven business groups and one proprietary company, which in turn were owned by thousands of Gorokan contributors. Recently, however, Gouna has been reorganized as a corporation to make it more flexible and to enable it to raise capital more easily.

In 1977, with the aid of bank loans, Gouna purchased two

expatriate plantations, including one with a thriving poultry and egg business. Since then, Gouna has expanded these ventures and gone on to acquire or develop a range of other enterprises. These include an auto and truck agency, a service station, and oil products agency, a sporting goods show, an insurance agency, a printing company, and the Gouna Centre itself, which rents space to two major banks, several retail stores, and other businesses. In addition, Gouna has developed a management service for coffee blocks and has recently acquired a majority interest in the second largest coffee exporting firm in the country. All these enterprises and assets have a value of at least K10,000,000.

Although ownership is totally Gorokan, the management is largely expatriate. Auwo Kitauwo (who, along with Hari Gotoha, was a prime mover in organizing Gouna) is chairman of the Gorokan directors of the corporation. He and Hari Gotoha closely monitor Gouna and ensure that the corporation's goals are being followed, but they leave the day-to-day management to a team of executives, accountants, and other professionals, all of whom are expatriates except the manager of their coffee block service who is from the Western Highlands Province.

Like Gouna, the Eastern Highlands Development Corporation (EHDC) had its roots in the local desire to purchase expatriate plantations. One of the prime movers was Akepa Miakwe, a business leader from the Bena region of Goroka. While serving as Bena's representative in the national House of Assembly during the early 1970s, Akepa became enthusiastic about the idea of buying out expatriate plantations. He returned home to Bena and started raising money to buy out the plantations there, but he collected only a few thousand kina. In the following years, after self-government had been granted and when the expatriates were leaving the country, Akepa was able to raise much more money. Akepa then organized the EHDC, and with the capital subscribed, plus government loans, he was able to buy out four plantations.

Now the EHDC owns nine plantations, three coffee factories, and an office building in town, all of which have a value of at least K5,000,000. Akepa and the other directors of the EHDC do not actively manage the corporation. Instead, they contract with the Angco Corporation, a large nationwide agricultural firm headquartered in Goroka, to manage the plantations and factories. The EHDC, in turn, owns a minority share in Angco.

First-generation entrepreneurs revisited

Many of the first generation of business leaders that I studied in the late 1960s were born in the Stone Age, i.e., before contact with the outside world and the introduction of metal tools and the money economy. Of the most prominent business leaders then, Bimai Noimbano and another have died, and most of the others are elderly and have not retained their business leadership. The exceptions are Sinake Giregire and Hari Gotoha, who were the youngest of the prominent entrepreneurs of two decades ago. They are no longer, however, indisputably the leading local businessmen. Each has encountered business problems over the last two decades, and both appear to have lost some of their initial enthusiasm for building up their businesses.

Since the late 1960s, when he was indisputably the leading businessman of the district, Sinake Giregire's business fortunes have declined. Among the business leaders of the 1960s, Sinake was the one most active in politics, both traditional and modern. From 1964 to 1977 he represented Goroka in the national parliament and twice served as a government minister during that period. The long periods he spent in Port Moresby and his dedication to local politicking when at home—with all the attendant visiting and drinking—led him to neglect his business affairs. As a result, in the mid-1970s his coffee factory and coffee buying business were in effect bankrupt, and production virtually ceased on his coffee plantation. Only recently, with the direct intervention of an aggressive coffee buying and exporting firm, have Sinake's plantation and coffee buying and processing business begun to flourish once more. However, although Sinake has plans for further business expansion, it is doubtful that he could ever regain his former preeminence in business, given the competition from the younger entrepreneurs who have come to the fore in recent years.

Hari Gotoha has virtually retired from the business ventures that made him prominent in the late 1960s and into the early 1970s. He tried to turn over the management of his restaurant and retail store to his younger brothers and other relatives, but the businesses have languished in part, he says, because his kinsmen were not up to the task. Other projects such as a piggery and a tire and battery store have been closed. Now Hari has put much of his money into rental housing, a business that he finds easy to manage and rather profitable, given Goroka's acute housing shortage and the number of firms and government departments that are obligated to house their employees. In addition, he enjoys handsome dividends from an investment he made during the early 1970s in a fledgling helicopter company headquartered in Goroka, which has since developed into a major enterprise that specializes in servicing the mineral survey and mining companies now active in Papua New Guinea and elsewhere in the southwest Pacific.

However, while he is now less active in private business, Hari still devotes a great deal of energy to the Gouna Development Corporation, the major group enterprise he helped to found in the mid-1970s. In Gouna he has been able to fulfill his longstanding desire to work for "all the people, and not just myself alone."

A new generation of business leaders

Gorokan society has continued to produce entrepreneurs. As the first generation of business leaders have aged, a new generation of entrepreneurs has emerged. These entrepreneurs are in their forties, and thus they are about 15 years younger than the mean age of the first Gorokan business leaders and are slightly younger than Sinake Giregire and Hari Gotoha, the two youngest of the original Gorokan entrepreneurs. Akapite Wamiri and Enoch Molle are two outstanding entrepreneurs in this new generation of business leaders.

Many Gorokans consider that Akapite Wamiri is the leading local businessman. An early indication of Akapite's drive came when as a boy he walked all the way to the port of Lae in order to find work to pay school fees required in the private religious school he was attending. After completing his schooling and then a teacher training course, Akapite worked as a teacher for several years. His ambition, however, was to become a successful businessman. Akapite had always admired his older neighbor, Sinake Giregire, and while teaching he began doing odd jobs in town during weekends and on vacations in order to save money for a business venture. In 1970 he resigned from teaching, took the A$1,6000 he saved, and, with an additional A$200 from a clansman, purchased a used Toyota Land Cruiser for hauling passengers. Within a few years he owned several vehicles, including a large truck that he used to haul freight between the coast and the highlands.

In 1974, taking advantage of the exodus of expatriate planters, Akapite pooled K42,000 he had saved from his passenger and freight hauling business, together with K8,000 solicited from about 50 of his clansmen, and bought a coffee plantation. In order to complete the transaction, he secured a loan of K60,000 from the local branch of the Westpac Bank, a major Australian banking firm.

Shortly after the transaction was completed, coffee prices rose sharply due to a severe frost in the coffee growing regions of Brazil. With the high prices, Akapite made so much money that within a few months he was able to pay back K30,000 of the loan. Three months later he returned to the bank with the balance of the loan, which meant that within the year Akapite and his clansmen owned their plantation free and clear.

The continued high coffee prices allowed Akapite to build a coffee processing factory on the plantation, to purchase a hotel in Lae, and to start a cattle ranch in the lowlands of Madang. Subsequently, he has bought land elsewhere in Goroka to start another coffee plantation and has developed a sugar plantation in the Markham valley in partnership with a local man. More recently, he has invested profits from the plantation and his other enterprises in property located in coastal Papua New Guinea and in Australia.

In addition, he has become the landlord of the Westpac Bank, the bank that first loaned him money. In 1984 he purchased the land in Goroka where Westpac was located, and then he bought the new bank building that Westpac erected for its activities. Because the bank loaned him the money for these purchases and pays him a handsome rent, these transactions have not tied up Akapite's capital, and he has recently purchased a large town property on which he plans to build a major shopping center.

All these enterprises and properties are worth in excess of K4,000,000, a substantial increase over the K50,000 down payment used to buy the original plantation, and a tremendous increase over the A$1,800 he paid in 1970 to buy a Land Cruiser and start his business career. However, although Akapite is proud of his entrepreneurial role in developing his business organization, he also stresses that he is not the sole owner. He estimates that his share is about 75 percent, with the rest belonging to his clansmen and various other partners. Nonetheless, Akapite is firmly in charge of the holding company, the Anego Company, and, although he employs expert managers and accountants, most of whom are expatriates, he still closely supervises the operations of the individual enterprises.

Several other Gorokan entrepreneurs, like Akapite, have built up large multimillion kina enterprises to buy out plantations.

Enoch Molle, a business leader in his mid-forties, is one of the new generation of business leaders. While still at school he grew vegetables for sale and even started a small trade store. After leaving school, Molle worked as a laborer in the coastal port of Madang and then at Kavieng on the island of New Ireland. Upon returning to Goroka in 1966, he reopened his trade store and also began working for an expatriate as a coffee buyer. After a couple of years, Molle pooled his savings of K800 from his wages and trade store profits, with K400 from two of his clansmen, to buy a used truck so that he could go into the coffee buying business himself. In 1973 he purchased an even larger truck to expand his business.

A few years later he heard Michael Somare, then newly installed as the first Prime Minister of newly independent Papua New Guinea, call for Papua New Guineans to pool their money and buy out expatriate plantations. Accordingly, Molle formed a business group with several people from the area of Goroka where he lived. The combination of their money, together with a bank loan, allowed him to buy out a well-run plantation in his neighborhood. Then in 1979, using profits from the plantation, he bought an expatriate farm supply firm specializing in farm equipment, fertilizer, and pesticides. This firm, like the plantation, has proved to be profitable, and Molle has gone on to acquire a service station in Goroka, a farm supply company in Lae, a welding firm with branches in several towns, rental real estate, and a large property at the eastern end of the province for agricultural development.

Although Molle is the driving force behind these enterprises, he is not the sole owner. He owns a little more than half the shares in his holding company; some 125 other shareholders own the rest. Molle employs expert managers to run his businesses, all expatriates except for one of his clansmen whom he recently promoted as manager of the plantation.

In many respects, Akapite, Molle, and the new generation of business leader entrepreneurs seem more "modern" than their predecessors. They live in large comfortable houses equipped with electricity and plumbing. Their enterprises are well run and highly profitable, and they seem to be able to strike an acceptable balance between traditional obligations and business activities. To be sure, as wealthy and important men they must still contribute to funeral and brideprice payments and assist their clansmen in various ways. However, they appear to be more successful than their predecessors in drawing a definite line between business and personal affairs in order to avoid draining business resources to fulfill social and political demands and ambitions. Perhaps significantly, unlike most of the business leaders of the 1960s, few of these men are active in politics.

One other characteristic relating to the success of these new entrepreneurs bears mentioning. Drinking is a growing social problem in Goroka and elsewhere in Papua New Guinea, and the businesses of several first-generation Gorokan entrepreneurs suffered because they drank to excess. Akapite, Molle, and other major entrepreneurs who have recently become prominent do not drink because of either religious proscription or personal choice. Many of my Gorokan acquaintances pointed to abstinence as one of the secrets of their successes.

Yet, however modern these new entrepreneurs may appear to be, they remain extremely Gorokan. Their behavior still reflects traditional Gorokan values about economic endeavor and achieved leadership. In their drive for business success, in their ability to start small and then develop sizable business organizations, and in the obvious pride they and their supporters take in their success, these entrepreneurs appear to be following, like their immediate predecessors, in the footsteps of the traditional big men.

Emerging business leaders

Several relatively young and well-educated Gorokan businessmen are now coming into prominence. Most are in their thirties, have graduated from a university or have had some tertiary education, and have had relatively sophisticated work experiences before going into business for themselves. In contrast to the first- and sec-

ond-generation business leaders, these men have not had to follow
the same slow path of advancement through menial jobs or a succession of small ventures. Instead, because of their educational
background, they have been able to obtain relatively responsible
and well-paying jobs, from which they have gained experience and
contacts that have enabled them to go directly into business.

Benais Sapumei is one of the most prominent of these new
entrepreneurs. One of the first graduates of the University of
Papua New Guinea, he then joined his country's Department of
Foreign Affairs. In 1978, however, he resigned from the government to take a management position with Angco, the large agricultural exporting firm headquartered in Goroka. While working
for Angco, he became a leader in the EHDC, the development corporation centered in his tribal area of Bena, and went into business
for himself. He has operated a supermarket in West Goroka, has
recently purchased one of the two hotels in town, and is now seeking other business opportunities.

Benais is married to a former Indian national, and he and his
wife live in an expatriate style. As a busy executive and a businessman who lives apart from his original tribal milieu, Benais has difficulty in coping with all the requests for contributions and assistance from his clansmen. Nonetheless, he still identifies himself
with his tribal area of Bena and works hard to defend the interests
of the EHDC within Angco. For example, during my stay in
Goroka in 1986 Benais was almost totally preoccupied in fending
off a takeover bid for Angco that threatened to weaken the EHDC's
position in the firm.

Pepe Gotoha, another young entrepreneur, is the younger
brother of Hari Gotoha. Hari sent him first to the government's
Cooperative College, then to the University of Papua New Guinea
to develop Pepe's business skills so that he could return to Goroka
and help its clansmen establish and operate businesses. Instead of
returning to Goroka, however, Pepe took a job in the national
government's Commerce Department where he worked in the
"straight fashion store" program. After working there for a few
years, he himself went through the program and was assigned to a
store in Lae, which he has subsequently purchased. Using profits
from this store, he bought another store in Lae and then a third
one in Port Moresby. In addition, he has been investing in rental
housing in Lae and also has started a growing vegetable business

at the eastern end of the Eastern Highlands Province. Pepe has thoroughly examined the business opportunities in Goroka, but has concluded that—due to a shortage of land in the township, the strong competition from other local entrepreneurs, and the inevitable problems he would have in fulfilling customary obligations were he to relocate back to Goroka—he can be more successful in Lae and Port Moresby. Pepe therefore represents what may be a growing trend among young and ambitious Gorokans: migration to the coast or elsewhere where the opportunities and potential are judged to be greater.

Gorokan entrepreneurship reconsidered

Although rivaled by some other groups in the Papua New Guinea Highlands, the speed with which the Gorokans have taken to commercial development is outstanding in the Pacific. That a favorable environment for growing coffee, a relatively benign colonial experience, and, most recently, positive government programs have aided this development is beyond question. But the Gorokan people themselves have not merely reacted to the economic situation. They also have brought to this abrupt juncture of tribal society and the world market economy those cultural resources that have encouraged them to seize the opportunities offered by the implantation of a commercial economy in their midst. Culturally, the Gorokans were preadapted for entrepreneurship.

Although the first entrepreneurs to come to prominence were not traditional big men, they came to be known as "big men of business" because of their commercial success and leadership. As such, they acted very much as modern analogs of traditional big men: they called upon their clansmen and others for aid, even cash contributions, and they, in turn, stood by to help their clansmen and other supporters in times of need. In addition, just as traditional big men used their economic success and leverage for political leadership, most of these early business leaders sought to convert their economic position into political capital by running for elective office. Many were successful; virtually all of the first elected officials in Goroka were also prominent businessmen.

Although the brevity of my two-week stay in Goroka in 1986 makes me cautious about drawing sharp distinctions between the entrepreneurial situation during late 1960s and now, it does appear that the most prominent business leaders now are somewhat less embedded in traditional society than were their predecessors. This is not to say, however, that the current business leaders ignore the need to contribute handsomely to brideprice collections and other traditional payments or to help clansmen who are less well off with cash for school fees and the like. It does appear, however, that these transactions are less important to them and constitute a smaller proportion of their cash flow than was the case with their predecessors. Although I have only a limited knowledge of the younger entrepreneurs who are in their 30s, they seem even less involved in these transactions than the current prominent business leaders.

If this trend is real, then the character of Gorokan entrepreneurship may indeed be changing: entrepreneurs may be becoming more "modern" in that they are less beholden to their clansmen for support and consequently share less of their wealth with them. Even if entrepreneurship becomes more and more divorced from traditional rights and obligations as Gorokans become increasingly enmeshed with the dynamic commercial economy and the national society, I doubt that Gorokan entrepreneurs will become completely divorced from their culture. The traditional emphasis on status mobility through economic accomplishment motivated the first entrepreneurs to try their hand at *bisnis,* and from what I have seen this cultural drive still motivates younger Gorokans to go into business. Unless Gorokan society were to be utterly transformed, and traditional cultural values completely rejected, we should still see more generations of ambitious Gorokan entrepreneurs coming to the fore.

This is not to say that the rise of wealthy business leaders has not caused tension in Gorokan society and will not do so in the future. While the success of prominent business leaders is widely admired by the Gorokans, many people think that some of the business leaders control too much land.

Several business leaders, however, are especially sensitive to these concerns and recognize that group economic advancement should be pursued together with individual achievement. The formation of the Gouna Development Corporation by prominent business leaders such as Hari Gotoha and Auwo Kitauwo, as well as the founding of the Eastern Highlands Development Corporation by Akepa Miakwe and others, concretely expresses this concern for group economic advancement. As such, the entrepreneurial style of these organizers would appear to stand in contrast to that of the more individualistic entrepreneurs such as Akapite Wamiri and Enoch Molle. Yet, while the types of organizations they founded may differ, in some respects these men are not all that different, however individualistic or group oriented they might seem. All played crucial entrepreneurial roles in seizing the opportunity created by the exodus of expatriate planters by raising money to buy out the plantations and then by creating business organizations to operate the plantations and to reinvest the resultant revenue to develop other ventures. In addition, whichever organizational way they have chosen to carry out their business plans, all these entrepreneurs have won the attention of their fellow clansmen for their business success, thus staking their claim to be big and important men.

Although no Gorokan women have attained equivalent prominence in business, a number do operate small businesses, and during the 1970s rural Gorokan women initiated a vigorous movement called "women's work" *(wok meri)* to promote greater female participation in business (Sexton 1986). So far, however, it would appear that the male bias in the gender role pattern in Gorokan culture (and probably also the male bias in the imported business culture) has prevented women from becoming prominent entrepreneurs.

During the late 1970s a number of writers, who were oriented from the perspective of the neo-Marxist dependency school, discovered the Gorokan entrepreneurs. They charged that these men had destroyed the autonomy of the local village economy and had helped to push the mass of the Gorokans into a vulnerable dependency on the world economy (Amarshi et al. 1979; Connell 1979; Fitzpatrick 1980; Gerritson 1979; Good and Donaldson, n.d.). To these dependency theorists, the Gorokan business leaders were "rich peasants," "big peasants," or "kulaks" who were exploiting their fellow Gorokans and turning them into a downtrodden, third world peasantry.

Their point of view, which seems to have run the course of its brief popularity in Papua New Guinea's academic circles, ignored the cultural roots of Gorokan entrepreneurship. With the partial exception of Gerritson (1979), these writers considered that the

Gorokans brought nothing to the encounter with capitalism other than, perhaps, their alleged avarice. To them, Gorokan entrepreneurs, and their analogs elsewhere in Papua New Guinea, were creatures of colonialism produced solely by the intervention of outside capital.

These writers not only failed to understand the Gorokan contribution to their own economic evolution but also lacked dynamism in their schemes of class formation. Once a man becomes a rich peasant, his lot seems to be both that of a servant to outside capital, on the one hand, and that of an exploiter of the mass of peasants below him, on the other hand. That Gorokan business leaders have gone on to form such large and group-oriented companies as the Gouna Development Corporation and the Eastern Highlands Development Corporation is either ignored by these writers or explained away. Furthermore, that individualistic entrepreneurs such as Akapite Wamiri and Enoch Molle could form their large and diversified business organizations does not seem to be taken into consideration by the neo-Marxist dependency schemes.

In addition, these writers failed to consider that the contemporary class situation may be as fluid as the traditional one. In traditional Gorokan society the big men did not form a permanent class. Although the son of a big man might have an advantage in the economic and status mobility system due to his father's wealth, hereditary privilege did not really exist; ultimately, it was what a man achieved on his own that counted. Furthermore, once a man had attained big-man status through his own accomplishments, he could easily lose it should his health fail or his motivation diminish. The crucial question then is whether the new economic structure is promoting the formation of a permanent capitalist class. Although the answer is not yet clear, the evidence available so far points toward a continuation of traditional fluidity.

The crucial test of any hypothesis concerning the fixed character of the contemporary entrepreneurial class is the disposition of the business organization upon the death or disability of the founder. Because of the recency of modern entrepreneurship among the Gorokans, there are not many cases to examine. However, regarding two of the prominent business leaders of the late 1960s who have since died, both of their business assets either have been split up among many heirs and contributors to their enterprises or have been dissipated while contending parties fought over them. Similarly, where business leaders have lost their vigor and have retired from active business affairs, in no case has a son or other heir been able to take over the entire organization or even operate part of it with great success. It could be argued that the business organizations of the young entrepreneurs who appear to be less beholden to tradition may escape this leveling process because they have a firm corporate structure or because the business leader is training his sons to operate the business. However, I suspect that the traditional pattern of entrepreneurial mobility—up and down—may prove more enduring than some outsiders might assume and indeed some current business leaders might wish.

That the sons or other favored relatives of wealthy business leaders might have an edge in going into business because of educational advantages and family wealth would seem a reasonable hypothesis. The two young entrepreneurs featured in this study Benais Sapumei, whose father was an early entrepreneur, and Pepe Gotoha, whose entrepreneur brother sent him to school expressly to study business, enjoyed such an advantage. However, they are not the only young entrepreneurs, the majority of whom do not appear to have been so privileged.[3] I believe that economic success in Goroka will continue to depend on personal qualities rather than familial position.

In summary, the Gorokan case provides an example about how —contrary to many stereotypes found in the development literature—indigenous values and institutions that evolved in a non-market context can promote rather than hinder adaptation to the modern economy. The "business mindedness" of the Gorokans stems from their traditional culture and is personified in those entrepreneurs who have perceived the opportunities presented by the new economy and have gone on to found a range of enterprises to take advantage of them. They are carrying on the big man tradition of their ancestral culture, but in the modern world of business.

NOTES

1. One Australian dollar (A$), the currency then used in Papua New Guinea, was worth around US$1.17 in 1967.

2. One kina (K), the main unit of currency now used in Papua New Guinea, was worth around US$1.07 in mid-1986.

3. During my limited stay in 1986 I chose to interview Pepe Gotoha and Benais Sapumei because I already knew them from my previous stay in Goroka, not because they are representative of any new privileged class. See Finney (1987:51–52) for information on a young Gorokan entrepreneur who does not come from a business family.

REFERENCES

Amarshi, Azeem, Kenneth Good, and Rex Mortimer
  1979 *Development and Dependency, The Political Economy of Papua New Guinea,* Oxford University Press, Melbourne.

Connell, John
  1979 "The Emergence of a Peasantry in Papua New Guinea," *Peasant Studies,* No. 8, pp. 103–137.

Finney, Ben
  1968 "Bigfellow Man Belong Business in New Guinea," *Ethnology,* Vol. 7, pp. 394–410.
  1969 *New Guinean Entrepreneurs: Indigenous Cash Cropping, Capital Formation and Investment in the New Guinea Highlands,* New Guinea Research Bulletin No. 27, Australian National University, Canberra and Port Moresby.
  1970 "Partnership in Developing the New Guinea Highlands, 1948–1968," *Journal of Pacific History,* Vol. 5, pp. 117–134.
  1973 *Big-Men and Business: Entrepreneurship and Economic Growth in the New Guinea Highlands,* University Press of Hawaii, Honolulu; Australian National University Press, Canberra.
  1987 *Business Development in the Highlands of Papua New Guinea,* Research Report Series No. 6, Pacific Islands Development Program, East-West Center, Honolulu.

Fitzpatrick, Peter
  1980 *Law and State in Papua New Guinea,* Academic Press, London.

Gerritson, Rolf
  1979 *Groups, Classes and Peasant Politics in Ghana and Papua New Guinea,* Ph.D. dissertation, Australian National University, Canberra.

Good, Kenneth and Mike Donaldson
  n.d. *The Development of Rural Capitalism in* PNG: *Coffee Production in the Eastern Highlands,* History of Agriculture Discussion Paper No. 29, University of Papua New Guinea and the Department of Primary Industry, Port Moresby.

Howlett, Diana
  1973 "Terminal Development: from Tribalism to Peasantry," in *The Pacific in*

Transition (edited by Harold C. Brookfield), St. Martins Press, 249–273, New York.

International Bank for Reconstruction and Development
  1965 *The Economic Development of the Territory of Papua and New Guinea,* Johns Hopkins Press, Baltimore.

Sexton, Lorraine
  1986 *Mothers of Money, Daughters of Coffee,* UMI Research Press, Ann Arbor, Michigan.

PART 3

Significant Issues in
Small Business Development

CHAPTER 9

Pacific Women in Business:
Constraints and Opportunities

S. Deacon Ritterbush and Janice Pearson

IN MOST Pacific island societies, women are—and have always been—a powerful force in the home and the community. They not only have primary responsibility for raising the children and managing the household but also provide important support for men in their political and professional endeavors. Women's stamina and skills are legendary, as demonstrated in traditional food production activities and the production of ritual wealth. Moreover, their ability to marshal, distribute, and reallocate resources is evident in women's groups that have been instrumental in earning the funds to build community halls and upgrade kitchen, sanitation, and water facilities; in assisting public health workers to improve the health and nutrition standards of villages; and in finding effective solutions to curb unemployment and youth-related problems.

Today, due to economic necessity or a desire to improve educational opportunities or simply to satisfy personal aspirations, women are channeling this energy and resourcefulness into the private business sector. Case studies documented by researchers in the Pacific Islands Development Program (PIDP) noted the increasing participation of Pacific island women in the wage force, especially as business assistants, managers, and owners. Indeed, although the numbers are still small, women are emerging as some of the most successful entrepreneurs in the region, their business successes equaling or exceeding those of their male counterparts. In Tonga, Fiji, Papua New Guinea, and American Samoa, for instance, women are operating successful ventures ranging from commercial farming and broiler chicken businesses; to manufacturing companies that produce soap, baked goods, and clothing; and to tourism and transportation services.

Yet, as an economic resource, women are still virtually ignored

195

in national development programs and encounter various constraints in both the policy-related and traditional spheres. Women
must contend with the same business obstacles as men, including
inadequate business skills, a lack of basic infrastructure, poor or
unstable transportation facilities, and inadequate financing. In
addition, many women also often find that their economic aspirations are either patronized or not taken seriously by policy planners, bankers, and businessmen. In some countries, this attitude
causes problems in establishing lines of credit, obtaining land or
capital financing, building the necessary business contacts, or
receiving even the most rudimentary business skills from training.

Because the merging of traditional practices with contemporary
policies is often inappropriate or discriminatory, these policies do
not address the special needs of businesswomen; moreover, they
are outmoded. This chapter discusses the constraints that many
women face in their attempts at business venture development, as
well as those factors that can facilitate their economic endeavors.

Due to a paucity of data on the subject, most of the information
is drawn both from the PIDP country studies (Finney's Chapter 8;
Ritterbush 1986; Hailey 1986) and from a recent business survey
conducted by the Economic Development Planning Office of
American Samoa (Schug and Zodiacal 1987).

Factors encouraging greater female participation in business

In general, the traditional status of Pacific women has been secondary to that of men. Women had few if any rights to land and
usually were not allowed to hold positions of rank. Their traditional roles centered on household and small-scale food production activities. Because they had to learn only the knowledge and
skills required of a daughter, daughter-in-law, wife, and mother,
any formal education for most young women was limited. Moreover, women were not usually allowed to voice their opinions or
participate in any official decision making affecting the community.

This situation, however, has been changing throughout the
Pacific islands region largely due to the medical, educational, economic, political, and professional opportunities accompanying the
modernization process. Education has heightened personal aspira-

tions and provided women with the skills necessary to fulfill these goals. For some, these changes have meant finding new ways to participate constructively in society through organized community activities or through women's organizations; for others, through professional or entrepreneurial activities.

Modern medical practices have enabled men and women to plan their families, thereby freeing women to pursue other areas of interest beyond the dictates of their biological function. Modern medicine has also greatly improved infant mortality rates and increased the lifespan of various population groups throughout the region. However, the end result for many nations has been increasing population pressures on limited land resources. The inability to obtain land for farming is a leading cause of urban and overseas emigration. In addition, because married women with children are often the last to migrate and the first to be abandoned, special needs arise that have to be met if the well-being of their families is to be ensured.

Finally, the increase in the cost of living as well as the desire for western goods has encouraged many women to seek income-earning activities either for individual use or as a supplement to their husbands' incomes. The predominance of wives and mothers in business is explained by emigration and the rising cost of living; some women have taken over the direction of households due to the absence of the husbands. The phenomenon of the unmarried, childless woman in business is still rare in the Pacific region.

The reasons for greater female participation in business vary from country to country and from culture group to culture group. In Tonga the primary reasons for a woman to start a business were to supplement a husband's income, to provide a service to the community, or to obtain income as the sole financial support (see Figure 9.1). American Samoan and Western Samoan businesswomen (based in American Samoa) cited service to the community, the need for independence, and the enjoyment of meeting people as the leading motivations for starting a business (see Figures 9.2 and 9.3).

Regardless of the motivations, however, trends indicate a greater female participation both in the work force and in business ventures in the future. Their attempts at business development, in particular, have met with varied results throughout the region. Reasons frequently cited include inhibiting cultural practices and

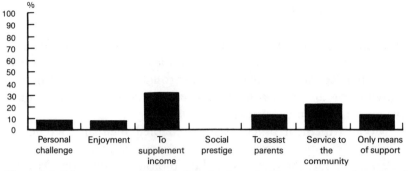

Figure 9.1. Primary reason for going into business for Tongan women (number of respondents: 22)

Source: Ritterbush, Entrepreneurship and Business Venture Development in Tonga, 1986.

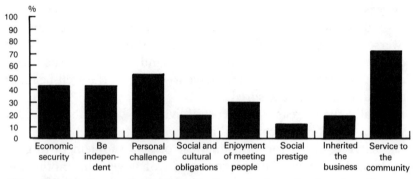

Figure 9.2. Leading motivations for starting a business for American Samoan women (number of respondents: 30)

Source: Economic Development Planning Office, Government of America Samoa, 1987.

Note: Tables add to more than 100% because many women gave more than one response; each category of response was taken as a percentage of the total number of respondents.

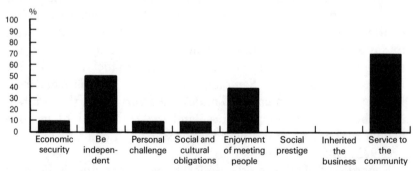

Figure 9.3. Leading motivations for starting a business for Western Samoan women working in America Samoa (number of respondents: 10)

Source: Economic Development Planning Office, Government of America Samoa, 1987.

Note: Tables add to more than 100% because many women gave more than one response; each category of response was taken as a percentage of the total number of respondents.

restrictions, lack of business acumen, and business policies that are inappropriate to the special circumstances of Pacific island businesswomen.

Cultural and technical constraints affecting female business initiatives

After a woman initially recognizes that she wants to enter into business and has an idea of her objectives, she then faces the problems of limited resources and lack of start-up finance. Many avenues are available for earning additional income such as saving the housekeeping money or starting a home-based cottage industry (making handicrafts, growing surplus crops for sale locally, and initiating other small-scale ventures), which require little initial capital. These small, usually single activity projects are sometimes used to secure the initial finance to start and expand a business goal. In rural areas, however, the women usually start their small ventures solely to supplement their husbands' income.

The process of saving sufficient revenue to initiate a formal commercial business is lengthy, and once the venture becomes operational, many problems are encountered that could contribute to failure including
• Cultural systems and values
• Lack of training opportunities
• Limited access to capital.

In addition to these difficulties, women often can neither find adequate child care facilities nor obtain credit. Other problems relate to the attitudes of social and business contacts. By not conforming to their traditional role, businesswomen often encounter severe criticism from other women as well as men in the society. Moreover, the male-dominated business world often regards businesswomen with suspicion, and even contempt, while bankers and business contacts treat them with reserve and skepticism.

Cultural constraints

Although different attitudes and economic opportunities are emerging through education and exposure, most Pacific island women have been traditionally conditioned to believe that they should not aspire to owning their own businesses. Some of the new, western-oriented values are often in direct conflict with traditional values.

In most traditional societies with mixed economies such as those in the Pacific region, the socioeconomic framework in which women function dictates the level of their participation in business-related activities. At its most fundamental level, village life generally revolves around the extended family or clan unit and consists of customary obligations, communalism, and corporately owned possessions. Generally, specific economic roles and duties are based on sex and age. Although these roles differ markedly throughout the Pacific, women in most societies are considered "support labor," and men are regarded as "managers." Women weed and tend the gardens that men cultivate, or they search the reef for small fish or crustaceans while men fish in deeper waters. Land resources are usually held corporately by the clan or by individual males while a woman's place centers around the home—as caretaker, cook, cleaning woman, and consoler. The pressures to adhere to these roles are extremely strong; the penalty being social ostracism, loss of status, and isolation if these roles are ignored.

Because rural areas tend to be more traditional, the rural-based businesspersons of both sexes encounter similar difficulties in operating businesses there. Often they are viewed as greedy, selfish, or too individualistic. The constant demands for loans (that often go unrepaid), lines of credit, employment, the use of business equipment, and the fulfillment of customary obligations can prove disastrous to a venture if not handled wisely. Fifty-four percent of all Tongan businesswomen considered that their social obligations had an adverse impact on their businesses (Ritterbush 1986) though others considered them beneficial to their businesses (Table 9.1).

These pressures are perhaps more profound for women because economic activity is so radically different from their customary traditional roles. Not surprisingly, the most successful indigenous female entrepreneurs tend to concentrate in urban areas—due to economic necessity, improved market opportunities, and more liberal attitudes. In urban areas, women are often spared from many of the traditional constraints encountered by businesswomen in

Table 9.1. Effects of social and customary
obligations on business ventures

Effects	Respondents	
	(N = 22)	%
Adverse	12	54.5
Neutral	7	32.0
Beneficial	3	13.5

N = number of respondents

rural areas. They engender less criticism, less suspicion, and less pressure to conform to a given set of behaviors.

Business education and training

Nevertheless, traditional attitudes can influence business-related national development policies. Although the equal status of women in most Pacific island nations has been recognized in certain legislation, even in the Constitutions, in practice women do not often attain equality in education, politics, employment, and business. For instance, the idea of women as "support labor" persists even though, as "support labor," women in business often handle details that include bookkeeping and billing, employee hiring and training, stock and materials purchasing, customer relations, and payroll. In fact, in many Pacific island nations, businessmen and policymakers alike admit that women are more efficient office workers and more adept at managing businesses than men. Where men tend to surpass women in initiating new ventures, women excel in performing detailed work and managing day-to-day operations. (This is perhaps less indicative of women's disinclination or disinterest toward entrepreneurial pursuits than it is of the lack of opportunity to practice their other business talents.)

But outmoded practices and policies continue, usually favoring businessmen over their female counterparts for training courses (both in-country and overseas), incentive programs, and loans for business development, expansion, and improvements. Essential business skills (particularly planning, marketing, management, and accounting) are vital to the continued development and eventual profitability of female-owned enterprises. Yet many new women entrepreneurs with strong motivation and sound economic support are still intimidated by the harshly competitive urban business world because they lack the confidence—born of limited business experience and training—to market their goods, their services, and themselves.

In those Pacific island nations where women do have equal access to educational facilities and are encouraged to pursue academic goals, there often exists little opportunity, support, or encouragement for them to train in business management. Instead, educational curriculums emphasize traditional female careers such as nursing, teaching, or secretarial work. Furthermore, even if in-country business training courses are offered, still a rarity in many countries, they are generally targeted on men or are scheduled at times that are inconvenient or incompatible with women's other responsibilities. Many women, who have no available family members to babysit the children or who lack or cannot afford daycare facilities, often have little choice but to remain at home. Evening courses are often held in urban centers where transportation, if available and affordable from rural areas, might be dangerous or culturally inappropriate for women to attend unescorted. The end result is that women remain severely handicapped by their lack of business management experience, business acumen, and bookkeeping—skills that are generally crucial to the ongoing success of any business.

Capital financing

Another business constraint is the inability to secure sufficient capital for business development and expansion. Although most female-owned businesses are primarily begun with funds derived from remittances, family members, or personal savings (obtained by budgeting household money or selling handicrafts or produce from household gardens), other women have limited access to capital, leaving them no alternative except bank loans. Many women entrepreneurs encounter discrimination because they are not accorded the same recognition as men when their business proposals are evaluated by the male-dominated loan staff of most banks.

Another factor is the lack of adequate security. Because women usually lack the necessary collateral, they often cannot receive loans without a male guarantor. Even women who have already proved themselves in business have difficulty in obtaining loans for capital improvements in some nations unless a male co-signs the note. The reasons are varied, but a major one concerns land.

In many Pacific nations, land is the most prevalent and often the only available form of collateral. But land laws often favor males, thus prohibiting individual women from leasing or inheriting land. Or they must appeal to their family for the use of clan-held land. Such appeals are often met with great resistance. Present land-related policies deny women not only a ready source of collateral but also the option to pursue a commercial farming career. Furthermore, for widows or women who are single heads of households (a phenomenon that is increasing due to male migration and rising divorce rates), the lack of ready access to farm land can be economically devastating. Because such women—usually rural based, undereducated, and untrained—often lack competitive skills in the market place, their talents are better suited to semisubsistence activities to provide for their families.

Profiles of successful women in businesses

Given the economic, technical, and sociocultural constraints, some women nevertheless manage to establish highly successful businesses. Despite the constraints, or perhaps because of them, several women have emerged in the past decade as leading businesswomen in their nations. Four of these women are described below (Hailey 1986).

Papiloa Foliaki owns one of the largest tourist resorts in the Kingdom of Tonga. Formerly trained as a nurse, she resigned her post in 1971 when her husband was appointed Director of Health. In search of a challenge, Foliaki used a bus she had inherited from her father as the catalyst for her future business empire. By carefully budgeting household expenses and selling gifts and garden produce, she saved enough money to renovate the bus. After an innovative market research exercise, she began a bus company, and by 1974 she operated ten buses in the Kingdom. She then diversified and established a motel, which now, through a program of planned expansion, boasts a squash court, a conference center, a restaurant, and a bar. Apart from her varied life as a mother, wife, and entrepreneur, she was elected Tonga's first woman member of Parliament. Foliaki's entrepreneurial vision, her determination, versatility, and articulate expression of ideas have contributed to her successes.

The Cook Islands boasts one of the South Pacific's most dynamic and versatile businesswomen. Marie Melvin owns and manages a range of businesses including a wood carving and timber operation, a handicraft shop, a flower center, and gift shop at the Rarotonga airport. Married with three children, Melvin attended only primary school, but after a career as a photographer in New Zealand, she returned to her native country and established a photography business. After purchasing the original Island Crafts store, she diversified into her present businesses. Melvin believes her personal success is due to her hard work, her family's support in the daily operation of the businesses, and domestic help at home. Her reputation as a businesswoman has been enhanced by her reliability and business consistency, which are exemplified by her ability to meet deadlines, pay bills on time, and work long hours despite personal inconvenience.

Mere Samisoni of Fiji is owner and manager of Fiji's popular Hot Bread Kitchen. The concept of a "bake on the premises" bread shop has proved so popular that Samisoni is on the verge of developing the first multinational company controlled by an indigenous Pacific islander. Although trained and employed as a nurse for many years, Samisoni became increasingly attracted to the challenge of creating her own business and quickly recognized the potential for hot bread shops in most Pacific island markets. She opened her first shop in 1982, and by early 1986 she had opened several branches throughout Fiji employing over 120 people. Through a well-planned franchising arrangement, she has since opened Hot Bread Kitchens in Solomon Islands and in Hawaii.

Even though Samisoni, the mother of three, initially experienced frustrations and business setbacks, including the refusal by the Fiji Development Bank to give her a loan, she credits sheer determination, hard work, a concern for quality, hygiene, and customer relations—qualities learned during her years of training and working as a nurse—as fundamental to the success of her business. More important, flexibility and the ability to adapt to her changing roles as wife, mother, entrepreneur, business manager, and community worker have proved invaluable.

The Od-N-Aiwo Hotel in Nauru is owned by Elaine Bailey who is a full-time primary school teacher, owner of an import-export business, a restaurant, a poultry farm, and a part-time taxi driver. A graduate of a teacher's training college in Australia, Bailey schedules her life around her teaching commitments and her business interests as well as her family. She attributes her business successes to family support, her father's business experience and advice, her ability to control customary borrowing *(bubati)*, and her determination to succeed.

Keys to successful entrepreneurship

Like their successful male counterparts, these businesswomen are shrewd, visionary, and tenacious individuals. And like entrepreneurs the world over, they are risk-takers and innovators and possess a marketing savvy that many women lack.

Other factors also work in their favor. Successful businesswomen are usually better educated than average. Many have lived and/or worked overseas, thus gaining exposure not only to a market economy but also to the greater socioeconomic mobility of foreign women. And they usually have some previous business experience. Such experience is invaluable, introducing them to the principles of savings and investment and teaching them how to control business resources, meet consumer needs, and develop customer relations. They also learn, through trial and error, how to effectively juggle the demands of business with traditional obligations.

A majority of successful businesswomen have also established important female networks, a source of support that cannot be overemphasized. Supportive women provide one another with new clients, ideas, information, and emotional wherewithal to carry on. Women's groups such as Papua New Guinea's *"wok meri"* have been important in initially exposing presently successful businesswomen to many rudimentary and important business skills. Other women establish joint ventures with foreign women, each bringing a different set of perceptions, expertise, and resources into the venture.

Finally, a large percentage of successful businesswomen enjoy the support—financial, technical, and emotional—of their spouses and male relatives. In Pacific island nations, where the economic and political realms are still dominated by men, the importance of male support is often crucial to the success of female-run businesses. The assistance from these men includes providing business advice, arranging financing, managing accounts, developing business contacts, providing overseas training opportunities, assisting in household and child care duties, and giving important emotional support. Such men are generally well educated themselves, hold government positions, or own businesses. Above all, they are practical, for if their women want to operate a business, let it be a success rather than a failure. Unfortunately, many of these men are not policy planners—because the same factors that benefit women in business will ultimately benefit them and the entire nation.

Summary

Increasing numbers of Pacific island women will enter the cash economy in the coming years. If the climate for female-owned and operated businesses is enhanced, the national economies will benefit from increased revenues, greater employment opportunities, and a more dynamic private sector. A more comprehensive and intensive effort is needed to eradicate many of the prejudices inherent in indigenous and western cultures. In so doing, the concept of women as competent owners and managers of businesses could be more widely accepted. Appropriate training programs could be initiated with formal and nonformal educational opportunities to train and advise women on business skills.

Unfortunately, this process is slow because the conditioning of attitudes about women is ingrained by generations of customs and taboos, and the current discriminatory attitudes and practices will probably continue until the new controls to counteract them can be enforced. Given this situation, a clear set of policy guidelines is needed in each national development agenda. These guidelines should first seek to remove current discriminatory policies and practices at both the village and national policymaking levels. These guidelines should be geared toward the special needs and situations of women in business, including flexible course scheduling, loan policies, and daycare facilities in areas where the extended family support system is no longer viable. In summary, these guidelines must be committed to refining the business acumen of women and thereby assisting them to achieve their full business potential.

REFERENCES

Government of American Samoa
  1987   Economic Development Planning Office, Pago Pago.
Hailey, John M. (ed.)
  1986   *Indigenous Business Development in the Pacific,* Final Report of Regional Workshop, Pacific Islands Development Program, East-West Center, Honolulu.
Ritterbush, S. Deacon
  1986   *Entrepreneurship and Business Venture Development in the Kingdom of Tonga,* Pacific Islands Development Program, East-West Center, Honolulu.
Schug, Donald M. and Alexander P. Zodiacal
  1987   *American Samoa Small Business Survey,* Economic Development Planning Office, American Samoa Government, Pago Pago, Xeroxed draft.

CHAPTER 10

Finance for Indigenous Business Development: An Appraisal

Te'o I. J. Fairbairn

IN ANY economy, access to a range of financial institutions and services is essential for maintaining the health of business enterprises, both large and small. Such services are critical for making available finance that can be drawn upon for the establishment or expansion of a business and for providing the operational capital. Yet among the small island countries of the South Pacific, the development of financial institutions and markets remains at the elementary stage, in some cases confined largely to the services of a development bank and a single trading bank. Predominantly because of their small size, Pacific island countries cannot hope to sustain the degree of sophistication found in the capital markets of the large developed countries; however, an examination of the present situation reveals ways in which the existing arrangements can be improved.

Background

This chapter examines the relationship between indigenous entrepreneurship and accessibility of development finance. Emphasis is on sources of finance at the time of initial business establishment, the nature and severity of problems encountered by entrepreneurs in attempts to raise outside finance, how these problems have been solved, and ways of improving access to outside finance.

The chapter draws upon the results of case studies of indigenous business development in six Pacific island countries carried out under the auspices of the Pacific Islands Development Program (PIDP) from 1984 to 1987. These studies were prepared for the

209

Cook Islands by Fairbairn with Pearson (1987), for Fiji by Hailey
(1985), for the Marshall Islands by Carroll (1986), for Tonga by
Ritterbush (1986), for Papua New Guinea by Finney (1987), and
for Western Samoa by Croulet and Sio (1986).[1]

Sources of funds

The combined evidence from the country studies noted above con-
firms that indigenous entrepreneurs in the South Pacific start off
with small capital investments. Typically, those businesses that
have been recently established started with an initial investment—
essentially, the proprietor's equity—of only several thousand u.s.
dollars. Many entrepreneurs—particularly in retail trade stores
and commercial agriculture—began with just a few hundred dollars. Among the few large investments, amounts of US$10–
20,000 were not uncommon, and these invariably relied heavily
on borrowed funds. On levels of investment by ethnic group, the
evidence from Fiji (Hailey 1985:67) shows that the amounts initially invested by indigenous entrepreneurs were significantly
below of other groups. Whereas the average investment in Fiji dollars totaled F$7,978 for Fijians, it amounted to F$21,174 for Indians and F$127,290 for part-Europeans and Chinese.

The low levels of capital investment observed for the majority
of indigenous entrepreneurs suggest two possible major deficiencies in the financial situation of this group. The first is insufficient
access to outside sources of finance. In this respect, Nafziger
(1978:107) noted the particular importance of lack of access to
financing from formalized institutions. The second is the failure of
the entrepreneurs themselves to take full advantage of the available financial institutions to meet their credit needs.

Whatever the reasons, the consequences can be drastic. The
resulting state of undercapitalization can seriously undermine the
enterprise's capacity to maintain liquidity and working capital,
not to mention its ability to survive the first few years of operation
when losses are usually incurred. The capacity to maintain adequate stocks and fixed assets and to undertake expansion is also
impaired. These shortcomings, as well as a failure to remedy
them, contribute to the high rate of alleged business failure among
indigenous entrepreneurs.

Table 10.1. Main sources of start-up finance for selected countries (%)

	Cook Islands (Rarotonga)	Fiji	Marshall Islands	Tonga	Western Samoa
Self-finance/owner's savings	61	61	67	78[a]	63[b]
Commercial bank loan	25[c]	3	11	–	9
Development bank loan	8[c]	36	4	8[d]	–
Combination–all or some of above	6	–	11	–	28[e]
Other	–	–	7[f]	14	–
Total	100	100	100	100	100

SOURCES: For the Cook Islands, see Fairbairn with Pearson (1987:39); for Fiji, see Hailey (1985:68); for Marshall Islands, see Carroll (1986:106); for Tonga, see Ritterbush (1986:110); for Western Samoa, see Croulet and Sio (1986:105).

[a]Applies to self-finance as a primary or principal source of funds.
[b]Includes a small element of bank finance.
[c]Includes some self-finance.
[d]This figure applies to both commercial and development bank loans.
[e]Major share from bank and other outside sources.
[f]Applies to "no response" cases.

The main sources of start-up finance for selected island countries are given in Table 10.1. The table is not altogether free of ambiguities arising from, among other things, lack of uniformity in the kind of questions asked and the ways that responses have been classified; nevertheless, the table clearly reveals the overriding importance of owners' savings as a source of start-up capital. As a general conclusion, approximately two-thirds of the entrepreneurs surveyed possessed their own start-up capital. Such savings are interpreted broadly to include not only the owners' savings and those of immediate family members but also money received in the form of wages from outside employment, profit from an ancillary business (if any), and other cash transfers such as rent and contributions from informal sources including money lenders. In some cases, they also include remittances from overseas relatives.

As Table 10.1 shows, the banks—both development and commercial—play a significant role in Fiji and the Cook Islands where funds were provided to at least one-third of the entrepreneurs. But for the other countries, notably Tonga and the Marshall Islands, these institutions appear to have played a minor role.

Details on finance sources other than the owner's own input and the banking system are available only for Tonga. In Tonga 6.4 percent of the entrepreneurs were able to obtain "primary" finance (i.e., the main source of funds used to start the business) from sources such as government, inheritances, remittances, and local family loans. This figure rises to 21.6 percent in the case of "secondary" finance (i.e., the largest source of funds obtained *subsequently* for purposes of reinvestment or for boosting operating capital), with 7 percent and 4.9 percent coming from remittances and local family loans, respectively (Ritterbush 1986:154). (If those who did not invest subsequently are omitted, the corresponding percentages are 27 for these miscellaneous sources and 9 and 6.) The extent to which entrepreneurs were able to use trade credit is not clear from the evidence in any of the studies, but this source of credit does not seem to be important in the initial stages of business establishment.

For the other countries, Table 10.1 indicates that these other outside sources are insignificant. With the possible exception of Tonga, the entrepreneurs' main source of mobilizing start-up finance is from their own funds and from their families. This situation contrasts with that found among many tribal groups in Papua New Guinea, where investment funds, often in large amounts, are raised through clan networks (Finney 1987:16).

In developing countries, reliance on self-finance as a source of capital investment is fairly common among small businesses during their initial establishment. The reasons are numerous and complex, but they relate to factors such as lack of access to formal lending institutions (as pointed out by Nafziger 1978:107), ownership patterns characterized by a large proportion of family operations, ignorance of potential loan sources, and the desire to maintain a degree of independence by "going it alone."

However, for most indigenous enterprises, the dependence on self-finance appears to be a onetime only phenomenon, confined essentially to the initial stages of enterprise formation. In time, as the enterprise becomes a growing concern, it is able to broaden its financial base through an ability to tap other possible funding sources including retained earnings. However, such an enterprise can still experience capital shortages, which the surveys show to be a continuing problem for most enterprises.

The rise in the importance of other sources of funds over the operational life of an enterprise is borne out by the experience of Tonga and the Marshall Islands. Thus, for Tonga, while initially 78 percent of the entrepreneurs relied on personal savings as the primary source of funds, only 9.2 percent subsequently did so for purposes of reinvestment (Ritterbush 1986:153–4). The latter proportion rises to 12.5 percent when adjusted to allow for the 26.5 percent of entrepreneurs who did not undertake reinvestment. At the same time, the proportion of entrepreneurs relying on bank loans rose from 9.7 percent to 40 percent while the relative importance of sources such as personal remittances, personal loans, and inputs from local family members also rose.

Fewer details are available for the Marshall Islands, but the survey data show a sharp fall in family savings as a source of funds between the time of establishment and subsequent development. Specifically, while 67 percent of enterprises relied initially on personal savings, only 10 percent (adjusted for "no investment" and "no response" cases) did so subsequently (Carroll 1986:106, 108). By contrast, profits assumed a major role, in most cases accounting for about one-half of the total investment/reinvestment.

The above evidence (not surprisingly) points to the importance of bank loans and profit in the evolution of a diversified credit base for small indigenous business. The data for the Cook Islands highlight another source that is particularly important for routine business operations—trade credit—normally a prominent element among small business in both developed and less developed countries (see Johns, Dunlop, and Sheehan 1983:110). About 70 percent of the sample indigenous entrepreneurs on the main island of Rarotonga relied on trade credit, and rather large amounts were usually involved. Details on trade credit are not available for other countries, but as in the Cook Islands, once an enterprise is an ongoing concern, its use of trade credit is likely to be fairly extensive.

Self-finance at initial stage of enterprise formation

As shown in Table 10.1 the initial degree of dependence on self-finance in the selected island countries is of overriding importance and probably is significantly above that experienced by small businesses in developed countries. (The latter point can be inferred from an Australian study by Johns, Dunlop, and Sheehan 1983: 110.) The reasons for such a high degree of dependence are not clear and are not analyzed in detail in the original country studies. However, the evidence presented in these studies does highlight certain factors that can initially limit access to outside finance.

First, except possibly for Fiji, the entrepreneurs face narrow and basically undeveloped capital markets. As noted earlier, the existing facilities in the formal capital market are typically dominated by a development bank, a few commercial banks (only one each in the Cook Islands and Tonga), and, in some cases, a provident or pension fund.[2] No formal market for equity capital exists in any of the countries surveyed though trading facilities for equities are provided in a limited way in Fiji, which also supports several government lending agencies as well as an active money-lending sector. Finance is largely undeveloped from non-bank sources that play an important part elsewhere, such as solicitors, credit unions, insurance companies, finance companies, and factoring operations (with the possible exception of Fiji).

The absence of a formal capital market is the most prominent factor in explaining the particularly high dependence on self-finance observed for Tonga. As Ritterbush states:

> . . . due in part to the lack of in-country lending institutions until 1974, since the average year for business establishment was 1969, most of the businesspersons were compelled to draw on their resources to finance any business venture they attempted (Ritterbush 1986:107).

The formal facilities for lending to entrepreneurs on outer islands and in remote rural communities were found to be particularly deficient and even non-existent. Procedures for making such loans tend to be centralized, with responsibility usually in the head office on the main island. Faced with these disadvantages, entrepreneurs residing in outer islands are forced to depend more on their own savings as evidenced, for example, by the study of Western Samoa (Croulet and Sio 1986:57), where the degree of self-finance on the outlying island of Savai'i was noticeably higher than on the main island of Upolu.

A second major factor limiting access to outside finance is the lack of expertise in preparing and submitting loan proposals. Often these proposals are presented to banks and related institutions without adequate detail on vital aspects of the business such as sales projections, required capital equipment and stock levels, markets, sources of material inputs, and expected profitability. As noted in the Fiji study:

> The problem of raising sufficient initial investment funds is not so much caused by a shortage of investment funds available in Fiji but

rather by the failure of entrepreneurs to prepare suitable proposals to attract these funds (Hailey 1985:101).

The study further pointed out that part of the problem is ignorance of what is demanded by the lending institutions and, in some cases, conflicting advice from support agencies.

A third constraint on access to outside finance relates to the lending policies and practices of formal financial institutions, particularly trading banks. Such institutions normally follow a set of established rules and conventions regarding priority lending areas, acceptable collateral, minimum loan size, and interest rate charges, which, in their overall effect, tend to discriminate against small businesses. This bias is likely to be even stronger for indigenous entrepreneurs who tend to be further disadvantaged by an unfamiliarity with banking institutions, lack of business experience, and inadequate understanding of English.

Trading bank restrictions of this kind were cited as a major factor contributing to the high rate of self-finance found in the Marshall Islands and Western Samoa. In the Marshall Islands the high interest rates charged by local banks coupled with the rendering of poor services to the local business community were said to be major influences causing an extensive reliance on self-finance (Carroll 1986:107). For Western Samoa the lending criteria applied by three leading formal lending institutions (other than the development bank) were considered to be "stringent"—a factor that led to the denial of funds to many entrepreneurs (Croulet and Sio 1986:49).

A final major factor is that during the establishment stage (but not confined to it) the indigenous entrepreneurs almost invariably lack suitable assets, including personal assets, that can be used as collateral to secure a loan from established lending institutions. Most indigenous groups live on and cultivate land that falls under customary tenure and hence cannot be pledged as collateral for loans. In the case of women there are also legal constraints. Few banks lend money without adequate security and are even less inclined to do so when they are confronted with additional risks arising from the entrepreneur's lack of credit rating, compounded by the relatively high cost of administering small loans.

Reinvestment of profit

Businesses that are ongoing concerns can draw upon earnings
(i.e., net profit plus depreciation allowance) as a major source of
funds for reinvestment either in the existing enterprise or in new
activities. The use of such internally generated funds has the
advantage of being obtainable normally at lower cost than outside
funds. These funds are also more amenable to control by the proprietor and, in some cases, can lead to tax savings, e.g., through
avoidance of tax payment on cash drawings or dividends.

The survey results for the Marshall Islands show that the practice of reinvestment was far from being entrenched. Among the
group of indigenous entrepreneurs who were classified as "more
successful" (27 in total), 33 percent had "no investment" subsequent to initial establishment, and for the "less successful" cases
(44 in all), 50 percent were similarly inactive (Carroll 1986:108).
These figures compare with 20 percent for the non-indigenous
group (15 in total).

However, with reference to those Marshall Islanders who did
invest, a total of 45 percent of the successful group as a whole
drew upon realized profits as a source of further investment. This
was well above the corresponding shares for the less successful
indigenous entrepreneurs and the non-indigenous group, which
were 11 percent and 35 percent, respectively. For the overall sample group—both investors and non-investors—the majority of
entrepreneurs, with the relatively less successful group dominat-
ing, did not utilize profits as a source of funds for subsequent
investment and expansion.

In assessing the above results, Carroll (1986:83) points to two
particular pressures that combine to encourage business owners to
spend earnings on personal consumption rather than to reinvest in
the business. One pressure is an apparently weak inclination to
save, deriving from the traditional subsistence system where
resources were generally plentiful and readily replenishable. The
second pressure was said to be a reflection of unrealistic expectations, especially in relation to the return on labor effort, deriving
partly from the colonial experience.

The pattern of business savings and reinvestment is less clear for
the other countries due to a lack of detailed information. However, for the Cook Islands and Western Samoa the propensity to

use business earnings for reinvestment purposes appeared to be fairly well developed. In the Cook Islands the desire to use realized profits to achieve business expansion or to start another business was found to be widespread (Fairbairn with Pearson 1987:73). With a few exceptions all the sample entrepreneurs (totaling 44) expressed the intention of using part of their profits for this purpose. (No evidence was available on the proportion of profits actually used in this way.)

For Western Samoa, data were available for 1983–84 on the distribution by sector of net profit for reinvestment, loan repayment, family upkeep, and sociocultural and "other" uses. These data showed that 29 percent of realized net profit in manufacturing was reinvested; while for the other leading sectors, 21 percent was for services, 32 percent for merchandising, and 13 percent for agrobusiness (Croulet and Sio 1986:139).

In the case study of Fiji, no clear pattern emerges from the evidence although only 50 percent of Fijian entrepreneurs saved any profits generated (Hailey 1985:80), which compares with 75 percent for Indians covered by the sample. This is not an impressive performance and, according to the survey, partly reflects a state of continuing "confusion" among Fijian entrepreneurs over the allocation of resources to meet business needs as opposed to social demands.

These fragments of information suggest that the practice of using business earnings for reinvestment is still undeveloped though there are some notable exceptions. While this practice has served to diminish the reinvestment capacity of an enterprise and hence its ability to expand, it also points to a significant potential for using business profits as a future source of funds for reinvestment. The realization of such a potential will depend on a variety of factors, including the attainment of greater entrepreneurial experience and sophistication and favorable trends in the capacity to generate profits.

Current problems

From the PIDP country studies, finance represents a leading constraint to the business life of indigenous entrepreneurs. Quantitative estimates available for three of the five countries surveyed provide an indication of the significance of finance as a constraint to the business. In the case of the Cook Islands, 19 out of 28 entrepreneurs admitted to experiencing "capital shortages," which, among other things, served to frustrate expansion plans (Fairbairn with Pearson 1987:109). For Tonga 72 percent of respondents stated that one of their three leading problems was related to finance (Ritterbush 1986:109).[3] For Western Samoa 43 percent of entrepreneurs perceived capital as a leading problem, and another 43 percent viewed it as a "moderate" problem (Croulet and Sio 1986:57).

The country studies provide a wealth of information about current problems facing entrepreneurs in the finance area, including narrow capital markets, stringent lending terms, inexperience in preparing loan applications and in approaching lending institutions, and lack of collateral with which to secure a loan. Poor access to outside finance due to inadequacies in existing capital markets is largely responsible for the widespread occurrence of undercapitalization. The result is that many entrepreneurs live a "hand-to-mouth" existence with respect to investment finance and suffer from the various symptoms of chronic undercapitalization. This struggle to survive all too often ends in failure.

As is evident from the surveys, considerable diversity exists among countries in the nature and severity of the problems and in the approaches used to address them. However, the comparative data can still be used to draw some major conclusions about the general financial situation of the region's indigenous entrepreneurs. The major conclusions, both general and specific, are as follows.

Major concerns

1. Narrow capital markets

The country surveys point to major inadequacies in the existing financial situation of indigenous entrepreneurs in gaining access to funds controlled by formal credit institutions. Several reasons are apparent. In most cases, indigenous entrepreneurs are constrained by the narrow range of lending facilities, essentially restricted to a development bank and one or two commercial banks. Opportunities to tap a variety of other lending sources such as those found in developed countries simply do not exist in the South Pacific.

In the case of Fiji and the Marshall Islands, a narrow range of facilities was not the sole factor responsible for their poor access to finance. In fact, both countries have a relatively diversified banking sector (Fiji has six commercial banks and the Marshall Islands three), as well as intermediaries such as insurance and finance companies. For Fiji, as noted earlier, indigenous entrepreneurs were judged to be handicapped not so much by a lack of access to outside finance as by a failure to prepare loan proposals that were acceptable to financial institutions. For the Marshall Islands "faulty" bank practices were said to be largely responsible for the "insufficiency of financial services" available to indigenous entrepreneurs (Carroll 1986:84).

Remote communities especially experience poorly developed financial facilities that restrict access to outside credit. However, in some cases, entrepreneurs have been able to compensate for this disadvantage. In the outlying island of Savai'i in Western Samoa, for example, entrepreneurs were able to obtain access to funds derived from other business activities, especially through the production of cash crops such as copra, taro, and bananas. Consequently, and somewhat paradoxically, capital was "more available" to them than to their urban counterparts in Apia who tended to be without alternative sources of business income (Croulet and Sio 1986:57).

The achievement of a more diverse financial structure depends on a variety of factors, including advanced levels of economic development, high per capita income, and a degree of monetization; but even small Pacific island countries have extensive scope for extending the range of financial facilities. In the case of the trading bank sector, circumstances may be conducive to the establishment of a new bank, as has recently occurred in the Cook Islands. (The Cook Islands government passed legislation converting the Cook Islands Development Bank into a central bank with power to carry out both development and commercial functions.)

In addition, the non-bank sector offers many opportunities for diversification. Those that seem to have the most potential include cooperative credit unions, savings and loan societies, and finance companies, as well as selected initiatives in the unorganized finance area such as individual money lenders. More sophisticated financial arrangements range from insurance companies, pension and retirement funds, building societies, leasing facilities, and discount houses to arrangements for securing access to equity capital. Some of these facilities (e.g., insurance and provident funds) are already in place in most of the island countries although the extent of these arrangements differs from country to country.

The existing financial institutions should be encouraged to become more actively involved in lending money to indigenous entrepreneurs. This is particularly relevant to trading banks whose role in this area tends to be characterized by rigid lending conventions established over time. Suggestions for encouraging more positive bank participation are outlined below, but existing practices can serve to severely penalize small indigenous businesses as opposed to large ventures, which are usually dominated by non-indigenous groups.

Access to outside finance can also be achieved by providing various special funds and facilities geared to the particular needs of indigenous entrepreneurs.

2. Development banks

Another area of concern revealed by the country studies relates specifically to the operation of development banks. Such banks are normally established by national governments to provide loans in priority areas as a means of promoting national development objectives. Apart from providing development finance, these institutions are also normally mandated to undertake complementary activities such as management training and technical advice, as well as equity capital, leasing, and loan guarantees. Special schemes can also be designed to serve the special needs of particular groups such as indigenous entrepreneurs.

The survey results show that development banks could be more effective in servicing the financial needs of indigenous entrepreneurs. Responses varied among countries, but a common complaint was that the development banks have neglected the needs of the indigenous entrepreneurs, and in this respect their behavior was viewed as similar to that of commercial banks.[4] In some cases (e.g., Western Samoa), respondents pointed out that a disproportionate share of the bank's loans had gone to a small number of large non-indigenous businesses (Croulet and Sio 1986:82). Estimates for Fiji show that between 1977 and 1983, only one-fourth of the money lent by the development bank for commercial and industrial ventures went to indigenous Fijians—which was considered to be a relatively small share (Hailey 1985:54).

Criticism of development banks for behaving essentially as trading banks was expressed by entrepreneurs in Fiji and the Marshall Islands. In Fiji it was said that the development bank showed more concern with generating a profit and ensuring regular repayments than with supporting ventures that promised to contribute to the national good as broadly conceived (Hailey 1985:54). For the Marshall Islands it was observed that the development bank was operating narrowly as a lending institution and was failing to carry out supporting advisory and training work (Carroll 1986:87).

Regarding mechanisms for lending, development banks were widely criticized for their processing procedures. The process of evaluating applications was lengthy and unnecessarily complicated. Repayment schedules for loans tended to be unrealistic and generally too short, while frequently the response to requests for rescheduling a loan was inflexible. Difficulties over repayment arrangements apply particularly to commercial farmers who cultivate long-term crops and who were expected to begin loan repayment before they could begin harvesting (Ritterbush 1986:61).

The country studies also show that many entrepreneurs feel that the interest rates charged by the development banks are too high. For Western Samoa an additional complaint was the marked disparity in the interest rates for agricultural and non-agricultural loans. This differential, ranging from 4 to 9 percent, was sufficiently high to generate criticism from non-agricultural entrepreneurs.

In consequence, some major areas need to be examined if development banks are to play their part in fostering indigenous businesses. Foremost are the needs to ensure that indigenous entrepreneurs obtain a fair share of loans, that loan procedures are simplified and accelerated, that realistic repayment schedules are designed (especially for commercial farmers), and that vital complementary advisory and technical services are provided, preferably in an integrated fashion (Carroll 1984:52). Development banks should also attempt to be more innovative in developing ways to relax existing collateral requirements and to intensify efforts to assist in the preparation of loan applications and the monitoring of projects once they reach the implementation phase. Finally, banks should encourage a greater use of loan guarantee facilities for entrepreneurs seeking loans from trading banks and related lending institutions.

3. Trading banks

The single most important financial institution in any country is the trading bank; these banks play a leading role both in providing investment funds and in facilitating the flow of business transactions. However, the country surveys revealed many criticisms of trading banks. In their lending activities, the banks were said to be "too restrictive" and "too stringent" and were accused of neglecting the small indigenous sector. Among the many specific sources of dissatisfaction cited were stringent collateral requirements, high interest rate charges, short repayment periods reinforced by strict requirements, and complicated application procedures. For indigenous entrepreneurs, all these factors, either individually or in combination, represent formidable barriers to gaining access to bank finance.

The bias against indigenous entrepreneurs was particularly evident among those respondents living on outer islands or in remote rural communities. Here, trading bank facilities either were limited to an occasional visit by bank officers from the central office or were non-existent. Thus the initial costs of these loans can be substantial because they usually require visits and/or protracted negotiations by mail.

The need for a diversified commercial banking structure was pointed out by entrepreneurs in Tonga and the Cook Islands, each of which had only one trading bank in operation. Entrepreneurs in Tonga referred to the absence of competition and its consequences, including a tendency to grant loans at levels below the legitimate finance needs of applicants (Ritterbush 1986:84). In the Cook Islands the disadvantage of having a commercial bank operating as a monopoly appeared to be widely felt and prompted many entrepreneurs to propose the establishment of a second bank (which is now in operation).

Granted, some of the complaints leveled at trading banks have to be treated with caution; but many are legitimate and point to the need for banks to play a more active part in providing development funds for indigenous businesses. This can be achieved through various means, but in their study of entrepreneurship in Western Samoa, Croulet and Sio (1986:79) suggest that one possibility is for trading banks to set aside a small share of their loan portfolio investment for small business loans. They also see the merit of overcoming strict collateral requirements by means of loan guarantees, which government or multilateral agencies can provide.

Trading banks can be encouraged to play a more positive role in other ways. These include a simplification of loan application procedures (and application forms written in the vernacular), more flexible collateral requirements, and improved outreach facilities for outer islands and remote communities. Trading bank performance in these areas is often improved by competition so that, where circumstances are favorable, possibilities for increasing the number of banks should be explored.

4. Special arrangements

The country studies elicited opinions on how the credit needs of indigenous entrepreneurs might be better served by the special schemes and facilities. Where these needs are not being adequately met, the establishment of such schemes can diversify the credit base for small indigenous businesses. One such scheme already exists in Fiji in the form of the Industrial and Commercial Loans to Fijians Scheme (CLFS) established in 1975 within the development bank to make special loans to Fijians. (However, it appears that CLFS has been rendered ineffective through insufficient funds.)

Among the various proposals formulated in the country studies are those to establish special funding schemes. For Tonga, Ritterbush (1986:135) argues for the introduction of three special funds: one to assist small farmers in purchasing tax allotments or subleasing farmland; another to provide loan finance to be used as collateral to obtain loans; and the third to be designated for small business grants. In the case of Fiji, Hailey (1985:107) sees merit in a compulsory savings scheme for Fijians as a source of additional investment.

Other opportunities include improving guarantee facilities as noted above. Government-owned agencies, including the development banks, can play an important part as guarantors. Various kinds of loan syndication schemes are an additional possibility. In Western Samoa, Croulet and Sio (1986:57) suggest that surplus church funds might be examined as a potential source of credit for indigenous entrepreneurs.

Finally, the obviously important role of informal sources of finance should be recognized and actively supported where they have proved to be particularly useful. From the limited evidence, it is apparent that many forms of informal credit practices are in operation, some of which could be upgraded as effective financing mechanisms.

Concluding comments

As is clear from the above analysis, access to outside finance is obstructed by several factors: limited credit institutions, stringent bank lending practices, lack of suitable collateral for loans, failure to prepare loan submissions in a manner acceptable to the banks, and remoteness in the case of outer islands and rural communities. Given these problems, indigenous entrepreneurs have been forced —particularly in the initial stages—to rely heavily on their own financial resources—a condition that all too often leads to under-capitalization and subsequent business failure.

If indigenous entrepreneurs are to have improved access to out-side finance, appropriate remedial measures must be directed at both widening the range of credit facilities and removing the unwarranted obstacles presented by the existing financial institu-tions. Because development and trading banks have a crucial posi-tion in relation to the supply of loans, priority should be given to their lending policies. Outside the formal banking sector, other ini-tiatives can improve the access to development finance. In some cases (e.g., guarantee facilities), such initiatives can be imple-mented with relative ease and little cost.

NOTES

1. The number of sample entrepreneurs studied totaled 44 in the Cook Islands, 80 in Fiji, 86 in the Marshall Islands, 185 in Tonga, and 70 in Western Samoa.

2. Coexisting with these leading institutions normally are a central bank authority, post office savings, and insurance agencies. Usually, several smaller institutions are also found, many of which operate in the unorganized finance sector.

3. In this case, the expression "financial difficulties" covers a wider range of problems than is true of the Cook Islands and Western Samoa studies. For Tonga the expression includes not only problems of capital shortage and lack of access to outside financial institutions but also problems connected with "poor investment" and "mismanagement of funds" (Ritterbush 1986:109).

4. However, one study of Western Samoa's development bank is critical of the bank's "heavy emphasis on small loans," most of which have been made to indigenous growers, fishermen, and village groups (Carroll 1984:52). According to the study, such loans have been bedeviled by a high rate of default and entail high fixed handling costs.

References

Carroll, J.
1986 *Entrepreneurship and Indigenous Businesses in the Republic of the Marshall Islands,* Pacific Islands Development Program, East-West Center, Honolulu.

Carroll, P. G. H.
1984 *The Development Bank of Western Samoa: A Profile,* Working Paper No. 39, Development Studies Centre, Australian National University Press, Canberra.

Croulet, C. R. and L. Sio
1986 *Indigenous Entrepreneurship in Western Samoa,* Pacific Islands Development Program, East-West Center, Honolulu.

Fairbairn, Te'o I. J. with J. Pearson
1987 *Entrepreneurship in the Cook Islands,* Pacific Islands Development Program, East-West Center, Honolulu.

Finney, B. R.
1973 *Big-Men and Business: Entrepreneurship and Economic Growth in the New Guinea Highlands,* University Press of Hawaii, Honolulu.
1987 *Business Development in the Highlands of Papua New Guinea,* Research Report Series No. 6, Pacific Islands Development Program, East-West Center, Honolulu.

Hailey, J. M.
1985 *Indigenous Business in Fiji,* Pacific Islands Development Program, East-West Center, Honolulu.

Johns, B. L., W. C. Dunlop, and W. J. Sheehan
1983 *Small Business in Australia–Problems and Prospects,* George Allen and Unwin, Sydney.

Nafziger, E. W.
  1978 *Class, Caste and Entrepreneurship: A Study of Indian Industrialists,*
        University of Hawaii Press, Honolulu.
Ritterbush, S. D.
  1986 *Entrepreneurship and Business Venture Development in the Kingdom of
        Tonga,* Pacific Islands Development Program, East-West Center, Hono-
        lulu.

CHAPTER 11

Finance for Indigenous Enterprises: The Case of Fiji and the Fiji Development Bank

Laisenia Qarase

THE EXTREMELY low rate of participation by indigenous Fijians in business is a well-known feature of the Fiji economy and one that is of considerable concern to the government. The reasons for this situation are manifold and complex and, as shown in Hailey's chapter on Fiji, they embrace historical, cultural, and educational factors as well as economic ones. However, two broad categories of constraints seem to be foremost in obstructing Fijian entrepreneurship. The first is the lack of business expertise that can be largely explained by limited experience, exposure, and know-how. The second is lack of monetary capital stemming from inadequacies in existing financial institutions, on the one hand, and a failure on the part of Fijians to take advantage of existing facilities, on the other.

This chapter examines the type and level of financing that are presently available to Fijians. The focus is on the role of the Fiji Development Bank (FDB) in the administration of certain preferential schemes to foster Fijian entrepreneurship. Lessons are drawn from Fiji's experience that may have a broader interest.

Sources of finance for Fijian entrepreneurs

Indigenous entrepreneurs in many recently independent countries often lack sufficient funds to implement seemingly viable projects. Therefore, loan finance is an essential ingredient for the finance package required for a business venture.

In Fiji institutional credit is available from several major sources, but funds for business enterprises are primarily confined

227

to the five commercial banks and the FDB. As of 30 June 1986 the commercial banks and the FDB had a current loan portfolio of $469 million equivalent to 43 percent of the total institutional credit outstanding at that date.[1] Most of the remaining institutional credit is made up by loans given through the Fiji National Provident Fund (FNPF), which had an outstanding loan portfolio of $561 million as of 30 June 1986. Sixty-seven percent of the FNPF's loan portfolio is invested in securities and in government, statutory, and non-statutory bonds; the remaining loans are nearly all for real estate development.

Fijians and other sections of the population have equal access to finance from both the commercial banks and the FDB. Only the FDB, however, has finance that is explicitly earmarked for Fijians and generally available with more flexible terms and conditions than that provided by commercial banks. Observers of the credit market in Fiji estimate that Fijians receive an extremely small proportion of finance from sources other than the FDB. Common problems confront indigenous entrepreneurs throughout the Pacific when they seek to obtain loans from the commercial markets. These include (1) difficulty in completing loan application forms together with supporting financial projects and viability analyses; (2) lack of securities that are acceptable to the commercial banks; and (3) stringent loan terms and conditions including repayment periods and interest rates.

As a result, development banks can help in the areas of project identification, feasibility studies, and loan applications. Special loan schemes can provide certain concessions such as lower interest rates, more flexible repayment terms, easier security requirements, and government guarantees.

Before a description is given of the concessionary loan schemes for Fijians implemented by the FDB, the FDB's general strategy, its objectives, and its constraints in a small economy are outlined.

Fiji Development Bank: strategy and objectives

The FDB was established by an Act of Parliament (Government of Fiji 1967) on 1 July 1967 following the FDB Ordinance of 1966. The bank is an autonomous statutory body with its own board of directors whose members are appointed by the minister of finance.

Paragraph five of the Act (Government of Fiji 1967) states that the FDB's overall policy directive is "to facilitate and stimulate the promotion and development of natural resources, transportation, and other industries in Fiji and in the discharge of these functions the bank shall give special consideration and priority to the economic development of the rural and agricultural sectors of the economy of Fiji."

The bank coordinates its operations within government policy as outlined in current development plans. At present the emphasis is on employment creation, foreign exchange savings, diversification of the economy, the reduction of income disparities, and the utilization of domestic raw materials. The bank uses four main instruments to attain these policy goals:

1. Direct, short-, medium-, and long-term lending, with subsidized interest rates currently ranging from 7 to 12.5 percent, with the degree of subsidization biased toward rural and agricultural lending.
2. Indirect assistance (through equity participation, guarantees, and underwritings) to stimulate investment in key areas where cash and asset liquidity are particularly short and immobile.
3. Subsidization of industrial and commercial loans to indigenous Fijians, currently by 1 percent in line with government's objective to create a racially equitable participation in commerce and industry.
4. Identification, appraisal, and direct implementation of investments that temporarily lack funds but that are judged to be in the national interest.

Fijian participation in the FDB loan portfolio is examined later in this chapter. Regarding loans in industry and commerce as of 31 December 1985, Fijians accounted for 856 out of 1,567 loans outstanding or 55 percent. However, in value terms, the picture is somewhat different, with Fijians claiming $7 million out of total loans outstanding of $45.6 million. In this sector, therefore, Fijians are poorly represented and average approximately $8,200 in loans compared with corresponding figures of $50,300 for Fiji-Indians and $70,000 for other races.

A major characteristic of Fijian loans is a high concentration in transportation, wholesale, and retail sectors—which combined account for 77 percent of the number and 47 percent of the value of total Fijian industrial loans. Specifically, most Fiji loans in this sector are for one- or two-person businesses such as a small taxi or retail operations. In contrast, Fijians are poorly represented in primary and secondary manufacturing activities. Only 24 percent of the number and 4 percent of the value of outstanding loans in this category are Fijian.

In carrying out its mandate, the FDB has not been free of criticism. This has been commented upon by other chapter authors in this volume (Fairbairn in Chapter 10). Among the perceived shortcomings are a failure to provide continuing support and advice, loan evaluation procedures that are too long and complicated, loan terms that are too stringent, and a general tendency to behave too much as a commercial bank. The FDB has also been criticized for being "racial" (Hailey 1985:54). The FDB has been addressing these aspects although it feels that some criticisms are ill based. It acknowledges that the advice and supervision given to many clients are inadequate (particularly those clients with smaller loans) in remote areas, and with little prior commercial experience. This situation is largely the result of the bank's lack of resources to cater to an increasing number of loan accounts.

Loan evaluation procedures are more detailed than those of commercial banks, which are concerned solely with repayment capability and have tight security requirements. The FDB also is concerned with the developmental elements of credit and thus is more prepared to lend for projects of marginal viability, to provide more relaxed terms of credit including security, and to reschedule accounts in difficulties. Clearly, less detailed appraisals are appropriate for smaller projects.

The criticism of racism is unjustified. In fact, in making loans, the bank focuses on project viability, developmental goals, and governmental policies with regard to particular encouragement to would-be indigenous Fijian entrepreneurs.

Preferential finance for indigenous Fijians is channeled through the FDB in two schemes:

1. The Industrial and Commercial Loans to Fijians Scheme
2. The Joint Venture Loans Scheme

These two schemes had an outstanding loan balance of $8.24 million at the end of June 1986. Approvals for the 1985–86 financial year totaled $3.19 million for the two schemes, equivalent to 15.7 percent of the value of the bank's loans for industrial and commercial purposes during that year.

In addition, agricultural finance, which will be discussed later, has been particularly focused on the development of Fijians in rural settings; in certain ways it can be judged to have had greater success than the small-scale projects under the Industrial and Commercial Loans to Fijians Scheme.

The Industrial and Commercial Loans to Fijians Scheme

In May 1975 the FDB established the Industrial and Commercial Loans to Fijians Scheme (CLFS) in response to a cabinet subcommittee directive to make special loans available to Fijians. The impetus behind the scheme was the lack of Fijian participation in the commercial and business sectors of the economy. It was felt that special credit facilities, which were subsidized and which could be given extra attention and supervision, would help to encourage indigenous Fijians to play a more active part in commerce and industry.

The scheme caters to indigenous Fijians who are registered in the Native Land Owners Register and to indigenous Rotumans. One-hundred percent-owned Fijian and/or Rotuman partnerships, companies, and cooperatives are similarly covered.

When the scheme was originally established, it was purported to offer four additional advantages over the bank's normal industrial and commercial lending guidelines:

1. Loans are available for a wider range of business opportunities including
   - Purchase of buildings and machinery
   - Purchase of existing businesses
   - Purchase by cooperatives of houses and flats for rent
   - Financing of working capital
   - Guarantee of repayment of loans to Fijians when finance is available from other sources.
2. Interest rates charged are lower than under the bank's industrial and commercial lending policy. The rate is currently subsidized by at least 1 percent.
3. For some types of lending the repayment period is extended.

General guidelines for repayment periods are as follows:

- For working capital, the period of repayment should not exceed three years.
- For loans to finance machinery and equipment, the repayment term should not exceed the reasonable working life of the machinery, with a maximum of ten years.
- For the acquisition or construction of a factory or other buildings, the repayment term should not exceed 20 years depending upon the age of the building and type of construction.
- For loans to be used for the purchase of shares in a business, the repayment period should not exceed ten years.
- For new utilities, vans and trucks can be financed only in exceptional circumstances and the repayment term should be short.
- For new buses, the repayment term should not exceed six years, and for reconditioned buses the term would be up to four years.
- For marine engines, the repayment term depends upon the nature of the engine being purchased, but for outboard motors the term shall not exceed 18 months.

4. The bank is able to adopt a more flexible policy toward security requirements. The difference between the client's security, as valued by the bank, and the loan amount is guaranteed by the Fiji government up to $50,000.

Since the introduction of the scheme, annual loan approvals peaked in the year ending 30 June 1980 when 546 loans were approved valued at $3 million. The following year approvals dropped substantially and have remained at an average of 325 approvals per year for the three years from 1983 to 1986 with an average value of $1.9 million per year. At the end of the 1985–86 financial year the CLFS had an outstanding loan portfolio of $8.24 million covering 1,231 accounts, which was seven and 14 percent of the total value and number, respectively, of FDB's outstanding portfolio.

The CLFS has encouraged a large number of Fijian individuals to seek small loans. For Fijian individual clients as opposed to Fijian-owned companies, the value of industrial and commercial loans outstanding on 30 June 1986 was $5.8 million, which was 71 percent of the total loans outstanding in the CLFS. The number of Fijian individual clients in the scheme at that date was 865. Fiji-Indian individuals had only 469 industrial and commercial accounts but a total value of $16.6 million. Therefore, the average loan size for Fiji-Indians was $35,529 whereas that for Fijians was much smaller at $6,764.

Industrial and commercial loans are given for the following purposes: primary and secondary manufacturing, construction, logging, transportation, wholesale and retailing, beverages and tobacco, hotels and catering, and other services. Fijian individual clients have a strong preference for loans in the transportation and wholesale and retailing sectors, with 76 percent of the number and 47 percent of the value of total outstanding individual loans in the scheme in these categories as of 30 June 1986. By comparison, Fiji-Indian individual clients had 47 percent and 35 percent of the number and value of Fiji-Indian industrial and commercial loans in these categories. Therefore, the average Fijian loan size in these two categories was $4,197 compared with $26,405 for Fiji-Indians and $31,280 for other races. This reflects the fact that most loans to Fijian individuals are for small enterprises such as small taxi and retail operations.

Another difference worth highlighting is in the primary and secondary manufacturing categories where Fijians are poorly represented in terms of both number and value. Only 40 out of 167 manufacturing loans (or 23 percent) were owned by Fijian individuals whereas 112 were owned by Fiji-Indians. In value terms, Fijian individual loans consisted of $332,000, which is only 4 percent of the total value of manufacturing loans at $8.3 million.

Thus Fijian individuals have more than a proportionate share in terms of the number of the total loans outstanding for industry and commerce, but most of these loans are small and invested in the transport and wholesaling and retailing sectors, which are now showing a fairly high degree of saturation in many areas. In addition, Fijian participation in manufacturing is negligible.

The CLFS has had its share of problems. A high proportion of the bank's accounts in arrears and bad debts written off originate in the scheme. Of the total bank arrears as of 31 December 1986, 18 percent by number and 12 percent by value were in the CLFS (compared with 14 and 7 percent of the number and value of loans outstanding).

The bad debts written-off under the scheme have averaged $300,000 per year over the three years to 1986. Seventy-eight percent of the value of total bad debt write-offs in 1985–86 were under the CLFS. From the bank's point of view, this scheme is costly, and severe doubts must exist about its developmental value when many clients are left with less than they had initially and with their entrepreneurial spirit somewhat destroyed.

Providing a taxi (or other capital assets) for a client who has no business experience and is not accustomed to planning and managing the cash needs of running a taxi and repaying regular installments may not be beneficial to the client unless there is some supervision in the early stages of the project. The lack of monetization and business experience of those people coming from a rural subsistence way of life cannot be overlooked. Therefore, in addition to providing concessionary credit for projects that are appraised and found financially viable, supervision and training by some agency are crucial in these situations.

The Joint Venture Loans Scheme, discussed below, recognizes this training need and seeks to cater to those people introduced to business management for the first time.

Joint Venture Loans Scheme

The Joint Venture Loans Scheme (JVLS) as announced in the 1984 budget was designed to enhance Fijian participation in business with that of other races. The scheme aims to assist joint ventures between Fijians and non-Fijians so that Fijians are able to combine their resources with those of non-Fijians who already have business experience. The scheme supplements the CLFS and broadly follows existing FDB lending policies but has certain advantages:

1. Loans are available for a much wider range of business opportunities. With the exception of retail and wholesale business, loans can be obtained for almost all types of industrial and commercial ventures assessed by the bank to be economically and technically viable and financially profitable.
2. Finance is available for up to 80 percent of the project cost provided that 80 percent of the total project cost does not exceed $200,000.

3. The Fijian partner can obtain equity capital finance in addition to the partnership's joint venture loan.

To qualify for a loan, a company or partnership must have a minimum of 25 percent Fijian shareholding or interest. As with the CLFS, the bank takes particular note of the structure and quality of the management proposed for the venture so as to ensure its success. Four special conditions are attached to loans from the JVLS:

1. No reduction can occur in the shareholding/interest held by the Fijian partner(s) during the currency of the loan without the bank's consent.
2. A Fijian shareholder who becomes a director of the enterprise will remain so until the bank agrees to his/her retirement, resignation, or removal from the board.
3. Companies or partnerships borrowing more than $100,000 are to submit audited accounts to the bank at the end of each financial year.
4. Formal management and employment contracts require approval by the bank.

In the three years of its operation to 30 June 1986, the JVLS had approved a total of 23 loans valued at $2.9 million. It is too early to effectively review the scheme, but one promising sign is that the average size of manufacturing loans over the three years is $148,000, which indicates that the scheme is enabling Fijians to become involved in a more sophisticated range of industrial activities.

The emphasis of approval has been on the manufacturing sectors. Eighty-eight percent of the total value of loans—$2.53 million—approved under the scheme since its inception has been in the manufacturing sectors, which include food processing. The idea behind the scheme is that where Fijians are unable as individuals to become involved in business, they can profit by becoming managers and part owners of businesses. Part ownership is considered a first stage in developing entrepreneurial experience through the participation of Fijians in working partnerships with people of other races. In this way, a level of Fijian business ownership is secured, and the appropriate business skills are developed as the

venture proceeds. One result is a mechanism that can enable preferential finance to be linked to a particular business experience
leading to successful enterprise.

Agriculture credit for Fijians

Fijians are well represented in borrowing for agricultural and fishing purposes, with 59 percent or 3,391 out of the 5,669 total agricultural and fishing accounts outstanding being Fijian as of 31
December 1986. In terms of value of accounts outstanding, 55
percent or $17.5 million out of $31.8 million are in Fijian
accounts.

In three subsectors Fijians have a fewer number of accounts
than other ethnic groups. These are in tobacco and vegetable
growing and dairy farming. Fijians are particularly well represented in livestock and fishing sectors where 71 percent of
accounts by number is Fijian. The average loan size for Fijian agricultural and fishing loans as of that date, 31 December 1987, was
$5,161 compared with $5,936 for Fiji-Indians and $10,314 for
other races.

Thus Fijians have a high degree of participation in agriculture
and fishing loans in relation to their share in the national population, though they also tend to have smaller loans on average than
other races. Some of this participation is because agricultural
schemes with special management supervision have been initiated
by the government to encourage Fijian farmers and fishermen to
develop cash-generating activities. The two main types of projects
have been cattle schemes and seaweed farming, which are described below.

Yalavou beef scheme

This scheme is one of two involving the development of Fijian
native land and is designed to increase Fijian participation in commercial agriculture, to narrow the growing divergence of wealth
between rural and urban sectors, and to substitute local beef for
imported beef.

The Yalavou beef scheme is an integrated rural development
project and involves the establishment of beef and goat farms, a

model farm, a community center, and roads, together with a large technical assistance input. The scheme is funded by the Australian and Fiji governments, with the FDB funding the individual farm development costs including purchase of stock, fencing, pasture development, etc., up to $1.65 million. The FDB uses the subsidized interest rates available for all agricultural loans.

As of 31 December 1986, the FDB has approved loans to 99 farmers valued at $1.43 million with $0.27 million undrawn. Accounts in arrears numbered 37 and totaled $23,773 at that date. Farmer performance has been below budget, and efforts are being made to improve herd numbers on both beef and goat farms.

Of the 99 individual farms established, there are 74 beef farms of 234 hectares each, 21 specialist goat farms, and four specialist cash crop farms. The construction of a kindergarten, a fully equipped nursing station with more than 140 km of road, and other infrastructural facilities have been completed. Unused land has been opened up, and the standard of living has improved for the people of Yalavou.

Seaweed projects

Loans of up to $3,000 are available for the purchase of a new boat and/or outboard motor for the purpose of cultivating seaweed. To be eligible for the loan finance, the applicant must be a bona fide seaweed farmer with a valid seaweed farming contract with Coast Biologicals (Fiji) Ltd. To obtain a loan, the seaweed farmer needs to contribute 20 percent of the loan. The balance is provided as a grant by the government and aid agencies. The usual concessionary interest rate of 8 percent is charged for all loans, and the repayment is amortized over 18 months with a grace period of six months. Payment is made by an assignment over the sale proceeds of the seaweed to the purchasing company and must not be less than 20 percent of gross sale proceeds. Security is a bill of sale on the boat, engine, and chattles plus assignment.

As of 1 March 1987, 75 loans totaling $212,319 had been approved to seaweed farmers, and the total area under cultivation was 17 hectares. Accounts in arrears numbered 35. Some farmers had their crops devastated by rough seas brought on by Cyclone Raja in 1986, and consequently many farmers chose to delay their

replanting until after the hurricane season. Also the appraisal
failed to take fully into account the socioeconomic situation and
preferences of farmers and assumed that they would wish to cultivate more than in fact they do; thus at present production levels,
the agreed minimum of 20 percent of gross sale proceeds is not
sufficient to pay off the loan. Supervision is also lower than
planned, with the agencies concerned unable to provide the agreed
necessary assistance due to staff constraints.

Despite these problems, which resulted in lower production
than predicted and insufficient repayment, farmers are now receiving a cash income and have an improved standard of living. They
have been provided with resources to enter the cash economy
without experiencing severe disruption to their way of life.

Lessons for development banks from the Fiji experience

A study was made of all loans written-off by the bank from January 1985 to December 1985. The number of Fijian loans written-
off during this period was 66, which was 88 percent of the total
number; the value of write-offs for Fijian loans was $502,333,
which was 86.6 percent of the total value written-off. Thus the
level of write-off of Fijian accounts was greatly in excess of their
proportionate participation in the FDB portfolio.

The study attributed the reasons for account failure. Thirteen
categories of reasons were used, and each written-off account was
given a score of six points to be allocated among the categories
according to the reason for failure. The three highest scoring categories were lack of maintenance, lack of commitment/loss of
interest, and inexperience; these categories accounted for over 60
percent of the reasons for failure among Fijian accounts.

These findings suggest that preferential finance available
through the FDB encourages Fijians to become involved in new
enterprises that require a certain level of support, advice, and
supervision that is not adequately being provided. Provision of
credit alone does not always encourage successful Fijian entrepreneurship.

Another lesson of the Fiji experience is that there must be a full
detailed project appraisal by the bank before granting credit. If the
client is not experienced, the bank cannot assume that the finan-

cial figures provided by the client are accurate and must necessarily be more thorough in its appraisal than when it deals with experienced professional entrepreneurs who would not undertake a project unless it were to be profitable and unless they were willing to put in the hours that they know will be required.

In the appraisal a full account must be taken of the socioeconomic context of the client and of the client's aims in undertaking the project. From the suggestions with regard to seaweed farming, the aim of clients may not be to maximize profit but rather to provide themselves with some cash income to meet certain cash needs. Taxis and small-scale retail operations receive small returns for extremely long hours, which may be unattractive relative to the subsistence farming alternatives available to many Fijians. The study found that loss of interest/lack of commitment relates directly to an unrealistic assessment by the client of the costs and benefits involved in the project.

In addition, the prior experience of cash management and business experience must be noted together with the availability of training and supervision—both financial and technical. Both seaweed farming and beef and goat farming are technical operations requiring advice and supervision. The need for financial management skills was recognized in the establishment of the JVLS to provide training for new Fijian business clients. For smaller-scale clients the FDB has set up a Management Advisory Service Department to help with the bookkeeping; however, the poor performance of Fijians in the small-scale commercial sectors clearly shows that greater technical assistance must be provided if they are to succeed.

Projects such as the seaweed and cattle projects—in providing the concessionary finance available for agricultural and fishing loans together with technical and financial supervision—are promoting development in the rural areas for people in their own environment. The seaweed project in particular allows people to remain in their home and village, continue with the same lifestyles, and yet enter into commercial activities. Despite the problems mentioned, which relate primarily to weaknesses in the appraisal and the lack of supervision, this project has raised the quality of life by enabling people to earn some cash so that they are better able to satisfy basic needs. Similarly, the Yalavou project has involved the provision of beef protein, health facilities, and educational facilities, as well as road access, which has opened up the areas for all inhabitants.

Finally, experience with regard to the urban commercial loans to Fijians suggests greater caution is required. Perhaps the bank has gone too fast in providing easy credit without ensuring that the client really understands all the costs involved in terms of time, hard work, money, and lack of family support and without providing the client with the requisite cash management skills. The client is often new to commercial activities and lacks the support system that exists in village life. Thus developmental agencies must provide effective guidance in new industrial and commercial enterprises to ensure that the credit provided does not incur a burden but rather promotes development and improves the lives of the clients.

Concluding remarks

In Fiji two races make up the majority of the population in almost equal proportions, and both races should be well represented in the various economic sectors. The schemes for preferential finance for indigenous Fijians, together with the loans in the government agricultural development schemes discussed above, have released credit to encourage a greater participation for indigenous Fijians in commercial activity.

Some of this credit has been used productively, some less so. The need for full detailed project appraisals, including the socioeconomic context and the prior experience of the client, is crucial. However, this chapter argues that the most important issue that needs to be more comprehensively treated by the bank and by others is the provision of training, advice, and regular technical and financial supervision for clients undertaking new ventures. This is the challenge now facing all those concerned with increasing indigenous Fijian participation in commercial enterprises.

Note

1. Throughout this chapter values are expressed in Fiji dollars. The exchange rates against the Fiji dollar for the relevant years are as follows: U.S. dollar

0.8065 for 30 June 1980; 0.8797 for 30 June 1986; and 0.8983 for 1 March 1987; the corresponding Australia dollar rates are 0.9325, 1.3091, and 1.3266.

REFERENCES

Government of Fiji
1966 *Census of Population 1966*, Bureau of Statistics, Suva.
1967 *Act of Parliament 1967*, The Laws of Fiji, Vol. XII. Government Printer, Suva.
1982 Fiji Employment/Unemployment Survey, Bureau of Statistics, Suva.
1985 *Fiji's Ninth Development Plan 1986–1990: Policies, Strategies and Programmes for National Development*, Central Planning Office, Suva.

Hailey, John M.
1985 *Indigenous Business in Fiji*, Pacific Islands Development Program, East-West Center, Honolulu.

CHAPTER 12

Government Policy in Support of Small Business Development in Australia

William James Sheehan

THERE are about 500,000 small firms in Australia, excluding those in agriculture, and they account for more than 40 percent of private sector employment.[1] They are, for the most part, relatively labor intensive and tend to generate more jobs per unit of capital invested than do larger firms.

The basis for government policies in relation to the small business sector is, broadly, that a vigorous and efficient small business sector is important to the economic and social health of Australia. It is argued that small firms are worth some encouragement because they have fewer needs for publicly provided infrastructure, they often use less energy in their operating processes, they usually have fewer adverse effects on the environment, and they often can locate closer to their markets and thus may have lower transportation costs.

In more general terms, small businesses provide a wider range of consumer choice and a more personalized level of service, their presence frequently results in a more competitive (and presumably more efficient) economic climate, they are essential for the provision of certain goods and services (market is too small or fragmented for large firms), and they provide an opportunity for enterprising people to exercise their talents and perhaps to develop entrepreneurial and technological innovations.

Unfortunately, the small business sector also faces problems and disadvantages. The major problem is related to the diffusion (or lack) of managerial skills within the firm. The Wiltshire Committee defined a small business as one in which:

> . . . one or two persons are required to make all the critical management decisions—finance, accounting, personnel, purchasing,

processing or servicing, marketing, selling—without the aid of
internal specialists, and with specific knowledge in only one or two
functional areas (Wiltshire 1971:11).

The result is often that one or more of these functions is not carried out skillfully, and the development and even the survival of
the small firm may be threatened. In a large firm the various functions can be spread among several persons each with appropriate
training and experience. The managers of a small business can, of
course, consult professional experts, but such consultations are
often expensive and may not be available at the time and place
they are required.

The disadvantages faced by the small business sector include (1)
lack of market power; (2) inability to exploit economies of scale;
and (3) the impact of government charges, regulations, and
administrative practices. Lack of market power may show itself in
difficulties of access to institutional credit facilities, an inability to
force debtors to pay promptly while not being able to delay payment to creditors, and difficulties in dealing with suppliers in relation to, for example, prices, delivery, quality, and range of goods
and services purchased.

An inability to exploit economies of scale may result from the
small absolute size of the market or from the size of the minor part
of it available to the small firm. In either case, the ability to compete with larger firms, either domestic or foreign, is impaired.
Where government charges (such as a license fee) or government
regulations (such as building standards) apply equally to both
small and large firms, there is likely to be an adverse differential
impact on the small firm.

For example, some government administrative practices related
to the purchase of goods and services seem to be quite disadvanta-
geous to the small business sector. Many government departments
and agencies buy only (or mainly) from a short list of potential
suppliers, and small firms often find it difficult to secure a place on
the list. Moreover, even when a sale is made to a government
body, the delay in receiving payment may be prolonged. This, as
remarked above, places a greater strain on the finances of small
firms than on those of larger businesses so that many small firms
are effectively limited in their access to the public sector markets.

One of the main aims of government policy in Australia in relation to small business development is to promote programs of assistance to help solve these problems and to alleviate the disadvantages. These policies are not generally aimed at treating the small business sector as a privileged part of the business community. Rather, the aim is to provide a range of facilities to help with efficient operation and development, which would be beyond the capacity of any individual firm to provide for itself.

Before the main features of the policies and programs are outlined, six preliminary points should be made:

1. All of the programs have suffered from a lack of publicity. This has resulted from a lack of money for this purpose and has meant that many small businessmen (particularly those in non-metropolitan areas) are unaware of available services and facilities.

2. Most programs are administered by state government agencies, and their impact seems to have been very uneven across Australia. New South Wales, Victoria, and Western Australia seem to have been the most active states and Tasmania the least active.

3. In addition to policies aimed at individual firms and potential entrepreneurs, there is also a research policy. Most research is carried out by the federal government through the Bureau of Industry Economics, but there is some research activity by state organizations, usually on matters of local significance.

4. Few of the government-sponsored programs of assistance are aimed at solving the problems or alleviating the disadvantages flowing from more general government policies—such as taxation and other fiscal measures, or the costs of publicly supplied goods and services or government regulations of an administrative or executive nature. This observation is also true of trade union policies. The responses (if any) of the small business sector to problems and disadvantages arising from these policies evidently arise from within the small business sector itself.

5. Criteria for judging the effectiveness of policies toward small firms have not yet been developed. This is principally because the ultimate aims of such policies have not been defined. Are they to encourage the emergence of more small firms? To help small firms to survive? Or to help them to grow?

6. It is not always easy to decide to which firms a particular policy or program should be applied. The question is one of the definition of a "small business" for the purpose at hand. There are no universally agreed upon criteria. Employment size (sometimes

including working proprietors, sometimes excluding them) is widely used, but this varies between states and between industries.

In Western Australia, for example, eligibility to participate in the state's programs of assistance for small businesses is apparently confined to those that are legally independent, are managed personally by the major investors, have a relatively small share of their market, and employ fewer than 20 people. In Victoria, on the other hand, a small firm seems to be defined mainly in terms of employment—less than 100 in manufacturing industry and less than 20 in non-manufacturing. In New South Wales some programs of financial assistance are not available to very small firms, usually those with fewer than five employees. This is evidently used as a rationing device but may be justified on the grounds that such firms have not yet shown a potential for survival and growth.

Policies and programs of state governments

Each of the states (New South Wales, Victoria, Queensland, South Australia, Western Australia, and Tasmania) and both territories (Northern Territory and Australian Capital Territory) have a policy of government assistance for small business and a series of programs designed to implement those policies. The federal government also has a policy and programs though, as indicated earlier and discussed below, the federal government's activities in this field differ from those of the states.

Some of the state organizations (e.g., the Office of Small Business in New South Wales) form part of the regular public service structure and report directly to a ministerial head. Others (e.g., the Small Business Development Corporation in Victoria) are statutory authorities and are not part of the formal public service structure. They report to a board as well as to a minister and, through this office, to state parliament. In Queensland the organization dealing with small business policy in the manufacturing industry is of the former type (it is the Department of Commercial and Industrial Development), but the organization dealing with tertiary industry is of the latter type (it is the Small Business Development Corporation). The advantage claimed for the statutory corporation is that it can more easily employ people of proven experience and mature years, especially where a limited-term contract of employment is desired by both parties.

Objectives

The objectives of the state organizations are sometimes set out quite briefly and sometimes outlined in detail. An example of the former may be found in Tasmania where the objectives of the Small Business Advisory Service are "The provision of counselling, information and referral services to small business enterprises and intending starters in business." By contrast, the objectives of the Small Business Corporation of South Australia (Government of Australia, n.d.) are stated more extensively and are as follows:

> Together with the relevant sectors of government, industry, commerce, and education to encourage expansion of long-term employment opportunities, strengthen the economic base of the state, develop a favorable investment climate, ensure effective use of labor and technical skills, and develop new products and markets. (In particular) the functions of the Corporation are:
>
> (a) to provide advice to persons engaged in, or proposing to establish, small businesses;
> (b) to promote awareness of the value of proper management practices in the conduct of small businesses and to promote, coordinate and, if necessary, conduct training and educational programs relating to the management of small businesses;
> (c) to disseminate information for the guidance of persons engaged in, or proposing to establish, small businesses;
> (d) to monitor the effect upon small business of the policies, practices and laws of the Governments of the state and Commonwealth and local government and to advise and make representations to those governments as to the interests of small business;
> (e) to consult and cooperate with persons and bodies representative of small business and, where appropriate, represent their views to governments;
> (f) to provide financial assistance to small businesses by way of the guarantee of loans or the making of grants;
> (g) generally, to promote and assist the development of the small business sector of the state's economy.

The first part of this statement of objectives is a reasonable outline of the broad parameters within which all the state organizations seek to operate. The second part is a reasonable outline of
the nature of the specific programs that most, though not necessarily all, state organizations seek to implement. To this end, they
all have policies on advisory services, education and training,
finance, promotion and publications, and the establishment of
committees for various purposes.

Advisory services

Advisory services are of two main kinds—counseling and consultancies. Counseling is available, usually free of charge, to owners
of existing small firms and to potential starters. It is available by
personal interview, by telephone, or by correspondence. In all
states, the small business organization is located in the capital city
(though some states have regional offices), and visits to country
towns are made either regularly or as required.

Counseling has proved to be very popular. By way of example,
in Victoria there were 1,748 inquiries in 1976–77, the first year of
operation of the Small Business Development Corporation. By
1980–81 the number of inquiries had increased to 7,500 and in
1984–85 to nearly 22,000. Just over one-half of these were from
existing businesses and just under half from new starters. Just over
one-half were from the retail and service sectors. About 83 percent
were from the state capital (Melbourne) and about 17 percent
from rural areas (Small Business Development Corporation (Vic.)
1985:10–11). Factors limiting further expansion have been a
shortage of suitable advisers and the costs of salaries and travel.

Consultancies are referrals made by the small business organization to experts in private practice. They are made when the solutions to the problems faced by a small firm are beyond the
resources of the state organization. Some consultancies may be
subsidized by the organization. They are usually available to assist
with management, technical, or financial difficulties for which
specialist professional advice is thought necessary. Most state
organizations also maintain an information service consisting of
manuals, brochures, technical data, audio-visual material, and
so on.

A National Industry Extension Service (NIES) was begun in

1986 as a joint federal-state initiative specifically aimed at small- and medium-sized enterprises with good growth and export potential. The service will provide information and advice to individual firms and will include consultancies and training. It is planned to include all current federal and state advisory services within NIES programs.

Education and training

Education and training programs are aimed at improving the competence of the owners and managers of small firms. Many of the programs are presented by the state organizations already mentioned, but most are conducted by educational institutions within each state—Departments of Technical and Further Education (TAFE), Colleges of Advanced Education (CAE), and universities. Courses are also presented by trade, industry, and professional associations such as the Australian Institute of Management and the Administrative Staff College.

The programs take many forms. They include courses on the general principles of management with emphasis on the applicability of these to small businesses; short courses, workshops, and seminars on particular aspects of small business management (e.g., accounting and finance, marketing, and personnel management) for managers in particular industries (e.g., hairdressing, catering, sheet metal fabrication, and news agencies); and courses forming parts of other programs, especially trade and post-trade courses for apprentices and other trainees. The state organizations support all these programs with advice on curriculum development, the provision of instructional materials, and promotion of the courses throughout the business community. The state organizations also offer some courses themselves, particularly in geographical areas where nothing else is available and for particular groups, notably those who, while not yet small business proprietors themselves, may be considering starting a small firm and may need information on the problems involved.

The state organizations also support the education and training programs in two other important ways. First, some of them provide, or provide assistance for, courses for the presenters of training programs—many of whom are not experienced teachers. Second, in most states, grants are available to provide relief management help for small business executives so that they can attend education and training sessions. These grants help to overcome one of the serious problems faced by small business managers— their difficulty in participating in such programs.

Finance

Policies of financial assistance for small firms are based on the proposition that the capital market may not be responding in the best possible manner to the needs of small business for a range of financial requirements. Access to adequate and appropriate forms of finance can be a severe hurdle for some small businesses. The variety of policies and programs in this area is extensive and is discussed in a separate section below.

Promotion and publications

Promotion and publication policies refer not only to activities publicizing the work of the state organizations but also to the cause of small business itself. Activities include radio programs and spot announcements, mainly directed at rural areas; the distribution of newsletters, press releases, handbooks, and brochures; the presentation of papers by members of the organizations' staff at seminars, conferences, and meetings of business and professional groups; and participation in "public" activities such as trade fairs and exhibitions. In Western Australia the Small Business Development Corporation held a Small Business Week in 1984 and again in 1985. This was aimed at increasing "the awareness of the collective importance of small business" (Small Business Development Corporation (w.a. 1985). Although the programs under this heading vary greatly in quality and coverage and although the policies they reflect are probably a minor part of the state organizations' rationale, they do form a useful way of achieving overall policy objectives.

Committees

Somewhat similar remarks can be applied to policies on the establishment of committees for various purposes—that is, they are useful ways of helping to achieve broader objectives. Most state organizations have established committees of either a permanent or an ad hoc nature to advise on the pursuit of specific objectives such as policy development, program evaluation, education and training, the provision of financial assistance, and the supply of advice to governments on, for example, the impact of regulations and legislation on the small business sector.

Federal government policies

The first significant initiative in Australia in the field of government policy on small business was taken by the federal government when it convened a National Small Business Seminar in Canberra in November 1973. The seminar was widely representative of small business interests and led directly to the establishment of the National Small Business Bureau early in 1974. From then until 1976, it was the only government agency (federal or state) dealing directly with the needs of small business.

The National Small Business Bureau began a counseling service, called the Small Enterprise Counselling Assistance Program, on a trial basis in Sydney and Perth. The bureau also issued a series of booklets and pamphlets designed to help the owners of small firms manage their businesses more effectively. It also promoted and financed several research projects in the small business area and arranged for the publication of the results of this research.

There was a change of federal government in November 1975, and since then developments in policy have meant an increased involvement by state governments in assistance to small business. Some of the state government policies have been outlined and discussed in preceding paragraphs. An agreement was made between the federal and state governments under which the Commonwealth (Federal)/State Small Business Program was implemented. This began in October 1976 and led to the closure of the Sydney and Perth offices of the National Small Business Bureau and eventually to the demise of the organization itself. The policies and programs of the federal government related to small business are now administered by the Small Business Branch of the Department of Industry, Technology and Commerce, Canberra.[2] Research in small business matters is carried out by the Bureau of Industry Economics within the Department; the bureau also produces an annual Small Business Review. The federal government's policies on finance for small business are administered through the Commonwealth Development Bank, which is a member bank of the Commonwealth Banking Corporation and established under legislation enacted by the federal parliament.

The Commonwealth/State Small Business Program resulted from agreement between the federal and state governments on a broad program of public-sector assistance to small business with an emphasis on cooperation between the two levels of government and a rationalization of the services and assistance provided. The basis for the rationalization was that the state governments assumed responsibility for the provision of direct services to the small business sector (such as counseling, education and training, and information). The federal government provides support services such as the preparation of training materials and publications and the promotion of research activities and also has a coordinating role.

Coordination is effected through a Small Business Working Party, which consists of senior officials, concerned with small business, from each state government and from the federal government. The latter provides the chairman of the working party and its executive staff. The working party mainly provides a medium for an exchange of views among the state organizations and a means to exert some pressure on the federal government for more (sometimes less) activity by that government in its designated fields of activity. It is not a policymaking body.

Thus the federal government provides a range of services to support the policies and programs of the state organizations. These are principally in relation to education and training, promotion and publications, research, and finance.

Education and training packages are available in several media—print, films and videos, audio cassettes, and slides with sound. They may be used by educational institutions and by trade, industry, and professional associations. They are actively promoted and supported by the various state small business organizations, some of which also make use of the packages in their own programs. A wide range of topics is available for a general audience (e.g., starting a small business), on specific topics (e.g., financial budgeting), and for specific industries (e.g., construction). Some packages are designed for group work and others for individual study.

The federal and state governments jointly have funded the Enterprise Workshop Program, which is designed to provide basic training for potential technological entrepreneurs and to draw to the attention of industry and academic institutions the need for such skills in Australia. Other jointly funded training activities include Innovation Centres to provide specialized assistance for the development of new ideas into commercial reality and the Centres for Development of Entrepreneurs to provide training in entrepreneurial skills.

The federal government's policy on promotion manifests itself mainly in the National Small Business Awards Program. This program is designed to highlight the contribution that small firms make to the economy and to provide a nationally recognized symbol of achievement for those firms that win awards. The federal government was also one of the major sponsors of the Seventh International Symposium on Small Business held in Melbourne in November 1980 and has, through the Commonwealth Development Bank, supported other conferences dealing with topics of relevance to small business.

As to publications, the Department of Industry, Technology and Commerce has issued a series of information booklets under the general title of "Managing the Small Business." There are now more than 40 of these booklets. Several have been translated into foreign languages for the benefit of owners and managers of small firms whose basic language is not English. The booklets are distributed through the Australian Government Publishing Service and are modestly priced.

The federal government also supports several national committees that provide a forum through which various groups and individuals can present and make known their views on aspects of small business policy and its development. These committees include the Small Business Working Party, referred to earlier; the Australian Small Business Council, a national advisory body on small business affairs; and the Small Business Management Development Committee of the National Training Council, which is concerned with policies and programs on education and training. The National Small Business Awards Program, referred to earlier, is sponsored by the federal government, which appoints a committee to act as a judging panel.

Research

Both the state organizations and the federal government undertake research programs into matters affecting small business. The federal government has supported research projects by the Bureau of Industry Economics into broader and longer-run issues of relevance to the environment within which small firms operate. Projects so far undertaken include small business finance (both generally and specifically in relation to the growth of the small business sector), small business failure (including the determination of rates of failure and the apparent reasons therefore), and the requirements for, and development of, entrepreneurial skills in small business. Some research is carried out within the bureau by its own staff, and some is carried out by independent consultants.

Not all the state organizations conduct research projects. Those that do mainly address local problems, often arising from requests for advice from the state government. In Victoria, for example, research has been undertaken and advice offered on retail tenancies legislation, workers' compensation insurance, debt recovery, occupational health and safety, and other matters. In Western Australia, there has been research on retail leases, statutory controls over the mobile food industry, the effects on local trade of planned freeway extensions, and electricity pricing in shopping centers. State organizations have also been concerned with somewhat wider issues, notably the establishment of databanks of information related to the small business sector in the state and its regions. These databanks will, it is hoped, form a reliable statistical basis on which more effective small business policies can be founded.

In addition to federal and state government research activities, many of the Australian universities, the CAE, and colleges within the TAFE system are more or less actively engaged in research on topics of importance to small business. Three research conferences have presented and discussed the results of or progress reports on such research. Two of these conferences were held at the University of Newcastle (N.S.W.), the first in May 1982 and the second in October 1984. The third conference was held at the Tasmanian State Institute of Technology, Launceston, in August and September 1986.

A wide range of research topics was examined at these conferences and, as noted above, is being pursued at both federal and state government levels. There are, however, three areas of considerable relevance to small firms that do not seem to have received the attention they deserve:

1. *Taxation.* Many taxes are levied in Australia, and although the effect of particular taxes on small business has been examined, no study of the impact of the tax system as a whole has yet been undertaken.

2. *Public sector activities.* Apart from taxation, the effect of the public sector on small business is mainly through the pricing of publicly supplied goods and services and the impact of government regulation. Although some research has been done in these areas, more is needed.

3. *Trade union activities.* The effect of these through, for example, national wage awards, occupational (as opposed to industry) wage awards, the basic wage concept, national (or industry) retirement schemes, and staffing practices is scarcely known. It is often claimed that they have adverse consequences for the development of small business, but evidence is lacking.

Finance

The small business sector in Australia often has great difficulty in obtaining finance, especially long-term finance. Small firms lack information about the most suitable sources of finance and frequently need advice and assistance on the best method of approach. These are deficiencies on the demand side. There are also deficiencies on the supply side. Institutional weaknesses result in an insufficiency in the volume of funds available to meet the special needs of small firms. There has been a particular lack of finance, both equity and loan, for young and innovative firms and for those in the ill-defined marginal area between "small" and "medium" in size.

The policies and programs of both the state organizations and the federal government have been designed to remedy the perceived deficiencies in the financial markets, at least to some extent. The policies and programs of the state organizations fall into three main groups:

1. Grants for specific purposes such as management training relief to enable the owners and managers of small firms to attend

appropriate courses, seminars, etc.; grants to implement management improvements within a firm; grants for viability studies to
establish eligibility for other forms of assistance; and grants for
research into the problems of small business. Subsidies to cover
part of the cost of professional counseling are also included in this
category.

2. Loans to small firms from funds provided by state governments. For example, in New South Wales there is a Small Business
Development Fund from which loans of up to $50,000 for up to
ten years may be made to existing and potential small business
owners.[3] The interest rate is normally below the current commercial market rate and may be further subsidized for up to two years.
In Victoria there is a Small Business Loan Program to supply
development finance for working capital purposes or for the
acquisition of plants and equipment. Preference is given to businesses with good prospects of growth and employment creation.
There are somewhat similar, though more modest, schemes in
South Australia, Western Australia, and Queensland.

3. Loan guarantee schemes. These schemes are now available
in five states and are designed to supplement the security available
when a small firm seeks to borrow from one of the trading banks
or from another approved financial institution. In general, a state
government will provide a guarantee for the repayment of a loan
made to an eligible small business where the borrower is unable to
provide suitable or adequate collateral security. The conditions for
eligibility vary among the states, as do the maximum amounts for
which a guarantee will be given and the maximum periods for
which it will operate. In general, the firm seeking the guarantee
needs to be established and demonstrably viable and to show a
potential for growth and an ability to generate sufficient cash flow
to service the guaranteed loan. In the case of Western Australia,
loan guarantees are available for new businesses as well as established ones (Small Business Development Corporation (W.A.)
1985).

The policies and programs of the federal government in relation
to small business finance focus on the activities of the Commonwealth Development Bank, though the Department of Industry,
Technology and Commerce monitors the financial markets and
provides advice to the minister on the supply of finance for small
business. As noted earlier, it also sponsors research in this area.

The Commonwealth Development Bank was established in 1959 and is part of the Commonwealth Banking Corporation, and the payment of monies owing by the bank is guaranteed by the Commonwealth (federal) government.[4] The functions of the Bank, set out in sections 72 and 73 of the Commonwealth Banks Act of 1959, are as follows:

(a) To provide finance for:
(i) the purposes of primary production; and
(ii) the establishment and development of business undertakings, particularly small undertakings, (i.e., where owners' equity does not exceed $5 million), in cases where, in the opinion of the Development Bank, the provision of the finance is desirable and the finance would not otherwise be available on reasonable and suitable terms and conditions.
(b) To provide advice and assistance with a view to promoting the efficient organization and conduct of primary production or business undertakings referred to above.

In determining whether or not finance shall be provided, the Commonwealth Development Bank is required to have regard primarily to the prospects of the operations becoming, or continuing to be, successful and not necessarily to consider the value of the security available in respect of that finance.

The Commonwealth Development Bank therefore complements the activities of the trading banks, which are the traditional primary sources of external finance for small business. However, where available security is not strong and extended repayment terms are sought, the proprietor of a small firm may have difficulty in arranging trading bank finance. The bank's main criterion for lending is the ability of the borrower to generate a cash flow to service the debt. Security comes second, and if the prospects of an adequate cash flow are good, the bank tends to accept whatever security is available. Moreover, the bank will lend for terms of up to 20 years and sometimes longer, whereas the trading banks and other financiers usually prefer to lend for much shorter periods.

The Commonwealth Development Bank provides funds for the purchase and leasing of plant and equipment as well as for general working capital purposes. Counseling is also available for customers and prospective customers on technical, financial, and managerial problems, and a thorough appraisal of the business is carried out before a loan is made. The bank has recently gained the power to make equity investments in small business, but it has not yet developed policies in this area, although several proposals are under consideration. The bank has more than 30 offices throughout Australia, and all the major banks act as agents for loan applications.

The relative quantitative importance of these various sources of finance for small business is difficult to measure because satisfactory data are not available. However, net loans approved by the Commonwealth Development Bank for business purposes (excluding primary production and equipment finance) rose from about $38 million in 1982–83 to $175 million in 1985–86 (Bureau of Industry Economics 1986:66). The state government schemes are much smaller. For example, the Small Business Loan Program in Victoria (which is thought to be one of the larger ones) seems to have lent only about $2.3 million in 1984–85 while the loan guarantee scheme (now with wider coverage) supported about the same volume of lending over a five-year period.

The relative lack of success of the loan guarantee schemes is of interest. Lobby groups within the small business sector argued strongly for some years in favor of the introduction of such schemes, but they have not been widely used. The criteria for acceptability of applications may be too narrow, or the form of guarantee required too restrictive, or the funds available under the schemes too small, or some combination of these may account for the low level of usage.

Of course, the main source of finance for small business is the trading banks, and rough estimates suggest that from six to ten times the amount of lending by the Commonwealth Development Bank is made available by the trading banks by overdrafts and term loans. A large volume of funds for the purchase of equipment comes from finance companies, many of which are subsidiaries of or are associated with the trading banks. The federal government's control over interest rates strongly affects the volume of finance available from all these sources, as well as the terms and conditions of its availability.[5]

Finally, two recent developments may be noted; both are of considerable interest. In late 1984 the Perth Stock Exchange began a "second board" market designed to cater to the buying and selling of shares in companies that are unable to satisfy the listing requirements for the "main board." Such companies are mostly of small to medium size and do not have a sufficiently large or widespread number of shareholders to be traded on the exchange in the usual way. There are also "second board" markets in Sydney, Melbourne, Adelaide, Brisbane, and Hobart though the last three are quite small.

Although it is perhaps too soon to judge the success of these secondary markets, they should help with the financing of small- to medium-sized businesses, especially those that are growing and showing profit potential. A listing on a market should make the business better known, and the possibility of selling shares more easily should make investment in such companies more attractive to prospective share buyers. Over 100 small companies are listed on the "second board" markets.

The second development refers to the encouragement by the federal government of investment in innovative companies of small and medium size. In 1984 the government legislated for the licensing of management and investment companies, and 11 such companies have now been licensed. The establishment of management and investment companies was recommended in a 1983 study by the Australian Academy of Technological Sciences. They are venture capital companies that are required to invest in eligible small- and medium-sized firms. To be eligible, the firm must satisfy several criteria including having not more than 100 employees or a net worth of not more than $6 million. In addition, the firm must not be more than ten years old, be using innovative technology, and have the potential for rapid growth.

The economic rationale for this development rests on the proposition that without some government intervention, a nation may devote too little of its resources to investment in research and innovation and to the adoption of new technologies. This is due to the nature and extent of the risks involved and to the difficulty encountered by a small- or medium-sized firm in limiting its average risk of loss from investment in invention and innovation. An additional problem arises from the fact that even when a new development is successful, the small firm may not always be able to capture all the rewards for the introduction of a new product or process. Not all patent systems are completely satisfactory and not all innovations are patentable anyway.

The licensing of management and investment companies is under the control of an independent Licensing Board established by the federal government to administer the program. The board also certifies businesses as being eligible for funding and management guidance by a management and investment company. For its part, the federal government provides an incentive to investors in management and investment companies by allowing a 100 percent tax deduction for capital subscribed to such companies in the year of investment. The amount subscribed may be deducted from the investor's taxable income so that its taxable value to the investor is the capital value multiplied by the maximum marginal rate of income tax. The federal government has indicated its willingness to forgo $20 million per annum in taxation revenue to support the program. As of 30 June 1986 the Licensing Board had approved capital raisings of about $123 million, of which about $120 million had actually been raised and about $82 million invested or committed in 91 different businesses. The remaining capital is held for follow-on investment in these businesses and for expected new investments.

Taxation

There is a great variety of taxes levied in Australia and at all levels of government. The most important is income tax, which accounts for more than 55 percent of total tax revenue and is imposed solely by the federal government. A range of consumption taxes imposed by both federal and state governments yields nearly 30 percent of all tax revenue. A payroll tax on labor inputs accounts for about 5 percent of total tax revenue. This tax is levied by the governments of the states and territories. Miscellaneous taxes, fees, fines, etc., yield the remaining 10 percent. All have implications for the small business sector, though it is not obvious that there is any overall policy in Australia relating to the taxation of small firms.

Clearly, income tax is quantitatively the most important tax and is the one that receives the most attention in discussions about the impact of taxation on small business. Legally, a small firm may be organized as a sole proprietorship, a partnership, a trading trust, a private company, or a public company, although extremely few are, in fact, public companies. The net income of each is taxable in different ways, and the effect of these differences has generated most of the debate about the impact of taxation on small business. These tax differences have also led to allegations of inequity and calls for reform of the tax system.

A sole proprietorship is not a tax accounting entity and is not taxable per se. The income arising from a business organized in this way is simply added to the owner's income from other sources and taxed according to the progressive scale of rates applicable to individuals. Partnerships and trading trusts are recognized tax accounting entities but are not usually taxed separately. The income arising from a business organized as a partnership or trust is distributed among the partners or beneficiaries, added to their income from other sources, and, as with a sole proprietorship, taxed under the progressive rate scale applicable to individuals.

The two company forms are both legal and tax accounting entities but are taxed differently from those discussed in the preceding paragraph. Both are subject to the same primary rate of tax, which is proportional rather than progressive in its impact. A company may retain as much of its after-tax income as it wishes without incurring any further liability for taxation. Dividends paid are, however, taxable in the hands of the shareholders, although credits are available in most circumstances for tax already paid by the company.

The fairly obvious differences in tax treatment between, for example, sole proprietorships and private companies have led to heated debates on taxation policy. The sole proprietor not only pays more income tax at most levels of income but also is less able to defer payment of tax in ways open to a private company and its shareholders. Neutrality of treatment suggests that business income of the same amount should be taxed at the same rate or rates, irrespective of the structure of the business by which it was earned. Whether this is administratively feasible or equitable or desirable on other grounds is another matter. As indicated earlier, more research is needed on the impact of the tax system generally, and this is not likely to be easy. Taxation policy is a particularly complex area.

Because consumption taxes are imposed on a proportional basis, they should not impose a relatively greater burden on small firms than on large. The same is generally true of the miscellaneous levies referred to earlier. The method of charging payroll tax does, however, positively favor small business. It is calculated as a percentage of wages and salaries paid, and there is a lower exemption limit until a level is reached at which the full rate of tax is payable. No doubt a policy of administrative convenience is partly responsible for this advantage to small business, but it is also one of the few examples of a policy of positive discrimination in favor of small firms. Details vary among the states and territories.

There is, however, another example in the area of taxation discrimination against small businesses, though it is probably unintentional. This is in the costs of tax compliance. A study (Johns, Dunlop, and Sheehan 1983:174–80) found that the costs of determining and discharging the firm's tax liabilities and of complying with other statistical requirements of the taxing authority were significantly higher for a small firm as a percentage of its wage and salary bill. The reason is that a substantial element of fixed costs occurs in preparing and submitting tax returns. Some extension of the policy of exempting very small firms from the payment of taxes other than payroll tax may be worth examining.

An additional point to emerge from the study mentioned above relates to sales tax, an important consumption tax levied by the federal government. Payment of this tax is required within 21 days from the end of the month in which the sale was billed. In many cases, a small business will not have received payment for the goods (including the tax) from its customer. This is an example of a small firm's lack of market strength when an additional burden is imposed on its financial position. It is also an example of a policy (a tax regulation) that is basically non-discriminatory but that has nevertheless had a more unfavorable impact on small business than on large. Yet another example could be given in relation to the investment allowance that was in effect in Australia from 1976 to 1985. This policy was designed to encourage investment in plants and equipment in manufacturing industry and to result in income tax concessions to those firms that did invest. The policy prescriptions did not discriminate between firms based on size, but in practice they did. A much lower proportion of very small firms benefited from the allowance than did the larger small firms and medium-sized firms (Johns, Dunlop, and Sheehan 1983:165).

The reason was that very small firms tend to be labor intensive and to use relatively less capital than do larger firms. It was also partly due to the fact that small firms generally benefit less from the incentives and concessions available under the Income Tax

Assessment Act 1936 (as amended). This Act is a complex piece of legislation and is subject to almost constant change. Most small business proprietors are unable to keep up-to-date with the effects of the changes and are unable to afford the costly expert advice that they need in this field.

Conclusion

Before 1973 there was really no official policy, government or otherwise, on the development of small business in Australia. There were some policies, particularly in the fields of taxation and finance, that had a differential impact on business firms according to their size. For the most part, these differences were unplanned and unintended (payroll tax is a probable exception), and in most cases the extent and the effects of the differences were unknown.

Since then, a great deal of activity in both the public and private sectors has been aimed at developing small businesses and at removing or at least alleviating some of the disadvantages from which they apparently suffered. This activity in the form of a series of policies and programs was undertaken for perceived sound economic, social, and political reasons. Occasionally, some policies and programs seem to have been responses to the fashionable trends of the time.

Certain difficulties have arisen. The division of policy control between the federal and state governments,[6] which is almost inevitable in a country like Australia (or Canada or the United States), means that it is not possible to speak of a uniform policy followed throughout Australia on the development of small business. This is not necessarily a bad thing. Not all parts of the country have exactly the same economic, political, or social structure, and experimentation with different policies (or indeed with none at all) may well maximize both local and national objectives.

But what are the objectives? There seems to be no agreement about this subject, and there also seems to have been a notable lack of discussion on the issues. At one level, the objective may be to achieve an optimum distribution of economic activity, within an industry or within the economy as a whole, between small firms and large. However, we do not know what this optimum distribution is, and, in a dynamic economy, it is likely to be constantly

changing anyway—so that the proposition is probably not quantitatively verifiable.

At another level (and the one that seems to have guided most
policies and programs in Australia), the objective seems to be to
improve the prospects for survival by small business. This, it is
held, can best be achieved by providing information, counseling,
and management training to improve the internal efficiency of
small business and to remove or lessen the institutional disadvantages faced by small firms. Much has been achieved but more
needs to be done if small business is to have a reasonably equal
opportunity to operate successfully. Some of the areas still not
tackled include the effects of the governments' own policies on
pricing, regulation, and procurement and the effects of the activities of trade unions.

The achievement of this objective is, theoretically at least, statistically testable. Time series data on the lifespans of existing
businesses, on bankruptcies, and on rates of closure should provide useful criteria by which to judge the success (or otherwise) of
policies aimed at improving the rate of survivorship of small business. It might also be possible to compare the cost of the policies
and programs with the savings resulting from a lower rate of small
business failure, though it is not easy to see how this can be done.
A difficulty associated with a "survival" objective relates to the
question of growth. That is, if policies are designed primarily to
assist small businesses to survive, are they also to be assisted to
grow? If so, the market will presumably sort out the better from
the worse. The better are likely to grow and the worse to remain
small and perhaps in more or less permanent need of counseling
and other assistance.

Although many (indeed most) of the policies and programs that
affect the development of small business in Australia have originated in the public sector, not all of them have done so. Some have
resulted from pressures within the private sector—for example,
the emergence of "second board" markets on the stock exchanges,
changes in retail shopping patterns leading to research on conditions in tenancy agreements and in franchising arrangements, and
so on. In addition, government policies and programs have frequently emerged from original representations by small business
lobby groups. The development of the small business sector is a
consequence of the interaction of several dynamic forces.

NOTES

1. I am indebted to my colleagues Mrs. K. M. Renfrew, Dr. W. C. Dunlop, Mr. G. P. Walker, and Dr. I. G. Wallschutzky for their comments on earlier drafts of this paper.

2. Small business programs for the Australian Capital Territory (which is still mainly a federal responsibility) are administered by the A.C.T. Small Business Bureau, which is part of the Department of Territories.

3. In this chapter values are expressed in Australia dollars: the Australian equivalent of one U.S. dollar was $1.05 in 1982–83; $1.15 in 1983–84; $1.31 in 1984–85; and $1.49 in 1985–86. These exchange rates represent the mean of the rates ruling at June 30 in each year and were supplied by the Reserve Bank of Australia.

4. Most of the capital of the Commonwealth Development Bank is derived from the federal government or is generated from within the Commonwealth Banking Corporation. The bank has, however, occasionally borrowed from the private institutional market. On 30 June 1985, about $566 million of such borrowings, of various maturities, were outstanding. The bank's subscribed capital was nearly $62,000 million.

5. The interest rate ceiling formerly imposed on trading bank loans of $100,000 or less no longer applies. The ceiling was supposed to favor small business, but the validity of this supposition is doubtful. For a discussion, see Johns, Dunlop, and Sheehan 1983:134–35.

6. There are also local governments (cities, towns, shires, etc.) in Australia, but few of these have active policies in relation to small firm development. They may distribute promotional material or help with the supply of water, drainage, and power services; or, more important, they may develop industrial estates, most of which are likely to be occupied by small firms. The powers of local governments to grant tax concessions are severely limited.

REFERENCES

Government of Australia
    1981 *Final Report of Committee of Inquiry on the Australian Financial System,* Australian Government Publishing Service, Canberra.
    n.d. *Commonwealth and State Programs for Small Business,* Department of Industry and Commerce, Canberra.

Australian Academy of Technological Sciences
    1983 *Developing High Technology Enterprise for Australia,* Parkville.

Johns, B. L., W. C. Dunlop, and W. J. Sheehan
    1983 *Small Business in Australia: Problems and Prospects,* George Allen and Unwin (2nd edn), Sydney.

Small Business Development Corporation (Victoria)
    1985 *Ninth Annual Report,* Melbourne.

Small Business Development Corporation (w.a.)
  1985 *Annual Report 1985,* no other publication details given.

Bureau of Industry Economics
  1986 *Small Business Review,* Small Business Research Unit, Canberra.

Wiltshire, F. W.
  1971 *Report of the Committee on Small Business,* Department of Trade and
        Industry, Canberra.

PART 4
Conclusion

CHAPTER 13

Assessment and Conclusions

Te'o I. J. Fairbairn

THE COUNTRY studies in this book have highlighted subjects of considerable practical importance: entrepreneurial characteristics, reasons for going into business, major problems encountered, factors making for success, perceptions of the role of government, and appropriate forms of financial assistance. The evidence presented in the country studies suggests that indigenous entrepreneurs encounter many difficult problems in business arising both from their own shortcomings and from limitations in the environment within which they operate. The data also show that entrepreneurs look to government to resolve many of these problems or at least to alleviate them.

Some general observations

The case studies generally confirm that indigenous entrepreneurs are highly motivated to succeed in business. They are driven by a desire to make money, to improve living standards, and to secure a livelihood for their families. They are also motivated by the reality that within their communities few other opportunities exist to earn money. These motives are clear from the responses of the entrepreneurs themselves when asked to give reasons why they went into business.

Success in business is also valued as a means of acquiring social status. The case study by Finney (Chapter 8) on the Highlands of Papua New Guinea shows that for Gorokans the acquisition of social and political status is a major goal. They value business suc-

269

cess not only for its own sake but also as a vehicle for acquiring so-called "big-man" status as a path to social eminence in the community. Croulet (Chapter 5) maintains that a powerful driving force among many entrepreneurs in Western Samoa is the desire to secure a chiefly *(matai)* title.

The country studies also show that Pacific island entrepreneurs are generally well educated—decidedly more so than the general indigenous population. A large proportion of entrepreneurs have completed high school, and many have undertaken tertiary-level education or have received advanced vocational training either at home or overseas. Their superior education (relative to that of the general indigenous population) combined with a high level of motivation can create a predisposition to success.

Two other sources of strength, which sustain the efforts of indigenous entrepreneurs, are (1) the ability to draw upon the resources of family members and (2) the opportunity to engage in more than one economic activity. Family assistance is especially important during the establishment of a business when finance is being mobilized and when family labor, especially of spouses, is needed. The involvement in other business activities—a somewhat distinctive characteristic of Pacific island entrepreneurship—enables entrepreneurs to spread business risk, to make an intensive use of scarce management skills, and, for those still active in the subsistence sector, to have a measure of security—or fallback—in the event of a business failure.

As the country studies amply illustrate, Pacific island entrepreneurs encounter many overwhelming obstacles to the achievement of their entrepreneurial goals. A major constraint is their lack of previous business experience or training in basic business principles and techniques. Many Pacific islanders became businessmen only after they had completed a career elsewhere, especially in government service—a fact that partly explains the prominence of Pacific entrepreneurs in the middle to advanced age groups (i.e., 35 years and over). And because few entrepreneurs had been raised in a business environment, they were further handicapped by the lack of an early exposure to business.

This lack of business experience and training is manifested in various ways: lack of confidence in dealing with formal credit and support institutions, inadequate appreciation of market forces, inappropriate pricing and stocking practices, over-extension of credit to customers, and a failure to take full advantage of existing technical assistance and training schemes. Consequently, entrepreneurial participation has been restricted to technologically simple small-scale ventures at the periphery of the commercial sector.

Another major shortcoming—which again reflects the lack of experience—is the tendency of entrepreneurs to start a business with inadequate capital. In general, the entrepreneur is forced to rely on his or her own limited financial resources (usually supplemented by contributions from immediate family members) simply because funds from alternative outside sources are not readily available. However, for many entrepreneurs the deficiency in start-up capital arises from unrealistic expectations and a failure to assess the real financial requirements of the new ventures. These severe capital shortages, unless remedied, can ultimately result in stagnation or bankruptcy.

Business problems

Additional major obstacles are imposed by the environment and include constraints on sources of capital funds, transportation, market facilities, sociocultural forces, and government support.

Capital shortages

Access to outside sources of capital is critical to the efficient operation and growth of the business sector. However, the access of entrepreneurs to the credit facilities of the formal financial market has been obstructed by complicated and stringent lending procedures, rigid collateral requirements, traditional institutional biases favoring large businesses, and even the lack of basic banking services for entrepreneurs in remote areas. Both limited access to capital funds and chronic shortages of these funds have debilitating effects on business performance.

Thus the credit situation of Pacific island entrepreneurs must be improved if they are to participate effectively in the commercial life of their countries. Governments need to initiate such improvements, as argued in Chapter 10, by broadening the range of credit facilities and by removing unwarranted restrictions practiced by existing financial institutions, especially trading banks. The case of Australia (Chapter 12) provides many useful guidelines.

Another hiatus is the absence of informal credit networks beyond those provided by the entrepreneurs and their kinsmen. The main exception is Papua New Guinea where, according to Finney (Chapter 8), the pooling of funds for business investment by the prospective entrepreneurs and their clansmen and followers is a common occurrence among Gorokan Highlanders. Informal credit systems have been prevalent in many Asian developing countries, and these should be examined for their potential in the Pacific.

Transportation

Indigenous entrepreneurs view transportation as yet another major constraint to their operations, and they identified numerous areas needing improvement—more regular overseas shipping, more frequent flights, and lower freight rates. Inadequate transportation was a particular concern of businessmen, especially commercial farmers located on outer islands and in remote rural districts. Entrepreneurs consider that an adequate system of shipping and/or road transportation is vital for the economic well-being of their communities—to deliver supplies, to export goods, and to facilitate travel. The solution to these transportation needs is expensive. Nonetheless, governments should be aware that inadequate transportation imposes a substantial burden on the business community (and ultimately the consumer); where possible (and feasible) government should take the necessary measures, including subsidization and privatization, to reduce this burden.

Marketing

The country studies identify the main market constraint as the small (and consequently weak) domestic markets. However, direct government intervention is not likely to be practical because this structural problem basically arises from the characteristically small and fragmented nature of Pacific island markets. However, where evidence does exist of market saturation due to an excessive number of competing ventures, government action can be taken to discourage new entrants.

The improvement of marketing systems, especially for produce, involves an appraisal of existing schemes and an examination of new possibilities. Many schemes now in operation are inefficient and constitute more of a hindrance than a help to suppliers. In such cases, efforts at rationalization are in order—an exercise that should not exclude handing over marketing functions to the private sector.

Traditional obligations

Another external factor that can threaten the viability of indigenous businesses is traditional customary and community practices. Because entrepreneurs operate within small closely knit communities, they are invariably exposed to pressures and obligations that emanate from customary practices and traditions. Entrepreneurs are expected to support community activities through contributions both in cash and in kind and to participate in church and local government activities. They are also expected to be generous in extending trade credit to their customers. If entrepreneurs choose to ignore these customary obligations, they risk social ostracism and loss of customers as well as loss of access to local labor and other community resources. To survive, entrepreneurs must seek to limit their involvement in these obligations to levels that do not jeopardize the financial viability of the business. As stressed by Finney (Chapter 8), entrepreneurs must develop the ability to balance the demands of the community (or clansmen in the Papua New Guinean context) against the requirements of sound business practice.

According to the country studies, most successful entrepreneurs have learned to live in relative harmony with these sociocultural pressures, and many have transformed them to their advantage. As Ritterbush (Chapter 7) observes of successful Tongan entrepreneurs and their responses to these pressures: "[they] were masters at manipulating the environment to suit their own needs" and were able to follow strategies that "turned potential obstruction to positive forces."

In his study of Western Samoan entrepreneurship, Croulet (Chapter 5) argues that an entrepreneur's ability to deal with sociocultural pressures can be strengthened by education and training. He suggests that Samoan entrepreneurs should be taught to plan and budget for traditional responsibilities requiring funds.

Government support

The country studies all point to the importance of government action to establish a favorable environment within which indigenous business can thrive. Participants at the regional workshop on Indigenous Business Development in the Pacific produced specific recommendations for possible government action (see Appendix).

Formal and nonformal education

The enhancement of business skills—at both management and technical levels—is essential if the level of indigenous entrepreneurship is to be strengthened. Training programs can be undertaken at both formal and informal levels and can be designed selectively to meet the needs of different sectors, as well as age and gender groups. Non-government organizations can also supplement official training programs. Practical subjects need to be taught that are directly relevant to the everyday business operations, for example, pricing and inventory policies, record keeping, budgeting, and forward planning.

The lack of business background can be partly remedied by teaching basic business principles and techniques in schools—an approach that may require a major redesigning of school curricula. The teaching of business subjects at school can not only enhance business skills at an early stage but also instill entrepreneurial attitudes and ethics.

Training programs can also provide opportunities for indigenous entrepreneurs to travel—both overseas and to other parts of the country to learn new ideas and gain experience. This author (Chapter 4) attributed much of the success of the Cook Islands' entrepreneurs to their extensive overseas experience either as trainees or as long-time employees. Croulet (Chapter 5) also stressed the value of overseas experience as a positive factor among Western Samoan entrepreneurs. To facilitate such visits, governments should create and expand opportunities for entrepreneurs to visit overseas businesses, attend business and trade seminars, and acquire experience through affiliation with overseas businesses.

Credit facilities

The banking sector in particular—both trading and development components—needs to be innovative in its lending policies and procedures, which can take many forms. One example is the preferential lending schemes established by the Fiji Development Bank for Fijian entrepreneurs as described by Qarase (Chapter 11). Another example, as described by Finney (Chapter 8), is the "Straight Fashion Stores" scheme administered by the Papua New Guinea Agricultural Bank to foster indigenous entrepreneurs through in-store training, loans, and ultimate purchase.

These examples, which are already in operation, have potential for application in other countries. But governments should examine other possibilities for their value in support of indigenous entrepreneurship.

Government coordination

Several country studies also emphasize that governments need a more cohesive and integrated approach toward the indigenous business sector. Two requirements are needed. First, policies and strategies must be clearly formulated concerning the role and importance of indigenous business. Second, these development measures must be provided in a coordinated fashion with one agency empowered to act as a central monitoring (and possibly coordinating) unit.

According to the data in the country studies, the main support agencies—those concerned with development finance, business advice, training, and marketing—have shown little inclination to coordinate their activities or even to consult with one another. This lack of cooperation has frequently resulted in duplication of effort, conflicting advice, and depletion of resources. Clearly, an integrated and coordinated effort can result in more effective support programs.

Women's participation

Another issue is the relatively limited participation by women in the business life of the region. Ritterbush and Pearson (Chapter 9) suggest several reasons why the participation of women in business has been limited, although women do in fact play a larger role than might be apparent through their support to their entrepreneur spouses. Apart from the conventional barriers such as restricted access to capital, women also face discrimination stemming from the prevailing perceptions about the traditional role of women in society. Specific areas of discrimination should be identified so that appropriate measures can be taken to reduce their debilitating effects on the economy.

Summary of entrepreneurial requirements

Ideally, the successful Pacific island entrepreneur needs to be highly motivated, to be reasonably well educated and trained, to be prepared to use family resources (including the aid of a spouse), to operate within a closely knit community (and meet his or her share of community obligations while maintaining sound business practices), and to have overseas experience. In addition, he or she should engage in more than one business activity in order to spread risk and to maximize the benefits from his or her management skills.

The indigenous entrepreneur must also be sufficiently knowledgeable to exploit institutional sources of development finance and to take advantage of existing government support measures. As the business begins to generate profits, the entrepreneur should have established a pattern of reinvesting a portion of the profits for improvement or expansion of the business.

Through appropriate policies and support programs, Pacific island governments can improve the institutional framework and environment to maximize the positive attributes of indigenous entrepreneurs. Such government support could catalyze Pacific island entrepreneurs, thereby contributing to private sector development and, in turn, to employment expansion and balanced economic growth in the nation and the region.

1986 Workshop on Indigenous Business Development in the Pacific: Principal Recommendations

AT THE 1986 regional workshop on Indigenous Business Development in the Pacific, participants made the following recommendations, organized into three categories:

Finance

1. That development banks or similar national institutions should provide services to indigenous entrepreneurs in the areas of project identification, project planning, feasibility studies, and loan finance proposals. Alternatively, a separate independent institution should be established for these purposes. Such services should be funded by government where necessary.
2. That development banks or similar development financing institutions should establish special loan schemes specifically for indigenous entrepreneurs. Such schemes should have concessionary features such as longer and more flexible repayment terms, lower interest rates, and government guarantees. Such concessions would require government commitment and financial support.
3. That development financing institutions should improve their loan appraisal procedures by undertaking market surveys and improved screening of clients to prevent or minimize the risk of failure.
4. That studies should be carried out to determine the extent of involvement (or lack of it) by commercial banks in promoting and assisting indigenous entrepreneurs.
5. That commercial banks should be required to provide special

278

assistance to indigenous entrepreneurs. This could be done via
the central banks using their regulatory powers to issue specific
policy directives regarding entrepreneurs.

6. That efforts should be made to encourage the use of alternative
sources of finance such as private venture capital, trustee holdings, and unit trusts.

Training

1. That agencies at the national level should be focused on small
business to coordinate resources, curricula, and advisory services in business management training. Appropriate nonformal
business training programs should supplement the work of
these national agencies.

2. That, wherever possible, training programs and training materials should be translated into the local vernacular.

3. That formal training programs in business management, which
are geared to all levels of expertise, should be sponsored by
governments and offered in both rural and urban centers.

4. That recognized programs of nonformal practical business
training should be established and should incorporate technical
and vocational business skills. These programs, which can be
run by non-governmental organizations and community-based
organizations, should have the continued and sustained support of government.

5. That a regional workshop should be convened to formulate
modules and curricula to support these business training programs. Apart from advising on the core business management
curricula, this workshop should address areas such as development of entrepreneurial skills, business leadership, the need for
thrift and frugality, and the interaction between business and
local cultural obligations.

6. That a complete register of training institutions and agencies in
the region should be assembled and disseminated. This register
would give details of business training programs, training
resources, and materials, as well as information on training fel-
lowships, grants, and exchange programs available in the
region.

7. That more extensive use should be made of successful entrepre-

neurs and the private sector in developing and monitoring business training programs. A register should be established of indigenous entrepreneurs who are prepared to offer their services and skills in the development of business training schemes or practical training opportunities.

Government policy and organizational support

1. That indigenous entrepreneurs should increasingly participate in the formulation and evaluation of national development plans and policies.
2. That there should be closer coordination among existing agencies and services involved in the development of indigenous business to improve their effectiveness and make the best use of national resources.
3. That there should be an evaluation of existing government procedures and management services involved in the administration of policies relating to indigenous business development.
4. That appropriate incentive schemes should be introduced and encouraged specifically for indigenous businesses.
5. That greater efforts should be made to disseminate information to indigenous peoples on
   • Entrepreneurial opportunities available
   • Support/incentive schemes offered nationally
   • Suitable forms of incorporation
   • Taxation regimes and exemptions where applicable
   • Organizations and agencies that can provide advice and assistance.
6. That such enterprise support organizations be established to assist indigenous entrepreneurs with
   • Incorporation and secretarial formalities
   • Preparation of business plans and feasibility studies
   • Negotiation for bank or other forms of loan finance
   • The search for joint venture partners
   • Preparation of tax returns, statutory forms, etc.
   • Establishment of appropriate record-keeping and information systems
   • General business and management advice.
7. That low-cost workshop, office, or warehouse space in urban

areas should be provided to indigenous entrepreneurs; that roads and shipping services should be improved to facilitate transportation of goods and produce to and from urban centers.

8. That organizational support should be provided to promote the distribution and marketing of local goods and produce, in particular, to facilitate the development of export markets overseas for the goods and services of indigenous business ventures.

About the Authors

Volume Editor

Te'o I. J. Fairbairn is a research associate at the East-West Center's Resource Systems Institute and former acting director of the Pacific Islands Development Program. Born in Western Samoa, Dr. Fairbairn has published extensively on the South Pacific including a 1985 book titled *Island Economies: Studies from the South Pacific* published by the University of the South Pacific. In addition to teaching economics at the University of Newcastle in Australia and at the University of the South Pacific in Fiji, he has served as senior economist with the South Pacific Commission in New Caledonia and as U.N. senior planning adviser in Western Samoa and the Cook Islands.

Contributors

John J. Carroll, economic advisor, Economic Development Authority of Pohnpei State, Federated States of Micronesia

C. Ross Croulet, evaluator, Income Generating Projects, Foster Parents Plan International, Rhode Island, United States

Ben R. Finney, professor and chairman, Department of Anthropology, University of Hawaii, United States

John M. Hailey, lecturer, Enterprise Development Centre, Cranfield Institute of Technology, United Kingdom

JANICE PEARSON, technical assistant, Asian Development Bank, South Pacific Regional Office, Vanuatu

LAISENIA QARASE, managing director, Fiji Development Bank, Fiji

S. DEACON RITTERBUSH, executive director, Pacific-Asian Research Associates, Hawaii, United States

WILLIAM JAMES SHEEHAN, member, Board of Management, Institute of Industrial Economics, Newcastle, Australia, and research associate, Department of Economics, University of Newcastle, Australia

Index